First
Certificate
GOLD

WITH KEY

exam maximiser

Sally Burgess with Richard Acklam

LONGMAN

Contents

Introduction to the *Exam Maximiser*

What is the *First Certificate Gold Exam Maximiser*?

The *First Certificate Gold Exam Maximiser* is specially designed to maximise students' chances of success in the First Certificate in English examination.

The Exam Maximiser offers:

- *further practice* with all the important vocabulary, grammar and skills that you study in the *First Certificate Gold Coursebook*.

- *the facts* on the papers and questions in the First Certificate exam. The *Exam overview* on page 6 gives you information on each of the five papers.

- *step-by-step guidance* with the strategies and techniques you need to get a good grade in the exam. There are also lots of **Hot tips!** to help you get extra marks.

- *exam-style exercises* so that you can practise using the techniques.

- *sample answers* to exam questions, showing you things you should try to do and things you should avoid doing in the exam. There are also typical teacher's corrections and examiner's comments as well as sample answers for you to grade.

- *practice with transferring rough work to answer sheets* used in the exam. This means that you know exactly what to expect in each paper and that there are no unpleasant surprises.

- *help with using time effectively* in the exam so that you can avoid the problem of losing marks because you run out of time.

- *a complete sample exam* which covers what you have learnt while using the *First Certificate Gold Coursebook* and the *Exam Maximiser*. This means that you know what it actually feels like to do the First Certificate exam. You can then get further practice in this by working through the *First Certificate Gold Practice Exams*.

Who is the *First Certificate Gold Exam Maximiser* for and how can it be used?

The *Exam Maximiser* is extremely flexible and can be used by students in a variety of situations and in a variety of ways. Here are some typical situations:

1

You are doing a First Certificate course with other students probably over an academic year. You are all planning to take the exam at the same time.

You are using the *First Certificate Gold Coursebook* in class. Sometimes you will also do the related exercises or even a whole unit from the *Exam Maximiser* in class, though your teacher will ask you to do exercises from it at home as well. You will use the entire *Exam Maximiser* or you and your teacher will use it selectively, depending on your needs and the time available.

2

You have already done a First Certificate course and you are now doing an intensive course to prepare for the exam.

Since you have already worked through the *First Certificate Gold Coursebook* or perhaps another First Certificate coursebook, you will use the *Exam Maximiser* in class. This, together with the *First Certificate Gold Practice Exams*, will give you a concentrated and highly focused short exam course.

3

You have a very short period in which to take the First Certificate exam.

The level of your English is already nearing First Certificate exam standard, though you have not been following a First Certificate coursebook. You now need examination skills. You will use the *Exam Maximiser* independently, that is to say without a coursebook, because you need practice in the exam tasks and how to approach them.

4

> You are re-taking the First Certificate exam as unfortunately you were not successful in your first attempt.

You may be having to re-take the exam because you were not sufficiently familiar with the exam requirements. You will not need to follow a coursebook, but you will use the *Exam Maximiser* to develop your exam techniques and build up your confidence.

5

> You are preparing for the exam on your own.

- Perhaps you are in a class where the teacher is using the *First Certificate Gold Coursebook* as a general English course. This means there are probably students in your class who are not actually taking the exam. Your teacher will recommend use of the *Exam Maximiser* for homework, so that everyone can revise and practise what they have learnt. However, you can also use it on your own to prepare for the exam. You can give yourself additional practice by using the *First Certificate Gold Practice Exams* just before you take the exam.

- You are not attending a First Certificate class, but wish to take the exam and prepare for it independently. You will get the practice and preparation by using the *Exam Maximiser* by itself. Near the exam time you may wish to use the *First Certificate Gold Practice Exams* as well.

Exam overview

Paper	Name	Timing	Content	Test focus
Paper 1	Reading	1 hour 15 minutes	4 long texts, or 3 long and 2 or more short texts; 35 reading comprehension questions.	Questions test your understanding of the general idea, the main points, specific details, the structure of the text and specific information.
Paper 2	Writing	1 hour 30 minutes	Part 1: compulsory letter Part 2: a choice of writing tasks	Questions test your ability to write letters, reports, articles and compositions for specific audiences.
Paper 3	Use of English	1 hour 15 minutes	5 sections with 65 questions altogether focusing on grammar and vocabulary.	Questions test your knowledge of grammar and vocabulary.
Paper 4	Listening	40 minutes (approximately)	2 longer recorded texts and 2 series of short extracts; 30 listening comprehension questions.	Questions test your ability to understand the main idea, the main points, detail or specific information.
Paper 5	Speaking	15 minutes (approximately)	A conversation divided into four parts between two candidates and an interlocutor. Another examiner will be in the room with you to assess your performance. NOTE: in certain examination centres there will be only one candidate and the examiner, but the format of the test remains essentially the same.	The four parts test your ability to exchange personal and factual information, to express your own opinions and attitudes and to find out about other people's opinions and attitudes.

1 A sense of adventure

Vocabulary: travel

Paper 3, Part 2

About the exam
In Paper 3, Part 2 you fill in the gaps in a text.

Strategy
Always read the whole text all the way through **before** you begin to fill in the gaps.

1 Fill in the gaps in the following text with an appropriate word or phrase from the box. You do not need to use all of the words.

canoe travelling liner missing trip
destination taking off visit checking in sail
hire maps fly catching departure travel

Welcome aboard the First Certificate Gold Exam Maximiser!

Imagine that you are about to set out on a rather complicated but exciting journey. Perhaps you are going to drive a jeep across the Sahara desert, (1)......................... across the Pacific Ocean or travel down the Amazon in a (2) ....

Naturally you will prepare for a journey like this very thoroughly. It is not just a question of (3)......................... at an airport and getting on a plane or (4)......................... a train or bus. You will need to consult (5)......................... and atlases, talk to people who have already been to the places you will (6)......................... and decide what to take with you.

Preparing to take First Certificate is very like going on a journey. You have to know what the examination will be like and what kinds of questions you will be asked. You need to learn how to answer the various kinds of questions well and what dangers to avoid.

Like (7)......................... alone through the desert or in the mountains, across an ocean or down a river, preparing for FCE on your own would be very difficult. But with a guide it is much easier. When you are travelling, a guide can help you make the most of your money and time so that you enjoy your journey and get to wherever you are going. In other words a guide can help you **maximise** your chances of travelling safely and arriving at your (8)......................... on time.

The *First Certificate Gold Exam Maximiser* is like a guide. It is designed to help you learn everything you need to know to pass FCE, in other words it **maximises** your chances of exam success. So welcome aboard the *First Certificate Gold Exam Maximiser*. We hope you have an enjoyable and safe (9)......................... and that you reach your final destination, FCE, with absolutely everything you need to do really well in the exam.

2 The following groups of words relate to *ships, trains, planes, cars* or *buses*, but there is one word or phrase in each group that does not belong. Circle this word or phrase and then write which type of transport the other words relate to.

EXAMPLE: a steering wheel   brakes   a boot

(a deck)   ....*cars*....

1 a dual carriageway   a platform
   the fast lane   a lay-by   ....

2 a cruise   a liner   a flight   a lifeboat   ....

3 a guard   a port   a platform   a track   ....

4 to check in   a single
   a departure lounge   to take off   ....

5 a parking meter   a driving test
   a seatbelt   an inspector   ....

6 an inspector   a stop   a fare
   a steward   ....

7 a cabin   a seatbelt   a cruise   a deck   ....

Learner training

When you learn new words, put them into categories, for example *Transport: ships; cars; planes.* Later, think of a category and write down all the words you can remember.

Reading: multiple matching

Paper 1, Part 4

About the exam
In Paper 1, Part 1 you match statements or questions to paragraphs. The texts usually give information about something.

Strategy
Read the text through quickly to get a general idea. Then study the questions. Read the text again and underline the relevant information in each paragraph.

1 Read the text opposite through once quickly. Which of the games would you like to play on a long journey?

from *Travel Games* by Lynn Guest

Travel Games

1 Long car journeys can be pretty boring – especially if you are using motorways. Before too long everyone is fighting over what cassette to put on or what radio station to listen to – Dad wants the football, Mum wants the classical music station, someone else wants heavy
10 metal and nobody can agree. One way to get over this problem is to play some kind of game as you are driving along. The following travel games might be just the thing when tempers are getting frayed or when you simply want to have some fun.

A OBSERVATION
20 With your partners, make a list of ten items you are likely to see out of the window on your journey such as a woman with a pram, a boy on a bicycle, somebody hitchhiking, a bank, a statue, etc. Each player has to try and spot the ten items first. When a player sees one of the objects, he or she shouts
30 out and claims it; it cannot be used by other players. The one to spot all the items first is the winner.

B CRAZY STORIES
Each player takes it in turn to be the story-teller. During the story he or she will make the occasional deliberate mistake which the other players will
40 have to try and spot. When they do, they must shout out and the first one to shout gets a point. An example of a mistake would be: 'I went to the football pitch and had a game of golf. While I was there I met a little girl who was my nephew.' There are two mistakes here as you do not play golf on a football pitch and
50 she was his niece, not his nephew. Now you have a go.

C ADDING UP
Each player picks a number between 10 and 20. The object of the game is to find car number plates which add up to your chosen number. For example, if you chose the number 17 then a number plate
60 of F458 GHU would be a success. However a number plate of D981 SYT would be of no use to you. The first player to spot his or her number wins the round. Everyone chooses another number and the game begins again. Continue until one player has won three rounds.

D ANIMAL,
70 VEGETABLE OR MINERAL?
One player has to think of an object, but all he or she tells the others is whether it is animal, vegetable, or mineral. Mineral can be used for all objects which are not animal or vegetable. For example, a horse or an egg would be
80 animal. A tomato or a loaf of bread would be vegetable. A diamond ring would be mineral. The other players have to try and find out what the object is by asking questions which the player is only allowed to answer with a 'Yes' or 'No'. If you think you know what the object is, you can ask a question like: 'Is
90 it a horse?'. If the answer is 'Yes', you win. If no one has guessed the object after 20 questions, the person who thought of the object wins.

E I WENT ON A TRIP
One player begins, 'I went on a trip and took a fishing net'. The next player says, 'I went on a trip and took a fishing net and
100 my bowler hat'. The next in turn says, 'I went on a trip and I took a fishing net, my bowler hat and a bucket and spade.' The game continues until one of the players forgets something on the list. Start again with a new list.

'The salesman said that this was the ideal car for life in the fast lane'

2 Now read the following questions and write the appropriate letter for each game in the gaps. Some games are used more than once. The first two questions have been answered for you. Look at the notes before you answer the other questions.

Which game:

would be best for people who enjoy guessing games?

1 ...*D*...

Notes: *the relevant information for this question is in line 84. It says the purpose of the game is to 'find out what the object is'. 'Find out' means almost the same thing as 'guess'.*

could only be played if you were travelling by car?

2 ...*C*...

Notes: *the important information here is 'find car number plates' in line 55.*

involves listening very carefully?

3 ....

could be played on a plane as well?

4 ....   5 ....   6 ....

must be played by more than two players to be effective?

7 ....

Word formation

Paper 3, Part 5

About the exam
In Paper 3, Part 5 you read a text with gaps. At the end of each line of the text there is a word in capital letters. You use this word to form a new word for each gap.

Strategy
Before you try to fill in the gaps, decide whether the missing word is an adjective (e.g. *beautiful*), an adverb (e.g. *carefully*), a noun (e.g. *information*) or a verb (e.g. *believe*).

1 The following sentences all come from the listening exercise on page 14 in the *First Certificate Gold Coursebook*. Look at the underlined words in each sentence and decide whether they are adjectives, adverbs, nouns or verbs.

1 And so began two hours and forty minutes of <u>disbelief</u> (......*noun*......), fear and finally horror for the 2,300 passengers of the '<u>unsinkable</u>' (...*adjective*..) Titanic.

2 For that was all the time that it took for the biggest and <u>supposedly</u> (....................) safest liner in the world to sink beneath the icy waters of the North Atlantic.

3 The myth of the *Titanic*'s unsinkability was only one of an <u>incredible</u> (....................) <u>combination</u> (....................) of human errors.

4 Although the *Titanic* struck the iceberg at 11.40 p.m., it was not until five minutes after midnight that the order was given, '<u>Uncover</u> (....................) the lifeboats!'

5 In one of the last <u>overcrowded</u> (....................) lifeboats to leave the *Titanic* stood Mrs Emily Richards, then twenty-four, and going off to join her husband in the USA.

6 The sea was full of <u>wreckage</u> (....................) and bodies.

7 One of the strangest aspects of this disaster was that it had been foreseen in <u>extraordinary</u> (....................) detail in a novel published fourteen years earlier.

8 The book, written by Morgan Robertson, told the story of the biggest and most <u>luxurious</u> (....................) liner ever built.

Hot tip!
Always read the whole sentence to decide if you need a **positive** or a **negative** word to fill each gap. For example, do you need the positive or the negative form of the word in this sentence?

.... we arrived late and missed the first ten minutes of the film. (FORTUNATE)

2 Now fill in the gaps in the following sentences with the correct form of the word in capitals. Decide what part of speech to use and whether you need a positive or a negative word.

1 The local people are sometimes rather
..*unfriendly*.. and often seem to want to avoid the tourists. (FRIEND)
Notes: *the missing word is an adjective. You know this because 'are' and 'rather' come before it. The idea of the sentence is negative.*

2 It's no use getting .... just because there's a long queue to check in. (PATIENT)

3 The man in the tourist information office was very .... and gave us lots of free maps and brochures. (HELP)

4 They decided to close the hotel because it had never been very .... (PROFIT)

5 We had lovely .... weather the whole time we were there. (SUN)

6 Don't .... the cost of hotel accommodation when you plan your next holiday. (ESTIMATE)

7 A dishonest waiter tried to .... us for our meal. (CHARGE)

8 Take an umbrella if you go in autumn as it is very .... to rain. (LIKE)

9 There are .... people in most of the world's big cities nowadays. (HOME)

10 The safari park was a bit of a .... as there were too few animals. (APPOINT)

Listening: gap fill

> **Paper 4, Part 2**

About the exam
In Paper 4, Part 2 you listen to a talk or conversation and complete short sentences with a word or phrase.

Strategy
Always spend at least one minute looking carefully at the instructions and questions before you listen.

1 Read the following instructions and notes and then mark the statements below **T** (true), **F** (false) or **?** (don't know).

Listen to a young traveller giving a report on a place she visited. Match the numbered phrases in Column A with a word or phrase in Column B. Write the appropriate letter in the gaps. There are two extra items in Column B which you do not need to use.

Reporter: Diane Pilgrim   **Destination:** Gozo, Malta

Column A

1 She got to Gozo by ....

2 To explore the island she ....

3 There is an old castle on the island that is used ....

4 Marsalforn, Ramla bay and San Blas bay are best for ....

5 The church in Tapinu has been used ....

Column B

a) as a disco.

b) plane and ferry.

c) in a film.

d) swimming.

e) hired a moped.

f) water-skiing.

g) restaurants.

Statements

1 You will hear more than one person speaking on the cassette. ....

2 You will hear somebody telling a story. ....

3 You only have to write in the letters 'a', 'b', 'c', etc. ....

4 The speaker will give her opinion about the place. ....

5 It would be a good idea to listen carefully for words for types of transport and the places mentioned. ....

2 Now listen to the cassette and do the exercise.

Writing: transactional letter

Paper 2, Part 1

About the exam
Part 1 of Paper 2 is **compulsory**. There is no choice. You always write a letter to ask for or give information of some kind.

1   A **formal** letter is a letter you write to someone you don't know or don't know very well, especially companies and institutions. An **informal** letter is the kind of letter you write to friends, members of your family and other people you know well. Which of the following phrases and sentences would you expect to find in a formal letter? Which would you expect to find in an informal letter? Mark them **F** (formal) or **I** (informal).

1   Dear Sir/Madam, ...

2   *Love,*
    Eleni   ....

3   *See you next week. I can hardly wait!*   ....

4   I look forward to receiving
    your reply.   ....

5   *Yours faithfully,*
    Ana García Herrera   ....

6   I am writing in reply to your
    letter of 15 May.   ....

7   Give my love to your parents.   ....

8   Should you require any further
    information, do not hesitate to
    contact us at the above address.   ....

9   *Write back soon and tell me all your news.*   ....

10 I'm sorry I haven't written
    for such a long time, but I've
    been really busy.   ....

11 *I would be most grateful if you could send*
    me any further relevant information.   ....

Strategy
Always read the instructions carefully and decide what kind of letter you are supposed to write. Formal or informal? To a friend or to someone you don't know?

2

1   Look at this task and the underlined words. Will your answer be formal or informal?

> Some <u>young people you met last summer</u> are planning to visit your country on holiday and have asked you to suggest some places of interest to see. Write a letter of reply using the notes below.
>
> – *when?*
> – *how long?*
> – *come and stay?*

2   Now look at this plan for the above task and put the points in a logical order. Write the numbers 1–7 in the gaps.

a) *Apologise for not replying sooner.* ....
b) *Thank them for their letter.* ....
c) *Ask when they will be coming.* ....
d) *Tell them to write again.* ....
e) *Invite them to stay for a few days.* ....
f) *Suggest places to visit/things to do.* ....
g) *Say why you haven't replied sooner.* ....

3   Think of ideas: a reason for not replying; places to visit; things they might enjoy doing and seeing. Is there a particularly good time of year to visit these places? What can your friends do there?

4   Write your letter in 120–180 words.

5   Check it carefully for any grammar, spelling or vocabulary mistakes your teacher has corrected in your written work before. If necessary, write your letter out again.

Strategy
Read the instructions very carefully, write a plan, think of ideas and check your work thoroughly.

Vocabulary: feelings

1   Match the following words with a definition below. Write the appropriate letter in the gaps. There is one definition which you do not need to use.

1	terrified	....	5	nervous	....
2	confused	....	6	cross	....
3	miserable	....	7	depressing	....
4	astonishing	....	8	thrilled	....

a) causing anger or impatience

b) very pleased or satisfied

c) making you feel very sad

d) causing great surprise

e) in a state of extreme shock or fear

f) worried about what might happen

g) uncertain about what to think or do

h) unhappy, tired and uninterested

i) angry, bad-tempered

2   Now look at this letter a student wrote in answer to the writing task on page 11 and find six mistakes with the form of adjectives. Write the sentences out again correctly in your notebook.

Dear Lucy and Tim,

I'm sorry I haven't replied to your letter sooner, but I've been too worried about my exams to think about anything else. I've just heard that I passed everything so I'm feeling pretty pleasing.

I was thrilling to hear that you are planning to come here. My family and I would be delightful to have you both stay.

You asked about interesting places to visit. The mountains are really amazed in spring with all the wild flowers. I went climbing there with some friends last summer, but one of them was terrified of heights so we had to come home early.

Another good place to visit is the provincial capital. There are lots of fascinated old streets with wonderful eighteenth century architecture. It's worth visiting at any time of year, though the summers can be a bit exhausted with the extreme heat.

Well, I had better finish. Write soon and let me know exactly when you plan to come.

Love,
Ruben

Grammar: questions

1   Put the words in the correct order to make questions. Write the sentences out in your notebook. Then match each question to an answer below and write the appropriate letter in the box.

1   people how learn do new words? ☐

2   do what we have do to? ☐

3   you do agree you don't? ☐

4   do you like in what spare doing time your? ☐

5   do you where want go to this weekend? ☐

6   why get you do nervous so? ☐

7   who you angry were with? ☐

8   what mean does 'miserable'? ☐

9   each you translate are word going to? ☐

10   you did definition write a 'cruise' of? ☐

a) The dictionary says 'very unhappy'.

b) My brother. He drives me crazy sometimes.

c) Yes. I copied it from the dictionary.

d) Playing basketball and going to the cinema.

e) By finding a good way of recording them.

f) I have to describe my photograph while you listen.

g) I think I'd like to stay here, actually.

h) I don't know. Exams always make me feel like this.

i) No, I'm afraid I don't.

j) No, just the important ones.

2 Fill in the gaps in the following sentences with an appropriate question tag. Then match each question to an answer below and write the appropriate letter in the box.

1   You're Polish, ... ? ☐

2   I've seen you somewhere before, ... ? ☐

3   Janusz is your older brother, ... ? ☐

4   Your sister studies English, too, ... ? ☐

5   You went on the trip to Oxford, ... ? ☐

6   Janusz really enjoyed it, ... ? ☐

7   He'd been there before, ... ? ☐

8   You used to live in Germany, ... ? ☐

9   You'll be at school tomorrow, ... ? ☐

10   You wouldn't know which bus I get to Piccadilly, ... ? ☐

a)   That's right. He went a couple of years ago.

b)   I think you get the number 14.

c)   No, I didn't actually. I hear it was really good.

d)   Yes. He wants to go again next weekend.

e)   Yes, I am. How did you guess?

f)   Yes, that's where my father's from.

g)   Maybe. You look slightly familiar, too.

h)   Oh, so you're a friend of his, are you?

i)   No, not any more. She's gone back to Poland.

j)   I'm afraid not. I'm taking my First Certificate exam.

3 Now listen to the questions Sam asks above and check your answers. Does his voice go up or down on the question tags? Is he fairly sure or not very sure that the information is correct? Mark the tags ↗ (up) or ↘ (down). Then practise saying them yourself.

4 Write indirect questions using the words given.

1   What am I going to do? (*I don't know*)
   I don't know what I am going to do.

2   Why did she say that? (*I wonder*)
   ....

3   How many tourists visit your country each year? (*I'd like to know*)
   ....

4   Does this bus go to Oxford Street? (*I wonder*)
   ....

5   Where is the tourist office? (*Could you tell me*)
   ....

6   Are there any museums near here? (*Do you know*)
   ....

7   What are we supposed to do? (*Would you mind telling me*)
   ....

8   Is she English or American? (*I don't know*)
   ....

Speaking: interacting

Paper 5, all parts

About the exam
Paper 5 is a conversation between you and another candidate and/or the interlocutor/examiner.

Strategy
In Paper 5 you have to answer questions, but you also have to **ask** them.

This transcript of two candidates doing Part 1 of Paper 5 contains five mistakes with questions. Find the mistakes and write the questions out correctly in your notebook.

EXAMINER: And what do you do, Sylvie?

SYLVIE: I'm a student.

EXAMINER: Katrina, ask Sylvie about her family.

KATRINA: How many brothers and sisters have you?

SYLVIE: I've got one older brother. He's studying art.

KATRINA: How is he?

SYLVIE: He's tall and handsome. And you? What you do?

KATRINA: I study too. At university.

SYLVIE: What you are studying?

KATRINA: Mathematics.

SYLVIE: And you have got any brothers and sisters?

KATRINA: No, I haven't.

UNIT

2 Work and play

Vocabulary: multiple choice cloze

Paper 3, Part 1

About the exam
In Paper 3, Part 1 you choose between four alternatives to fill gaps in a text.

Strategy
Sometimes the correct alternative is a word that goes with the word after the gap. Here is an example:

First Certificate Exam success .... on adopting the right strategies.

A consists   **B** revolves   **C** depends   **D** results

Alternative C is the correct choice because the verb *depends* is the only one that goes with the preposition *on*. The other verbs go with these prepositions: *consists **of**, revolves **around**,* and *results **in**.*

Always look at the words before and after the gap. They will help you choose the correct alternative.

1 Fill in the gaps in the following sentences with *on, from, of, for* or *to*.

1 At the beginning of my English class, I spent ages searching .... my favourite pen, but I couldn't find it anywhere.

2 Eventually I borrowed one .... the girl sitting next to me.

3 However, I was still worrying about the pen and I couldn't concentrate .... the lesson properly.

4 When I got home I saw my brother using a pen that reminded me a lot .... mine.

5 'Don't use things that don't belong .... you!' I said, taking the pen.

6 'And don't accuse me .... things I haven't done!' he said. 'This is *my* pen. Mum bought it for me this morning.'

2 Fill in the gaps in the following sentences with an appropriate word from the box.

| ashamed good responsible proud suspicious |
| satisfied keen terrified |

1 Don't ask me to climb up there. I am .... of heights.

2 In this house I am .... for making sure everyone helps with the washing-up.

3 You must be very .... of her for doing so well in the examinations.

4 I was not very .... with my results in the test.

5 He is not .... on high risk sports.

6 The guard seemed to be .... of the museum visitors and never took his eyes off them.

7 I think athletes who use drugs should be .... of themselves.

8 She speaks five languages, but she is not very .... at mathematics.

3 Read the following job advertisement and then choose the correct alternative to fill in the gaps.

1 **A** seeking
  B looking
2 **A** interested
  B keen
3 **A** qualified
  B good
4 **A** keen
  B interested
5 **A** in charge
  B responsible
6 **A** capable
  B suitable
7 **A** specialised
  B satisfied
8 **A** join
  B belong

WANTED Young People
We are (1) .... for young men and women to work as tour guides. We are (2) .... in interviewing young people of all nationalities who are (3) .... at communicating with people of all ages and (4) .... on travelling. Successful candidates will be (5) .... for meeting our clients at the airport and escorting them on tours of the area. You will be (6) .... for the job if you have finished secondary school and have (7) .... in foreign languages. Applicants who (8) .... to the Association of Professional Tourist Guides will be given preference.

14

Reading: gapped text

About the exam
In Paper 1, Part 3 you look at some sentences that have been removed from a text. You read the text and decide where the sentences fit. There is always one extra sentence which you do not need to use.

Strategy
Look at words like pronouns (e.g. *it, she*) demonstratives (e.g. *this*, *that*) and possessive adjectives (e.g. *my*, *her*) in the sentences that have been removed from the text and decide what they refer to.

1 Read these paragraphs from the article '**Why do we risk it?**' (*First Certificate Gold Coursebook,* page 8) and decide what the underlined words refer to. Write the word or phrase in the gaps.

RISK SPORTS are one of the fastest-growing leisure activities. Daredevils try anything from organised bungee jumps to illegally jumping off buildings. These people never feel so alive as when <u>they</u> are risking their lives. (1) ....

Some say that people who do risk sports are reacting against a society which <u>they</u> feel has become dull and constricting. (2) .... David Lewis, a psychologist, believes that people today crave adventure. In an attempt to guarantee safety, our culture has eliminated risk. 'The world has become a bland and safe place,' says Lewis. 'People used to be able to seek adventure by hunting wild animals, or taking part in expeditions. Now <u>they</u> turn to risk sports as an escape.' (3) ....

Risk sports have a positive side as well. <u>They</u> help people to overcome fears that affect them in their real lives. (4) .... This makes risk sports particularly valuable for executives in office jobs who need to stay alert so that <u>they</u> can cope when things go wrong. (5) ....

2 The following sentences have been removed from the text below. Read the text and decide which sentence goes in each of the numbered gaps.

A Since starting his new firm – Rent-A-Call – Mr Benz has received hundreds of calls from potential clients.

B One man wanted to be telephoned by a woman asking him out to the theatre in order to make his wife feel jealous.

C This idea came to him earlier this year after noticing how many Germans have mobile phones – but that very few ever get called on them.

Rent-A-Phonecall

Joachim Benz, a German businessman, will telephone customers on their mobile phones when they want to talk about whatever they want.

(1____) Mr Benz, who is twenty-nine, said, 'It struck me that although the reason for displaying these phones was to create an impression of being incredibly important and busy, there was no point in having one if it never rang.'

(2____) Most have been businessmen anxious to impress colleagues or clients by having their mobile phone ringing at a vital moment in the negotiations.

Inquiries have also come from people wanting to put on an act for a new boyfriend or girlfriend. **(3____)**

from *The Age* newspaper

🎧 Listening: note taking

Paper 4, Part 2

About the exam
In another type of exercise in Paper 4, Part 2 you listen and complete notes.

━ Hot tip! ◀━
DON'T write more than three or four words in note-taking exercises!

Listen to an interview in which a woman talks about an unusual occupation and complete the following summary of what she says.

Occupation: (1)
....

Father's occupation: (2)
....

She compares racing to (3)
....

(4)
....
comes to the track to watch her race.

(5) Boyfriend's nationality:
....

(6) Boyfriend's occupation:
....

Word formation

Paper 3, Part 5

1 The following sentences come from the interview with Meregan Turner. Look at the underlined word in each sentence and decide if it is an adjective, adverb or noun.

1 I just couldn't believe that anything could be so <u>wonder*ful*</u>. (.........................)

2 It's <u>complete*ly*</u> (.........................) taken over my life.

3 Were men <u>protec*tive*</u> (.........................) of you on the track?

4 But sometimes you get real <u>hostil*ity*</u>. (.........................)

5 When I <u>final*ly*</u> (.........................) succeeded, he <u>actual*ly*</u> (.........................) turned into my wheels.

6 I suppose because he understands what it's actually like he's less likely to think it's <u>danger*ous*</u>. (...................)

2 A suffix is added to the end of a word to change it to another part of speech. Study the suffixes in *italics* in the words in Exercise 1 and complete the following information.

1 If you add *-ly* to adjectives like ...., ... or ...., you make adverbs.

2 If you drop the -e and add .... to adjectives like *hostile,* you can make nouns.

3 If you add .... to verbs like *protect* that end in *-tect,* you can make adjectives or nouns (e.g. *detect*........).

4 If you add *-ous* to nouns like ...., you make adjectives.

3 The following extracts come from the listening *Hated jobs* on page 17 of the *First Certificate Gold Coursebook.* Read the extracts and then fill in the gaps with an appropriate form of the words in capitals at the end of each line.

PRIVATE INVESTIGATOR	
It can be quite a (1) ..... job and you can meet some really nasty types. I suppose it's not really very (2) ....., but some people don't like it much if they find out you've been spying on them ... – they can get pretty (3)	**DANGER** **SURPRISE** **PLEASANT**

DEBT COLLECTOR	
I think it's very (4) ..... that this kind of work has such a bad reputation. In fact, we all have to be licensed and follow strict guidelines. The worst part about the job? Well, I've had several (5) ..... phone calls in the office. ... What do I like most about it? ... lunch hours probably ... no, (6) ....., I think it's the fact that there's lots of (7) ..... . I'm certainly always busy.	**FAIR** **ABUSE** **SERIOUS** **VARY**

Vocabulary: jobs/employment

1 Match the jobs in Column A with a phrase from Column B. Be careful! The word *conductor* has more than one meaning. Write the appropriate letter in the gaps.

Column A

1 Bouncers   ....

2 A traffic warden ....

3 A stockbroker   ....

4 The conductor   ....

5 Referees   ....

6 An editor   ....

7 A plumber   ....

8 The dustmen   ....

9 Nurses   ....

Column B

a) doesn't drive the bus. S/he collects the fares.

b) prepares books and newspapers for printing.

c) are always leaving the lid off our rubbish bin.

d) buys and sells stocks and shares.

e) are always awarding penalties against our team.

f) keep troublemakers out of clubs or discotheques.

g) checks that vehicles are not parked in the wrong place.

h) are going on strike next month over conditions in hospitals.

i) is coming round to fix the leaking tap in the bathroom.

j) is picking up her baton and looking at the first violinist.

2 Mark where the main stress falls in the following jobs then check your answers in the dictionary.

EXAMPLE: commercial · artist

1 debt collector   6 nightclub bouncer

2 social worker   7 plastic surgeon

3 traffic warden   8 bus conductor

4 private investigator   9 senior librarian

5 tax inspector   10 newspaper editor

3 Find words in the grid below to match the following definitions. The first letter of each word has been given to help you.

1 money paid for professional job   s...................

2 announce formally that you are going to leave a job   r...................

3 a period of time when workers stop work to try to get better pay and conditions   s...................

4 money paid to a salesperson for each sale s/he makes   c...................

5 stop working because you are old   r...................

6 an amount of money added to your usual pay usually because you have worked hard   b...................

7 dismiss from a job   s...................

8 the ability to do something well   s...................

9 a person who is paid to work for somebody or a company   e...................

10 get money by working   e...................

C	B	X	H	S	K	I	L	L	C
L	O	N	R	S	A	P	Q	S	O
M	N	M	O	T	P	C	C	D	M
E	U	S	M	R	C	R	K	K	M
A	S	F	T	I	Z	E	C	R	I
R	G	U	B	K	S	T	X	E	S
N	W	H	V	E	Y	I	F	S	S
S	A	L	A	R	Y	R	O	I	I
K	I	J	X	E	D	E	G	G	O
E	M	P	L	O	Y	E	E	N	N

17

Speaking: prioritising

Paper 5, Part 3

About the exam
In Paper 5, Part 3 you talk to the other candidate or the examiner about some pictures, maps or plans. Often you talk about putting things in order of priority.

Strategy
Ask the other person what s/he thinks and say whether you agree or disagree with what s/he says.

Hot tip!
DON'T make a speech!

1 Listen to some students doing a task in Paper 5, Part 3 and look at the pictures. The first student is working on her own with the examiner. The other two students are working as a pair. Which students did well in this part of the exam? Anna *(Interview 1)*? Petra and Stefan *(Interview 2)*?

2 Now listen to Petra and Stefan again and complete the following questions which they ask each other.

1 .... put dustmen after nurses?

2 What shall we .... ?

3 .... editors?

4 Let's see. .... ?

5 .... to put them before editors?

3 Listen once more and write down three words or phrases they use for agreeing and one word or phrase they use for disagreeing.

1 ....

2 ....

3 ....

4 ....

Grammar: present tenses

1 Fill in the gaps in the following sentences with the correct Present Simple or Present Continuous form of the verbs in brackets. Put the adverbs in the correct position.

1 I .... *(not/like)* getting up in the morning.

2 My brother and I .... *(have)* to get up quite early to get to school on time.

3 Our father .... *(sometimes/drive)* us, but on other days we .... *(get)* the school bus.

4 We almost .... *(never/get)* to the bus stop on time and the bus .... *(always/wait)* when we .... *(turn)* the corner.

5 The bus driver .... *(tell)* us to hurry up and we .... *(jump)* on the bus.

6 We .... *(not/go)* to school next Monday because it's a holiday.

7 Instead all the people from my class .... *(meet)* in the mountains for a picnic.

8 I .... *(make)* a chocolate cake, my friend Ioanna .... *(bring)* a salad and the others .... *(bring)* meat, bread and soft drinks.

9 Ioanna .... *(ring)* me up every evening and asks, 'What .... *(have)* to do for homework?'

10 She .... *(not/listen)* when the teacher .... *(give)* us our homework for that night.

11 She .... *(always/talk)* in class which .... *(drive)* all the teachers crazy.

12 When Ioanna .... *(ring)* me up, she .... *(always/say)*, ''What .... you .... ?' *(do)*

13 And I .... *(answer)* ' I .... *(talk)* to you, silly!'

2 Look at Column B in the jobs vocabulary on page 17 again and write the numbers of the sentence or sentences that:

● are complaints about an irritating situation that occurs regularly. 1 .... 2 ....

● are explanations of the meaning of the word. 3 .... 4 .... 5 .... 6 .... 7 ....

● is said by a radio announcer while watching what is happening on stage. 8 ....

● are statements about events that will definitely take place in the future. 9 .... 10 ....

3 Now look at what Luca, an FCE candidate, said about the two photos he was asked to describe in Part 2 of Paper 5. Look at the photos and fill in the gaps with the correct Present Simple or Present Continuous form of the verbs in brackets.
In Picture A I can see some people on a beach. Some of them (1) .... *(sunbathe)* and some (2) .... *(walk)* along the beach. There is a yacht – I think they (3) .... *(come back)* from a boat trip. In the background there is a mountain and some apartment blocks. It (4) .... *(look)* a bit like Brazil.

I (5) .... *(like)* the other photograph better. I (6) .... *(think)* it could be in Switzerland or somewhere like that. There is a woman in the foreground. She (7) .... *(ski)*. I've never been skiing, but I'd like to try it.

A

B

Writing: transactional letter

Paper 2, Part 1

1   Look at the following task. Are you asked to write a formal or an informal letter?

Look at the advertisement and the notes you have made below it. Then write a letter of **between 120 and 180 words** in an appropriate style asking for more information covering the points in your notes. Do not write any addresses.

> ## WANTED
> ## NEW MEMBERS
>
> For water sports club. Water-skiing, scuba diving, jet ski, windsurfing! You name it – if it's a watersport, we offer instruction and facilities for it. Plenty of opportunity to practise your chosen sport with other enthusiasts at Club Aquarius! For your membership application form write to:
> *The Secretary*
> *Club Aquarius*
> *P.O. Box 312*
> *Littlehampton*
> *Sussex, SU3 9JT*

– *Membership fee?*
– *Annual or monthly payment?*

2   Are the following statements true or false? Mark them **T** (true) or **F** (false).

In a formal letter:

1   you include your name in your address.   ....

2   you include the name and title (Managing Director, Head Teacher, etc.) of the person you are writing to in her/his address.   ....

3   you write the whole date in words, like this: 'fifteenth of November, nineteen ninety-nine'. ....

4   if you begin the letter *Dear Sir/Madam,* you finish it with *Yours faithfully,* .   ...

5   you can begin your letter with *Dear* + the addressee's title, for example *Dear Secretary,* . ...

3   Now write the letter in Exercise 1 in 120–180 words. You should follow this procedure.

1   Look at the instructions and underline the words and phrases that tell you exactly what you have to do.

2   Think of four questions you want to ask in your letter.

3   Decide what order you want to put them in.

4   Write your letter. Use linking words such as *first of all, also, as well as this, finally.*

5   Check your letter carefully for any grammar or spelling mistakes. Make sure your letter is properly laid out.

> *Strategy*
> You have 1 hour and 30 minutes to write two answers.
> Spend **45 minutes** on each question. Divide the 45 minutes like this:
> • **5 minutes** reading the instructions very carefully, underlining key words and checking how many things you have to do.
> • **10 minutes** thinking of ideas and writing a plan.
> • **25 minutes** writing your answer.
> • **5 minutes** checking your work carefully and correcting any mistakes.

> **▬ Hot tip! ◄**
> DON'T waste time writing your answer out again! Write on every second line so that you can make corrections easily. If your work is clear and easy to read, it is not necessary to write it out again.

3 Nearest and dearest

Vocabulary: describing people

1 Match a word in Column A with a word with the opposite meaning in Column B. Be careful! There are two extra words in Column B which you do not need to use. Write the appropriate letter in the gaps.

Column A		Column B
1 hard-working	....	a) mean
2 kind	....	b) silly
3 generous	....	c) well-behaved
4 stubborn	....	d) lazy
5 naughty	....	e) tough
6 sensible	....	f) cruel
7 modest	....	g) flexible
		h) narrow-minded
		i) arrogant

2 Fill in the gaps in the following sentences with an appropriate word from Exercise 1.

1 He's rather .... and never stops telling you how wonderful he is.

2 If you don't stop being ...., you won't get an icecream.

3 I wish you weren't so .... Why can't you pay for the coffee for once?

4 Going out in the middle of winter without a jacket was a rather .... thing to do.

5 They're very .... They let us stay in their house and lent us a car.

6 There's no need to be so .... You deserve to be proud of yourself.

7 If you were a bit more .... and tried to see his point of view, I'm sure you'd get along.

8 People who live in small communities can be a bit .... and afraid to accept new ideas.

Listening: multiple matching

Paper 4, Part 3

About the exam
In Paper 4, Part 3 you hear short extracts. You listen to people speaking about a theme. You select information from each extract to go with statements or questions.

Strategy
Note key words and phrases when you listen to the cassette for the first time.

1 Listen to four people talking about how their position in the family has affected their personality. Which of the following adjectives are used to describe each position in the family? Mark them **E** (eldest child), **M** (middle child), **Y** (youngest child) or **O** (only child).

1 open-minded	....		6 ambitious	....
2 serious	....		7 aggressive	....
3 independent	....		8 adaptable	....
4 self-confident	....		9 relaxed	....
5 selfish	....		10 responsible	....

2 Listen to the speakers again and answer the following questions. Write the number of the speaker (1, 2, 3 or 4) in the gaps.

a) Who tries to do what people expect? ....

b) Who probably works best in a team or group? ....

c) Who probably had the most freedom as a child? ....

d) Who may try to dominate others? ....

e) Who may be a bit irresponsible? ....

f) Who may blame other people for her/his own mistakes? ....

Reading: multiple choice

Paper 1, Part 2

About the exam
In Paper 1, Part 2 you choose between four alternatives to answer questions about a text.

Strategy
- Read the text once quickly.
- Read it again.
- Answer the questions without looking at the alternatives.
- Find an alternative that is like your answer.

1 Read the following article and decide which of these adjectives best describes Janet Jackson.

A unhappy **B** positive **C** aggressive **D** sophisticated

The *Other* Jackson

Janet Jackson, the youngest of nine children, was born in 1966. She became a child star of American TV soaps after being spotted in a television appearance with her brothers, The Jackson Five. In the past ten years she has recorded five albums, the last two of them providing her with twelve American Top Five singles.

Initially overshadowed by her brothers and sisters, she has now become famous in her own right. As a female singing star, only a handful of other artists – Madonna, Whitney Houston and Gloria Estefan, for example – provide her with serious competition.

Janet has managed to create a new art form, a mixture of music, dance and fashion which is perfect for the video age. She is small and rather shy which makes her seem vulnerable. She is also much more natural than many of today's stars.

Janet was born in Gary, Indiana, but moved with her family to the West Coast when she was two. She was brought up in the deluxe Jackson compound in Encino, California, with its own zoo and private cinema. She would turn on the TV to find cartoon likenesses of her brothers dancing to 'ABC' and 'I want you back'.

By the age of seven she was performing in the family's live stage act. Janet and her brother Randy would do impressions of Sonny & Cher, W.C. Fields and Mae West. Then came her enrolment in Valley Professional, a school for children in the entertainment business, small parts in TV series and a recording contract with A&M Records.

At the age of eighteen she moved away from the family to live in New York. She then secretly married Motown singer James DeBarge. The marriage only lasted sixty days and ended in annulment. 'All my life I had people telling me what to do. I wanted to do something on my own. So I ran away to get married.'

Janet came from a large, tight-knit family with a dominant and ambitious father who turned from his own minor music career to direct those of his children. Trying to become independent and gain control of her life must have been very difficult. It would be understandable if she had had to give up some things. Does she have any regrets?

'No. None. If I had my life to live all over again, I'd do it exactly the same. Everything I experienced, good or bad, was for a reason, and that was to prepare me for today and tomorrow.'

from *The Observer* magazine

2   Write answers to the following questions using information from the text.

1   How did Janet Jackson become a TV star?

....

....

2   Why was her childhood unusual?

....

....

3   Why did she move away and get married?

....

....

4   How does she feel about her life so far?

....

....

3   Now look at these alternative answers to each of the questions above and choose the correct answer, A or B.

Question 1
A Someone saw her performing with her brothers on TV.
B Her brothers saw her performing on TV.

Question 2
A It was exciting because her family moved so often.
B It was unusual because her family were very rich and famous.

Question 3
A Because she wanted to be independent.
B Because she didn't want anyone to come to the wedding.

Question 4
A She feels that the things that have happened to her have prepared her well for the life she leads.
B She feels sorry about some things that happened in the past and wishes she could change them.

4   Alternative B in Question 1 is wrong. The text says she was 'spotted in a television appearance *with* her brothers' NOT *by* her brothers. Look at the other questions again and match the following statements to the incorrect alternatives. Write the question number and the letter of the incorrect alternative in the gaps.

1   This is wrong because it says the **opposite** of what the text says.   ....

2   This is wrong because it says something that might be true which is **not** in the text.   ....

3   This is wrong because it says something the text does **not** say.   ....

┌─ **Hot tip!** ◄─────────────────────┐
If you don't know which alternative is correct, guess! NEVER leave a question unanswered!
└──────────────────────────────────────┘

5   Look again at the text and find words with the following meanings.

1   made to appear less important *(para. 2)*

....

2   a small number (of people) *(para. 2)*

....

3   can be understood *(para. 7)*

....

'I bet other people's parents don't put their kids under this much pressure.'

23

Word formation

Paper 3, Part 5

Learner training
Pay attention to the beginnings and endings of words. You can often work out the meaning of new words if you can break them up into parts. For example: *un-believ-able*.

1 Look at the words in Exercise 5 on page 23 that you found in the text on Janet Jackson and find:

1 a suffix that can be added to a verb to make an adjective. ....

2 a suffix that means 'the amount contained in'. ....

3 a prefix that means 'from above' or 'too much'. ....

2 Read the following text and then fill in the gaps with an appropriate form of the word in capitals at the end of each line.

Strategy
- Read the text all the way through once quickly.
- Decide what part of speech goes in each gap.
- Think of possible words to fill each gap.
- Form words from the words in capitals.
- Check that each word is the right part of speech.
- Check that each sentence makes sense, for example that you have used a negative prefix in a sentence with a negative meaning.

Although my two sisters and I have (0) ......*different*.....	**DIFFER**
mothers, we are definitely (1)	**LIKE**
This is not just a matter of (2) ...., though	**APPEAR**
we are all small with curly hair and a (3)	**TEND**
to (4) .... and put on weight. The resemblance	**EAT**
goes much further than that. Throughout our (5)	**CHILD**
we were brought up to be very (6) .... and our	**ADAPT**
ability to accept change is another (7)	**CHARACTER**
we share. Another would be (8) .... We all hate	**SHY**
parties where you have to walk into a (9)	**ROOM**
of strange faces. Being (10) .... like this means	**CONSCIOUS**
we are all interested in wearing (11) .... clothes.	**FASHION**
We often share our clothes. (12) .... this causes	**FORTUNATE**
arguments. We really should come to some (13)	**AGREE**
about who can borrow what from whom – and when.	

Grammar: making comparisons

1 Read the article opposite. Which of the families is most like your own?

2 Read the article again and mark the following statements **T** (true) or **F** (false).

1 Peter Menzel and his team visited the same number of families as countries.

2 The Carballo family is smaller than any of the other families.

3 They have fewer domestic appliances than the Pfitzners or the Ukitas.

4 The Ukitas have the same number of children as the Pfitzners.

5 The Ukitas' daughter Miyo is older than both of the Pfitzners' sons.

6 The Pfitzners seem to have a bit more free time than the other families.

7 In some ways the Carballos seem to be happier than the other families.

8 They seem to be more concerned about the future of their country than the other families.

3 Now write five more sentences like the ones in Exercise 2 comparing the families in the text.

FAMILIES AROUND THE WORLD

In 1994, the International Year of the Family, Peter Menzel, an American photographer, decided to take photographs to show the many different ways families live around the world. With a team of photographers and journalists he visited thirty average families in thirty different countries. They got to know the families and took photographs of them outside their homes surrounded by their possessions. Here are some of the results:

The Carballo family, Argentina

Family members:
Juan Carlos, husband, 42
Marta Elizabeth, wife, 31
María Pía, daughter, 6
María Belén, daughter, 8
Nahuel, son, 9

Mr and Mrs Carballo both work as photographers. They are not rich, but they could afford to buy a new stereo, television and video recently. But times are not easy and they have had to move in with one of Mrs Carballo's aunts. Sunday afternoon is their favourite time of the week. They all get together round the barbecue to eat, dance and laugh.

Size of family home: 3 rooms in Mrs Carballo's aunt's house.
Working week: husband 30 to 35 hours, wife 40 hours.
Domestic appliances: 1 radio, 1 telephone, 1 television, 1 video, 1 stereo.
What they want for the future: a more stable situation in Argentina.

The Ukita family, Japan

Family members:
Kazuo, husband, 45
Sayo, wife, 43
Miyo, daughter, 9
Maya, daughter, 6

Mr Ukita and Mrs Ukita and their children have very busy lives. Miyo, the older daughter, dreams of taking part in the Olympic games. Five days a week she rides her bicycle to the local sports centre where she spends two hours swimming lengths of the pool. She also goes to extra classes to prepare for the difficult national exams. This leaves her a little time left for watching television and the Ukitas have one with a special button so that they can watch foreign programmes in the original language.

Size of family home: a flat measuring 132 square metres, including living room, dining room, kitchen and bathroom.
Working week: husband 40 hours, wife 60 hours (housework).
Domestic appliances: 3 radios, 1 telephone, 1 television, 1 video, 1 microwave oven, 1 computer.
What they want for the future: a bigger house with more space.

The Pfitzner family, Germany

Family members:
Bernhard, husband, 38
Brigitte, wife, 36
Manuel, son, 7
Christian, son, 4

Bernhard Pfitzner works as a physiotherapist in Neuss, a city near Cologne. He works hard, gets home late and is often tired. He would like to be able to spend more time with his sons and dreams of owning a house in the country. Mrs Pfitzner works hard, too. She is very concerned about environmental issues. She does not want her two sons to grow up heavily influenced by television so she only lets them watch for between half an hour and an hour a day.

Size of family home: a rented flat measuring 83 square metres with four bedrooms, kitchen, hallway and bathroom.
Working week: husband 40 hours, wife 50 hours (housework).
Domestic appliances: 3 radios, 1 radio cassette, 1 television, 1 video, 1 video camera.
What they want for the future: a bigger fridge, a house in the country and a cleaner natural environment.

▲ The Carballo family

The Ukita family ▶

The Pfitzner family ▶

Writing: transactional letter

> **Paper 2, Part 1**

Hot tip!

DON'T waste time in the exam counting words! Work out how many words you normally write on a line and multiply this by the number of lines you have written.

1   Read the following task and the answers that two candidates wrote.

> Your younger sister/brother is going to visit relatives in an English-speaking country. Your relatives have not met her/him before. Write telling them about her/his travel arrangements and explaining how they should recognise her/him.
>
> Include these notes in your answer:
>
> – *check flight times*
> – *describe clothes*
> – *gift from here?*

Candidate A

Dear Susan and Nick,

We collected Stavros's ticket yesterday so I'm writing to give you his travel details.

He leaves Athens on December 13 on Flight OM 197 and arrives in Melbourne the next day at 11.20 in the morning. The airline says there are sometimes delays so it's worth phoning them at the airport to check the flight is on time.

I've enclosed a recent photograph, but just in case you have problems recognising him, he's quite tall for his years with a straight light brown hair and green eyes. He'll be wearing a light grey T-shirt, jeans and black trainers.

Is there anything you would like him to bring from Greece? The honey is delicious, you know it, and so are the olives. I ask you to tell us what would you like.

I think that's all for the moment.

All the best,

Giorgos

Candidate B

Hello my friends,

I writting inform you about my sister travel. She is leave on fly IB 264 from Barcelona and arive your country at 6 o'clock.

She is very pretty with a blonde hair and blue eyes. She is good student. She is studying very hard every day. Sometimes she uses glasses but she will use contact lens this day. She will be dressing a blue trouser and a yellow bluse. I send you one foto.

Do you want that she bring you a gift? She can bring a tipical food or clothes. You must say me what do you like.

Goodbye,

Carlos

2 Now look at the following examiner's reports and decide which is for Candidate A and which is for Candidate B.

Report 1

Candidate: ....

Grade: **unsatisfactory**

* Some points in instructions not covered.
* Beginning and ending of the letter are inappropriate.
* Letter is quite well-structured.
* Basic errors (spelling, grammar and vocabulary).
* Inappropriate vocabulary for an informal letter.
* Not enough information about flight details.

Report 2

Candidate: ....

Grade: **very good**

* Clear paragraphs covering all the points in the instructions.
* Appropriate beginning and ending to the letter.
* Some good structures.
* Wide vocabulary.
* Some poor expression, but almost no errors.
* People reading letter would know exactly what to do.

3 Find five spelling mistakes in Candidate B's letter and write the words out again correctly in your notebook.

4 Find five sentences in Candidate B's letter which contain mistakes with verb forms and write them out again correctly in your notebook.

5 Find five sentences in Candidate B's letter which contain mistakes with articles (a/an, the) and write them out again correctly in your notebook.

6 What verb normally goes with the words *glasses, contact lenses* and *trousers?* ....

7 Rewrite the unsatisfactory letter using the good letter as a model.

Learner training
Do extra writing exercises and exchange them with a friend. Get your friend to correct your mistakes. Correct your friend's mistakes.

4 Seeing is believing

Reading: multiple matching

Paper 1, Part 1

About the exam

There are always two matching tasks in Paper 1. They are tasks 1 and 4. In one type of task you choose headings from a list for each paragraph in the text.

Strategy

Learn to recognise the structure (like a plan) of the text. This will help you decide on the paragraph headings.

1 Read the following article about computer errors and decide which of these two plans the writer followed.

A

- *Describe the situation.*
- *Describe a problem.*
- *Describe unsatisfactory solutions.*
- *State the problem again.*

B

- *Ask a question.*
- *Answer the question.*
- *Give specific examples.*
- *Ask another question.*

When a computer error is a fatal mistake

Our lives depend on computers. They control our money, transport, our exam results. Yet their programs are now so complex that no one can get rid of all the mistakes.

(0 _G_)
Life without computers has become unimaginable. They are designed to look after so many boring but essential tasks – from microwave cooking to flying across the Atlantic – that we have become dependent on them.

(1___)
But as the demands placed on computers grow, so have the number of incidents involving computer errors. Now computer experts are warning that the traditional ways of building computer systems are just not good enough to deal with complex tasks like flying planes or maintaining nuclear power stations. It is only a matter of time before a computer-made catastrophe occurs.

(2___)
As early as 1889, a word entered the language that was to become all too familiar to computer scientists: a 'bug', meaning a mistake. For decades bugs and 'de-bugging' were taken to be part of every computer engineer's job. Everyone

accepted that there would always be some mistakes in any new system. But 'safety critical' systems that fly planes, drive trains or control nuclear power stations can have bugs that could kill. This is obviously unacceptable.

(3____)

One way to stop bugs in computer systems is to get different teams of programmers to work in isolation from each other. That way, runs the theory, they won't all make the same type of mistake when designing and writing computer codes. In fact research shows that programmers think alike, have the same type of training – and make similar mistakes. So even if they work separately, mistakes can still occur. Another technique is to produce back up systems that start to operate when the first system fails. This has been used on everything from the space shuttle to the A320 airbus, but unfortunately problems that cause one computer to fail can make all the others fail, too.

(4____)

A growing number of computer safety experts believe the time has come to stop trying to 'patch up' computer systems. They say programmers have to learn to think clearly and to be able to demonstrate through mathematical symbols that the program cannot go seriously wrong. Until programmers learn to do this, we will probably just have to live with the results of computer bugs.

(5____)

Of course, more often than not the errors are just annoying, but sometimes they can come close to causing tragedies. On the Piccadilly line in London's Underground a driver who was going south along a track got confused while moving his empty train through a cross-over point. He started to head north straight at a south-bound train full of people. The computerised signalling system failed to warn him of impending disaster and it was only his quick human reactions that prevented a crash.

from *Focus* magazine

2   Now read the article again and choose a heading for each paragraph from the list below. There is one extra heading which you do not need to use. The first one has been done for you.

A An old problem with serious consequences.
B Two new approaches, but can they solve the problem?
C A potentially tragic error.
D But are they here to stay?
E Experts say 'Bring back maths!'
F Old methods are no longer satisfactory.
G We couldn't live without them.

3   Find words or phrases in the text with the following meanings:

1   impossible to imagine (*para. 0*)   ....

2   needing support from (*para. 0*)   ....

3   long-established, conventional (*para. 1*)   ....

4   sudden great disaster (*para. 1*)   ....

5   often seen or heard (*para. 2*)   ....

6   not good enough (*para. 2*)   ....

7   separately (*para. 3*)   ....

8   support (*para. 3*)   ....

9   terrible events that cause great sadness (*para. 5*)   ....

10   about to happen (*para. 5*)   ....

Grammar: *like*

Paper 3, Part 3

About the exam
In Paper 3, Part 3 you read sentences and complete new sentences so that they have a similar meaning. You have to use a word that is printed in **bold** to complete the new sentence.

Hot tip!
Check for third person singular 's' in the Present Simple.

1 Complete the second sentence so that it has a similar meaning to the first sentence. Use the word in **bold** and other words to complete each sentence.

EXAMPLE: I am very similar to my brother.
  like
  My brother .... *is very like* .... me.

1 Do you want me to help you tidy up?
like
Would .... you tidy up?

2 Can you describe him for me?
tell
Can you .... like?

3 I think it must be a dog barking.
like
It .... a dog barking.

4 She plays racket sports, such as tennis and squash.
like
She .... tennis and squash.

5 They enjoy going to the beach at the weekends.
like
They.. at the weekends.

6 I think I can smell smoke.
like
That .... smoke.

7 My sister and I are very alike physically.
look
I .... my sister.

8 Can you tell me about the course?
like
I .... know about the course.

2 The following dialogue contains nine mistakes with the use of *like*. Find the mistakes and write the sentences out again correctly in your notebook.

JOAQUÍN: How is your sister like?
HEIDI: She's the same height like me and she's blonde, too. She looks so much like me you'd think we were twins.
JOAQUÍN: By the way, would you like going to the cinema at the weekend?
HEIDI: That sounds as a good idea.
JOAQUÍN: Do you like to see anything in particular?
HEIDI: Let's see something funny. I'd like comedies.
JOAQUÍN: OK. I'll come round to your house at five, if you like it.
HEIDI: Fine. Are you as your brother, always late?
JOAQUÍN: No. I like my mother, always on time.
HEIDI: Good, I like punctual people. I'll be ready at five o'clock.
JOAQUÍN: Perhaps your sister would like to come, too.
HEIDI: No, I don't think so. She's already going out on Saturday night.
JOAQUÍN: OK. See you on Saturday.
HEIDI: See you then.

Vocabulary: phrasal verbs (*take*)

1   Match the first half of the sentence in Column A with the second half of the sentence in Column B. Write the appropriate letter in the box. Then fill in the gaps with *on, off* (x3), *up* (x2), *in* or *over*.

Column A

1 I really should take a day ....

2 The manager said they were not taking ....

3 I'm sorry to have taken ....

4 My older sister was always taking ....

5 It was hilarious! He was taking ....

6 Take ....

7 We thought these virtual reality things would really take .... here,

8 I wasn't taken ....

Column B

a) for a moment when she said she had been ill.

b) volleyball. It'll do you the world of good.

c) so much of your time.

d) work and paint the kitchen.

e) our games when we were children.

f) but they've been a complete financial disaster.

g) any more bar staff for the time being.

h) one of the teachers when she walked in.

2   Fill in the gaps in the following sentences with an appropriate phrasal verb from Exercise 1.

1 You can use ...., with words like *a sport* or *a hobby* or names of specific sports and hobbies.

2 You can use .... with the word *staff* or with words for specific jobs.

3 People who study or work can .... *a few days, two weeks, a month,* etc.

4 Activities, things or people can .... *too/so much/a lot of time/space.*

5 Bossy people often .... other people's *jobs/games/conversations/meetings,* etc.

3   There are mistakes in four of the following sentences. Find the mistakes and write the sentences out again correctly in your notebook.

1 She took off me so well I had to laugh.

2 The meeting had only been going for a few minutes and he'd taken it over completely.

3 The doctor said I should swim, so I've taken up it.

4 They've already made them redundant and they only took on them a month ago.

5 We won't be very busy this week so why don't you take off it?

6 She's such a clever liar she always takes me in.

☎ Listening: multiple matching

Paper 4, Part 3

About the exam
In Paper 4, Part 3 you listen to short extracts. You match each extract to a question or statement.

Strategy
Once you have matched a statement to a speaker, cross it out and concentrate on the others.

You are going to hear five people talking about problems they have had with machines and electronic devices of various kinds. Listen and match one of the following statements **A–E** to one of the speakers. There is one statement which you do not need to use.

A She/he was frightened.
B She/he found herself/himself in the wrong place.
C She/he disturbed some other people.
D She/he said something she/he didn't mean to say.
E She/he asked someone to help her/him.
F She/he almost forgot where she/he was.

Speaker 1 ....

Speaker 2 ....

Speaker 3 ....

Speaker 4 ....

Speaker 5 ....

Writing: narrative

Paper 2, Part 2

About the exam
In Paper 2, Part 2 you choose one question to answer out of four. One of the questions may ask you to write a story.

1 Below are the first two paragraphs from a story, but the sentences are in the wrong order. Put the sentences in the correct order. Write the numbers 1–11 in the gaps. Use the words and phrases in bold to help you.

Paragraph 1

a) A search party went out to look for **the men** and found **them** two hours later more than 100 kilometres away. ....

b) **In 1970 an army battalion** were doing basic training on an enormous plain in the north-west of China. ....

c) **They** seemed dazed and confused and their uniforms were badly torn. ....

d) One morning a thick fog came down and **three soldiers** became separated from the others and were reported missing at about ten o'clock. ....

e) **They** gave **the following** explanation of what had happened to them during their two-hour absence. ....

f) **Nevertheless**, they were in perfectly good health and did not have any physical injuries. ....

Paragraph 2

g) Apparently the three men lost consciousness **at this point** though they all reported feeling they were inside some kind of aircraft and they all remembered seeing coloured flashing lights. ....

h) **Suddenly** they heard **a loud whirring noise** as if an enormous helicopter were somewhere overhead. ....

i) **As the three soldiers looked around for the rest of the battalion** they realised they were alone though they felt as if someone or something was watching them. ....

j) **Moments later** they felt themselves being drawn upwards towards **the light** by an irresistible force. ....

k) When they looked up to see where **the noise** was coming from they were almost blinded by **an intense yellow light**. ....

2 Here is the last paragraph of the story, but it contains six mistakes with verb tenses. Find the mistakes and write the paragraph out again correctly in your notebook.

The captain has not believed their story at first. After all they could have easily hitched a ride with a passing lorry driver. What was more difficult to explain was the fact that even though they have been missing for only a few hours, when they had been found they all have long beards as if they have not shaved for six months or more. They had all been absolutely clean shaven when they had disappeared.

3 Read the following task.

> Write **a story** that begins or ends with the following words:
>
> *I stared in amazement as the strange object disappeared beneath the surface of the lake.*

1 Decide whether you want to begin or finish your story with the words provided.

2 Think of ideas. Ask yourself questions like: *What disappeared? Where did it come from? Who else saw it?*

3 Write a plan with your ideas in order.

4 Write your story in 120–180 words.

5 Check your work very carefully for errors with verb tenses.

Strategy

If you can't think of any ideas, ask yourself questions like:
● When did it happen?
● Where did it happen?
● What happened first?
● What happened after that?

'For heaven's sake Maureen, not everybody wants to see photographs of our grandchildren.'

Vocabulary and grammar:
open cloze

> **Paper 3, Part 2**

Strategy
Remember to read the text all the way through first. Then decide what part of speech is missing from each gap.

Read the following text and then fill in the gaps with an appropriate word. You have been given the first three letters of each word to help you.

> When you read magazine articles about
> (1) sci.................... discoveries or
> (2) tec.................... advances, you can get a very false impression of the way scientists and technicians actually work in (3) lab.................... .
> Of course the (4) res.................... they do solves
> (5) pro.................... or leads to the
> (6) dev.................... of new theories. But it is not all as carefully planned as we might imagine. A lot of the discoveries that have (7) rev.................... the way a disease is treated or a crop grown were made by chance. A chemist might add a
> (8) che.................... to a test tube and
> (9) pro.................... a new substance. A professional (10) inv.................... might try out all sorts of unsuccessful designs before coming up with a brilliant invention almost by accident.

▶ Hot tip! ◀
If you don't know what word goes in the gap, think of any word which is the right part of speech. NEVER leave a gap blank! You cannot lose marks for wrong answers.

Learner training
Make your own gap filling exercises. Use the reading texts and tapescripts from this book. Get a friend to take out a word every six or seven words.

Speaking: picture prompts

> **About the exam**
> In Part 2 of Paper 5 you talk about some photographs and say how you feel about them.

> **Strategy**
> If you do not know the English word for something in the picture, paraphrase. Say things like: 'It's a thing you use for ...' or 'It's a kind of ...'.

1 Listen to two candidates doing this part of the interview and look at the photos below. Which candidate did well, Laura or Ahmet?

1

2

4

2 Listen to the first candidate again and complete the following sentences with the words Laura uses.

1 .... a 'parabolic antenna' or aerials.

2 .... dish.

3 .... receiving satellite TV.

> ┌─ **Hot tip!** ◄─
> DON'T say things like 'That's all. I don't know what else to say.'! The examiner wants to hear you speak.

5 All you need is love

Grammar: reported statements

1 Read the following conversation between a doctor and a young patient and then complete the doctor's notes below.

DOCTOR: Well, what seems to be the trouble?

LAURA: I feel fine, but my parents are worried about me. They think I'm acting strangely.

DOCTOR: Are you sleeping well at night?

LAURA: I sleep well, but I wake up very early.

DOCTOR: And what about meals? Are you eating normally?

LAURA: No. I haven't eaten a full meal for a week. I never feel hungry.

DOCTOR: And has anything happened to upset you? A problem at school or perhaps at home?

LAURA: It's not really a problem. But there's a new student at school and ... well, doctor, he's the most wonderful person I've ever met. He's kind, intelligent and so good-looking. I can't think about anything else. His name's Steve and he's got a motorcycle ...

DOCTOR: Well, young lady, I don't think there's really very much the matter with you.

Case notes

The patient said she (1)_____ , but that her parents (2)_____ . She said they (3)_____ . When I asked about her sleeping patterns, she said she (4)_____ , but (5)_____ . Her eating patterns are also irregular. She said (6)_____ a full meal for a week and that she never (7)_____ . When I asked if something was worrying her, she said there (8)_____ at school. My diagnosis is that the patient is in love.

2 Read the following extract from a letter Laura wrote to her friend Suzie and complete the dialogue.

I couldn't believe it. He came up to me as I was getting on the school bus. He asked me if I was doing anything next weekend. I said I had to go out to lunch with my parents on Sunday, but that apart from that I didn't have any special plans. Then he asked if I'd seen the new Harrison Ford film. I said I hadn't, but that my brother had told me that he had really enjoyed it. He asked if I wanted to go and see it with him on Saturday night and I said that sounded great. He asked what time I wanted to go to the movie and I said I thought the 6.00 session was usually less crowded, so he suggested we meet at the cinema at about 5.45 and that we could have a pizza afterwards. I haven't decided what to wear yet, but Nicki says I can borrow her new top.

STEVE: Hi, how are you?

LAURA: Oh, hi. Fine.

STEVE: Listen. I was wondering ... Are you doing anything next weekend?

LAURA: Well (1).., but apart from that (2).. .

STEVE: Have you seen the new Harrison Ford film?

LAURA: No, (3).., but my brother (4).. .

STEVE: Yes, everyone says it's brilliant. Would you like to go and see it on Saturday night?

LAURA: That (5).. .

STEVE: What time do you want to go? At six or at eight?

LAURA: (6).. the six o'clock session (7).. .

STEVE: OK. Shall we meet at the cinema at about 5.45? Perhaps we could go for a pizza after the film.

Grammar: reported questions

Laura got home from her evening out with Steve very late and her mother was angry. Read their conversation and then complete Laura's diary.

MOTHER: What's his name?
LAURA: Steve.
MOTHER: Steve what? What's his surname?
LAURA: I don't know.
MOTHER: Well how did you get to know him?
LAURA: He goes to school.
MOTHER: What year is he in at school?
LAURA: Err ... I'm not sure. He's a bit older than me.
MOTHER: How much older is he?
LAURA: A couple of years. I think he's about sixteen or seventeen.
MOTHER: I see. So he's a lot older than you. And where did you go?
LAURA: I told you. We went to see a movie.
MOTHER: What time did the movie finish?
LAURA: At about eight o'clock.
MOTHER: And what did you do after that?
LAURA: We went to have a pizza.
MOTHER: How long were you in the restaurant? It doesn't take four hours to eat a pizza!
LAURA: It took quite a long time to get home.
MOTHER: And how did you get home?
LAURA: On Steve's motorcycle, but it broke down on the way.
MOTHER: On Steve's motorcycle! Listen my girl – that's the last time you go out with this Steve. Just think yourself lucky your father hasn't heard about this!

Dear Diary,
Mum is really angry with me. She says I'm not allowed to go out with Steve ever again and all because I got home a bit late. The next morning she wouldn't stop asking me questions. Honestly it was just like a police interrogation! She asked me what (1)_____. and how (2)_____ . When I said he went to school, she wanted to know (3)_____ . I didn't want her to find out that he's eighteen, so I just said he was a bit older. But she wasn't happy with that, she wanted to know (4)_____ . And then we started on what happened that night. She questioned me about where (5)_____ , what time (6)_____ and what (7)_____ after the movie. When I said we went to have a pizza, she asked (8)_____ . And of course she wanted to know how (9)_____ . When I told her Steve had a motorcycle, she nearly had a fit!

'Mum'll be down in a minute. While you're waiting would you like to see the video of her first wedding?'

Grammar: key word transformations

Hot tip!

DON'T change the word given! You must use the same form of verbs and nouns.

Complete the second sentence so that it has a similar meaning to the first sentence. Use the word in **bold** and other words to complete each sentence.

EXAMPLE: 'I'm sorry I got home so late,' said Laura.
apologised
Laura ..*apologised for getting*.. home so late.

1   'I won't tell anyone about it,' said Suzie.
promised
Laura's friend Suzie .... anyone about it.

2   'Laura, you should try being honest with your parents,' said the doctor.
advised
The doctor .... honest with her parents.

3   'Don't go out with that boy again!' said Laura's father.
warned
Laura's father .... go out with Steve again.

4   'You've been meeting your boyfriend after school, haven't you?' said Mum.
accused
Laura's mother .... her boyfriend after school.

5   'Lend me your gameboy, or I'll tell Mum and Dad,' said Laura's brother.
threatened
Laura's brother .... her parents unless she lent him her gameboy.

6   'I haven't seen Steve since Saturday night,' said Laura.
denied
Laura .... Steve since Saturday night.

7   'But I tried to phone him yesterday,' said Laura.
admitted
Laura .... him the day before.

8   'Perhaps I could meet your parents,' said Steve.
suggested
Steve .... Laura's parents.

9   'No, I will not speak to him,' said Laura's mother.
refused
Laura's mother .... Steve.

10   'Try being a bit more understanding, Mrs Carter,' said the doctor.
encouraged
The doctor .... a bit more understanding.

11   'I've made up my mind. I'm going to ask Steve to lunch on Sunday,' said Laura's mother.
decided
Laura's mother .... Steve to lunch on Sunday.

12   'Would you like to have lunch with us on Sunday, Steve?' said Laura's mother.
invited
Laura's mother .... lunch with them on Sunday.

13   'I think you're right. Laura is too young to stay out so late,' said Steve.
agreed
Steve .... too young to stay out so late.

14   'Next time we could take Andrew with us,' said Steve.
offered
Steve .... Laura's younger brother with them the next time.

15   'Perhaps it would be better to go out in the afternoons,' said Laura's father.
recommended
Laura's father .... in the afternoons.

Grammar: error correction

Strategy

If you see any of the following in a line, check that they should be there:

- definite and indefinite articles e.g. I go to school by (the) bus.
- auxiliaries (*do, have, are*, etc.) e.g. She asked me where (did) I put the keys.
- the word 'more' e.g. He is (more) taller than me.
- prepositions e.g. My parents gave (to) me a book.
- pronouns e.g. The man who (he) told me to come back today sounded German.

Read the following text and look carefully at each line. Some of the lines are correct, and some have an extra incorrect word which should not be there. If a line is correct, put a tick (✔) at the end of the line. If a line has a word that should not be there, circle the word. There are two examples at the beginning (**0** and **00**).

0	I (have) received a really nice long letter last week
00	from a girl called Laura I met on holiday last summer. ✔
1	In the letter she told to me about her new boyfriend.
2	He goes to her school, but is quite a lot more older.
3	At first her parents did not like to him very much
4	because they went out together and she got home late.
5	When she told her mother he had a motorcycle, she was
6	very upset and refused that to allow Laura to go out with
7	him again. Laura was very upset and went to the family doctor
8	for to discuss her problem with her. The doctor suggested
9	that Laura should to be more honest with her parents. She spoke
10	to my friend's mother and advised her to be more of understanding.
11	Eventually my friend's parents met her new boyfriend and
12	got on quite well with him. He promised to make sure Laura
13	always gets at home before eleven o'clock and suggested
14	taking Laura's younger brother when they go out.
15	Laura says me her parents really like her boyfriend now.

Vocabulary: love and marriage

Read the following letter to a problem page. Then fill in the gaps with an appropriate word or phrase from the box. Use the correct form of the verbs.

best man   infatuated
get married   fall in love
anniversary   go out
get engaged   choir   vicar
aisle   have an affair
bridesmaid   bouquet
have a baby   have rows
get a divorce

Dear Madge,

Tom and I met at a dance about five years ago. We started (1)............................. together and although at the beginning I thought I was just (2)............................. with him, before long we both realised we (3)............................. .

We wanted to wait until he had finished his military service before we (4)............................., but we (5)............................. anyway, before he went into the army.

The wedding was all the more wonderful because we had had to wait. Tom asked his oldest friend to be (6)............................. . As I walked down the (7)............................. I felt so happy I thought I would die. When the (8)............................. said, 'I now pronounce you man and wife.' and the (9)............................. sang 'Ave Maria' everyone could see how happy I was. Outside the church I threw my (10)............................. as high as I could and my sister Mary caught it.

But not long after that things started to go wrong. We started to (11)............................. about silly things and not long after little Lucy was born I found out that Tom (12)............................. .

I don't know what to do. I still love him, but he wants (13)............................. . Should I agree?

Yours,
CONFUSED

🔊 Listening: multiple choice

Paper 4, Part 1

About the exam
In Paper 4, Part 1 you will hear people talking in different situations. You choose the best of three answers to questions.

Strategy
Listen for clues about:
- what the people are talking about.
- how they feel about what they are saying.
- the relationships between the people e.g. friends, business colleagues.

Listen to the extracts on the cassette and choose the correct alternative to complete the following statements.

1 You are watching television. You hear this woman talking. She is talking about

  A a film she didn't enjoy very much.
  B a play that she didn't think was very good.
  C a book that she found very exciting.

2 You are listening to the radio. You hear this man speaking. He thinks people listening

  A speak Spanish.
  B may not speak Spanish.
  C do not speak Spanish.

3 You overhear this girl talking on the telephone. She is

  A politely refusing to go out with the person who phoned her.
  B accepting an invitation from the person who phoned her.
  C inviting the person who phoned her to go out.

4 You hear this woman talking about her husband. They met

  A in a cinema.
  B on a picnic.
  C in class.

5 You overhear these two boys talking on a bus. The first boy

  A doesn't mind meeting the girl's parents.
  B is afraid of meeting the girl's parents.
  C has met the girl's parents before.

Writing: background reading texts

Paper 2, Part 2

About the exam
In Paper 2, Part 2 there is always a question on the background reading texts. This question is **optional**.

Hot tip!
DON'T attempt this question if you have not read any of the books! Reading a summary is **not** enough.

Strategy
Read the book once all the way through. Then read the book again and keep notes of:
- what happens in the story.
- the characters.
- the places.
- the way you feel about the things that happen.
Read the book again quickly a week or two before the exam.

Think of a book or story that you have read recently in English or in your own language. Write a composition retelling the story in your own words so that a friend of your own age could decide whether to read it or not.

1 Underline the important words in the instructions.

2 Make a list of the important events in the story.

3 Plan your composition. Decide how many paragraphs you are going to write and which events you will mention in each paragraph. Will you write about what happens at the end?

4 Write your composition in 120–180 words.

5 Check your composition for spelling and grammar mistakes. Be particularly careful with reported speech.

Learner training
There are film versions of many of the books that are set as background reading texts. If you see the film (preferably in English) before you read the book, it will make it easier to understand. Remember that it will still be **absolutely necessary** to read the book several times as well.

Reading: multiple choice

Paper 1, Part 2

About the exam
In another type of multiple choice question in Paper 1, Part 2 you say what words like pronouns (e.g. *it, she, they*) and possessive adjectives (e.g. *his, our, their*) in the text refer to.

Strategy
To work out what a word refers to:
- look at the sentences before or after the word.
- remember that words like 'it' and 'this', or 'do' and 'so' can refer to verbs, nouns, adjectives and adverbs, or to phrases and clauses.

1 The following lines all come from Elton John's *Your Song* (page 47 of the *First Certificate Gold Coursebook*). Look at the underlined words and write what they refer to.

1 It's a little bit funny,
This feeling inside,

....

2 Don't have much money,
But boy if I did,

....

3 And you can tell everybody this is your song.
It may be quite simple, but now that it's done,

....

4 But, the sun's been quite kind while I wrote this song,
It's for people like you that keep it turned on.

....

5 So excuse me forgetting, but these things I do,

....

2 Read the article opposite and then choose the best title from the list below.

A So, love, this is your song.
B The successful pop song: a recipe.
C What's in a name?: what to call your baby.

---

1 THE WORLD is divided into the 'haves' and the 'have nots': those who have had their names used in popular songs and the rest. The 'haves' include anyone named Eleanor, Carol, Bernadette, Maria, Frankie or Johnnie. Girls called Sue or Suzie are especially fortunate, what with 'Wake up Little Suzie' and so on. The 'have-nots', a large and unhappy group, include people named Graham, Bruce, Jacqueline and a great many others. Anyone
10 with a name like these is likely to go through life without ever hearing their name in a song on the radio or anywhere else.

But help is at hand. Serge Romano has started a business called 'Songs for You' in Melbourne, Australia. Anyone can have a song written, recorded, preserved and presented to fit their specifications.

Serge got the idea for 'Songs for You' about a year ago when he and his wife Cathy were at a
20 wedding. 'The groom had got a song done for his bride. The reaction from her and the bridesmaids and other guests was fantastic. A little while later I was discussing it with friends, and it struck me that this could really take off.'

Aiming at the wedding and engagement market, the Romanos advertise on cards in florists and photographers' studios, but they will also take requests for songs for birthdays, Christmas and anniversaries. The minimum fee is $300. For this,
30 clients get a recorded version of their song on cassette (a CD is extra), plus a framed copy of the lyrics.

The creative process begins with a client filling out a questionnaire: About your song. This seeks details of the special occasion, relationship with the person to be immortalised in song, how they met, habits and most memorable moments. The musical style can be tailored to suit the client. For lovers, something romantic; for a younger listener a heavy-
40 metal feel might be more appropriate.

Each client gets a different song, though Serge admits that they may repeat a line from time to time. They try to avoid this as there is always the danger that two clients may meet and compare songs, but most songs are so personal, they couldn't be about anyone else. They might include nicknames or references to some special habit.

Most of Serge's customers are very satisfied with their songs. 'Yesterday I met a girl who'd had a song
50 done for her for Christmas. She played it in the bank where she works. She was nearly crying, explaining to me how much it meant to her. She knows the words by heart,' says Serge. 'To anyone else', he suggests, 'it might seem just like any other song, but Mary certainly doesn't think so.'

Are there any situations that Serge and his songwriters couldn't deal with? For example a woman about to split up with a man who wants to leave him a song to remember her by? Could Serge
60 and his team come up with something appropriate? 'Sure. We could do that. Though it's not a situation we've ever been presented with. Thank goodness!'

from The Age newspaper

3 Choose the correct alternative to answer the following questions.

1 Does the word 'these' in *line 10* refer to

   A names like Maria, Frankie or Johnnie?
   B names like Graham, Bruce or Jacqueline?
   C names like Eleanor, Carol or Bernadette?
   D names like Sue or Suzie?

2 Does the word 'her' in *line 21* refer to

   A Serge's wife Cathy?
   B the groom?
   C Serge?
   D the bride?

3 Does the word 'this' in *line 43* refer to

   A repeating a line from time to time?
   B two clients meeting?
   C writing different songs for each client?
   D clients comparing songs?

4 Does the word 'so' in *line 55* refer to the fact

   A that there are situations that Serge and his songwriters couldn't deal with?
   B that it meant a lot to her?
   C that it seems just like any other song?
   D that she knows the words by heart?

5 Does the word 'that' in *line 61* refer to

   A leaving him with a song to remember her by?
   B coming up with something appropriate?
   C being presented with a situation?
   D dealing with the request?

Learner training

You can improve your English and do well in FCE if you read newspapers, magazines and books in English. When you read widely like this, you will see words that are new to you. Sometimes it is necessary to look them up in a bilingual dictionary. Sometimes it is better to work out the meaning using your general knowledge and the words and sentences around the new word.

---

4 Use your general knowledge and the context to work out what the following words from the above article mean. Circle the correct alternative.

1 Often people have ideas very suddenly. So 'struck' *(line 23)* means

   A hit sharply or forcefully.
   B came immediately to the mind.

2 A song is a combination of words and music. So 'lyrics' *(line 32)* means

   A the words of a song, especially a modern popular song.
   B a musical instrument.

3 Something that only friends usually know about a person is the special name they like to be called. So 'nickname' *(line 47)* means

   A the same as surname.
   B a name used informally instead of a person's real name.

4 If you listen to a song a lot you eventually remember the words. So 'she knows the words by heart' *(line 53)* means

   A she has memorised the words.
   B she feels strongly about the words.

5 Find words in the text *So, love, this is your song* with the following meanings.

1 A word meaning 'man about to be married'.   ....

2 A word meaning 'woman about to be or recently married'.   ....

3 A word meaning 'unmarried girls who help the woman getting married at a marriage ceremony'.   ....

4 A word meaning 'agreement to marry'.   ....

5 A word meaning 'a date that is remembered because it is an exact number of years after an event'.   ....

6 It's all in the mind

Grammar: gerunds and infinitives

1 The following sentences come from a story called *Lady Musgrove's necklace.* There are grammatical mistakes in seven of them. Find the mistakes and write the sentences out again correctly in your notebook.

1 At first Mary denied to steal the necklace.
2 Even when her fingerprints were found all over Lady Musgrove's dressing room, she continued to claim she was innocent.
3 She pretended not to hear when they asked her where she had been the evening the necklace vanished.
4 But eventually she admitted to take it.
5 The astonishing thing was that she refused saying where she had hidden it, even when Lord and Lady Musgrove offered to drop the charges.
6 Finally, when the police were arranging take her to the station, she agreed returning it.
7 She seemed to be genuinely sorry, and Lord and Lady Musgrove promised to let her keep her job.
8 However, she said she would prefer to work as a shop assistant and that she intended to go to London.
9 She hoped finding a job there.
10 Lady Musgrove said she would try helping her find work.
11 Mary stopped to cry and thanked her for her kindness.

2 Fill in the gaps in the following sentences with the correct form of the verbs in brackets.

1 If they're too big, try .... *(wear)* them with thicker socks.

2 I'd like .... *(know)* more about how the brain works.

3 I remember .... *(wake up)* very early on my fifth birthday.

4 Try not .... *(make)* mistakes with verb tenses in the exam.

5 I was late for class because I stopped .... *(talk)* to a friend I met on the way.

6 Today is a holiday, but luckily I remembered .... *(go)* to the bank yesterday.

7 I stopped .... *(smoke)* three years ago.

8 I like .... *(go)* to the beach at the weekends, but it's seldom warm enough.

Listening: note taking

About the exam
In this type of exercise in Paper 4 you listen for:
● the main points.
● specific information.

Strategy
Study the incomplete notes before you listen to work out what kind of information you need to listen for.

1 You are going to hear a scientist talking about the body clock. First look at the notes and think about the kind of information you need to complete them.

---

1 It is only when our normal routine is interrupted that we notice *our physical or psychological rhythms.* ......

2 We can perform better if we ....

3 Short term memory works best at ....

4 and *until 9 o'clock in the morning.* ....

5 In the late morning we are best at ....

6 It would be best to learn a poem by heart at about ....

7 A splash of cold water and .... can help you wake up in the morning.

8 The main idea is that we are better at specific activities *at different times of day.* ...

---

 2 Now listen and complete the notes.

Hot tip!
REMEMBER! You don't have to write complete sentences.

Grammar: key word transformations

Complete the second sentence so that it has a similar meaning to the first sentence. Use the word in **bold** and other words.

1 He didn't want to take the books back to the library.
feel
He .... the books back to the library.

2 That overcoat costs too much.
afford
I .... that overcoat.

3 He hates it if he has to study on Saturday afternoons.
stand
He .... on Saturday afternoons.

4 She said she would accept my FCE registration a few days late.
agreed
She .... my FCE registration a few days late.

5 Do you think I should buy a bilingual dictionary?
suggest
Would you .... a bilingual dictionary?

6 She wouldn't lend me her notebook.
refused
She .... her notebook.

7 The burglars said they were plumbers.
pretended
The burglars .... plumbers.

8 Do you think you will pass the exam?
expect
Do you .... the exam?

9 'Why don't you do the exam again?' he said.
encouraged
He .... the exam again.

10 I haven't smoked for three years.
gave
I .... three years ago.

Vocabulary: multiple choice cloze

Paper 3, Part 1

About the exam
Apart from adjectives and verbs that are followed by prepositions, you will be tested on your knowledge of which words to use in particular contexts.

Strategy
Check that each of the alternatives can be used in the context. For example, look at these words:

A agenda   **B** timetable   **C** programme

All of the words refer to time that is planned. But 'timetable' is the most likely alternative in a text about classes in a school, 'agenda' would be best in a text about meetings and 'programme' in a text about concerts.

Read the following text and then choose the correct alternative below for each of the numbered gaps. Remember that in the exam there will be **four** alternatives for you to choose from.

1 **A** attend   **B** assist   **C** go
2 **A** brought up   **B** educated   **C** trained
3 **A** personal   **B** private   **C** particular
4 **A** matters   **B** courses   **C** subjects
5 **A** succeed   **B** pass   **C** approve
6 **A** degree   **B** curriculum   **C** career
7 **A** pupils   **B** trainees   **C** students
8 **A** lectures   **B** conferences   **C** talks
9 **A** lectures   **B** reading   **C** training
10 **A** lecturer   **B** professor   **C** teacher

EDUCATION IN AUSTRALIA

In Australia most children (1)..................... primary school from the age of five. Only two per cent of children of primary school age are (2)..................... at home. Some children who go to school also take up extra activities such as learning to play a musical instrument or dancing, and they go to (3)..................... classes for these and for school (4)..................... they find difficult or particularly interesting, such as languages, mathematics or computing. Ninety-five per cent of the population go on to secondary school, but a much smaller percentage (5)..................... the final year of secondary school examinations and complete a university (6)..................... . At the moment university (7)..................... and graduates make up less than a third of the total population. Australian universities are modern and well-equipped. Most teaching is by a combination of (8)....................., tutorials and practical classes. The humanities courses like History and Philosophy, usually involve a lot of extra (9)..................... in the library. To become a primary or secondary school (10)....................., it is usually necessary to study at a university for three years or more.

Learner training
'False friends' are words in English that look very similar to words in other languages, but mean something different. 'Sympathetic' is an example. If you say: 'She was very sympathetic.' in English, you mean: 'She showed that she understood someone else's suffering.' In many other European languages it would mean that you thought she was a nice person. It is a good idea to make a list of 'false friends'.

Hot tip!
The incorrect alternatives are sometimes 'false friends'.

Vocabulary: education

1 Find ten words in the grid below to do with education. Then write a definition of each word.

EXAMPLE: *truant*: a student who stays away from school without permission

C	A	P	R	C	H	E	A	T	L
L	M	T	G	M	B	A	F	Z	R
A	Y	E	S	E	C	K	P	K	P
S	B	R	M	Q	W	M	A	R	K
S	O	M	T	O	T	X	S	E	L
B	H	V	D	I	R	Z	S	V	E
G	F	V	H	Q	U	I	P	I	S
C	N	A	E	D	A	Y	S	S	S
W	J	F	I	X	N	J	N	E	O
R	Y	K	O	L	T	M	Z	X	N

2 Match a word in the box below with an object in the picture.

bookcase   calendar   lamp   stapler   pencil
sharpener   highlighter   calculator   notebook
waste-paper bin   paper clips

Speaking: short responses

Paper 5, Part 1

About the exam
At the beginning of Paper 5 the interlocutor encourages you to give personal information about yourself.

Strategy
Make sure you know how to talk about:
- levels in the education system in your country.
- subjects you study/studied at school/university.
- free time activities.
- your family.
- the area where you live.
- your plans for the future.

1 Here are some examples of candidates doing the first part of Paper 5. Who gives the best response in each case?

1
INTERLOCUTOR: Well your names are Daniel and Nilgün. Is that right? Now tell us a little bit about yourselves. What do you both do?
DANIEL: I study ... I don't know how to say it in English ... informatic?... in an academy.
NILGÜN: Well, I'm still at school. I'm in my third year of secondary school. I like maths and science subjects. Chemistry is my favourite.

2
INTERLOCUTOR: Oh really? And what do you both hope to do when you finish?
DANIEL: I'd like to go to university to study engineering or computer science.
NILGÜN: I don't know.

3
INTERLOCUTOR: Tell me, Nilgün, what do you like doing in your free time?
NILGÜN: I play handball for a local team. I enjoy that very much. I like listening to music and going to the cinema, too.
DANIEL: Nothing in particular.

2 Now roleplay this part of Paper 5 with two friends. You should each take it in turns to play the part of the examiner.

Writing: discursive

About the exam
In Paper 2, Part 2 you may be asked to write an article expressing your opinion about something.

1 Look at the following task and the answer one candidate wrote. He has made six mistakes with the language of giving opinions and agreeing and disagreeing. Find the mistakes and write the sentences out again correctly in your notebook.

An international magazine has asked you to write an article expressing your opinion about the following statement:

Co-education is a disaster for girls.

Write a short **article** for the magazine, based on your own experience.

I am not agree with the statement 'Co-education is a disaster for girls.' On my opinion co-educational schools have both advantages and disadvantages for both sexes.

It is often suggested that girls do not do as well because they are more self-conscious in the company of boys. But girls and boys will never learn to get over their shyness unless they actually have a chance to get to know people of the opposite sex.

I am agree up to a point that girls learn to be more passive in co-educational schools, but the two sexes are not normally separated in society and young women must learn to compete with men.

Another argument against co-education is that boys mature more slowly than girls and that this holds the girls back. This is truth up at a point, but surely the boys compensate for this in other ways. The sexes are different after all and as far as I am concerning these differences are a good thing.

So let's not separate boys and girls in our education system. In my point of view we are denying them important opportunities if we do so.

2 Rewrite the following letter with correct punctuation.

1   *dear mr lewis*

....

2   *my daughter helen will not be able to attend school tomorrow morning*

....

3   *she has an appointment with the dentist at nine oclock*

....

4   *dr melroses surgery is about twenty minutes from the centre of cambridge*

....

5   *it is unlikely that i can get helen to school before midday*

....

6   *i would be grateful if you would excuse her from english and mathematics classes*

....

7   *yours sincerely jane warburton*

3 Read the following task and then write your answer in 120–180 words. Use the language of agreeing and disagreeing from Exercise 1 and make sure you use correct punctuation.

> You have been asked to write an article for an English language newspaper aimed at parents with young children. Your article should be a response to the following statement:
>
> *Foreign languages should be taught at nursery school level.*

1   Underline key words in the instructions.

2   Make two columns: one headed FOR, the other AGAINST. Think of arguments for or in favour of the statement. Write them in the first column. Think of arguments against and write them in the second column.

3   Choose one of these two plans. (They are <u>both</u> good plans.)

PLAN A
- Introduction: my opinion.
- Paragraph 1: point for the statement; argument against this point.
- Paragraph 2: point for the statement; argument against this point.
- Conclusion: state opinion again.

PLAN B
- Introduction: my opinion.
- Paragraph 1: arguments in favour of the statement.
- Paragraph 2: arguments against the statement.
- Conclusion: state opinion again.

4   Write your article.

5   Check carefully for mistakes with verb forms.

Strategy
If you cannot think of arguments for *and* against, imagine what people you actually know would think about the question. What would your mother think? How about your best friend? And your grandparents?

Reading: multiple matching

Paper 1, Part 1

Strategy
Find the sentence that expresses the main idea in each paragraph. The headings you choose from will also express the main idea.

Read the following article and choose a heading from the list below for each paragraph. The first one has been done for you. There is one extra heading which you do not need to use.

A A very powerful mechanism.
B Two ways of remembering.
C Why we forget our earliest memories.
D Short term and long term memory.
E Healthy body; healthy mind.
F An old approach but a good one.
G Are you forgetful?

Learner training
Label real objects in your room or house with small pieces of paper with the English words written on them. You can learn other words in this way as well. For example, if you want to learn all the words for school subjects, stick pieces of paper with these words on objects in your room. Try to associate the word with the object. When you want to remember the words, imagine yourself walking round the room and seeing the various objects with the labels.

How to boost your memory

(1 _G_)
Perhaps you do badly in exams because you can't recall facts and figures or words and structures in a foreign language. Are you always losing things or forgetting the books you need for school that day? Or do you forget what Mum wanted you to get at the corner shop? Relax! Help is close at hand. There's a tremendous range of methods to boost your memory.

(2___)
Your memory is like a brilliant, but unreliable computer storing a vast amount of information. In fact the memory's capacity is theoretically unlimited. The brain can record more than 86 billion bits of information every day and our memories can probably hold 100 trillion bits in a lifetime.

(3___)
Nevertheless only about 20 per cent of our daily experience is registered, and of that only a tiny proportion is loaded into long term memory. Most of the images and ideas that pass through our minds during a day are held for only 25 to 30 seconds. This is just long enough for us to be able to keep the words of a sentence in our head as we read it so we understand its meaning.

(4___)
We also remember different things in two different ways: declarative and non-declarative. Declarative memory deals with concrete things, specific events and facts such as what we have been doing and our recall of things that have happened. Non-declarative memory includes knowledge of general things, how to ride a bicycle, how to behave and so on. Someone with amnesia will almost always remember how to ride a bike, but may well forget her own name. One sad victim of this type of amnesia announces every ten minutes that he has 'just woken up'. Every time his wife walks into the room he throws his arms around her as if he has not seen her for years, even though she has only been gone for a few minutes. Yet this man, formerly a highly-talented musician, is still able to play the piano and conduct a choir through a long and complicated concert piece.

(5___)
Normal, healthy people can improve their memories very easily. First of all learn to relax if you're trying to memorise something. You may miss important items if your mind is on something else or if you weren't paying attention because of anxiety – you retain information best when you are alert and concentrating. If you're having trouble concentrating, increase the flow of oxygenated blood to the brain. Despite its small size the brain uses 20 per cent of the body's oxygen requirement. So try to combine study with exercise, particularly the kind of exercise that gets you breathing faster. Keep your mind fit as well as your body by doing mental workouts. Crosswords, Scrabble and quizzes all help to keep the mind in shape.

(6___)
You can also train your memory in certain ways. The ancient Greeks invented memory systems called mnemonics, and they still work today. Most systems involve associating the things you want to remember with something you already have safely stored in your head, and the most effective systems make use of visual imagery, smell, touch and sound. If you want to remember someone's name, try to find something distinctive about their hair, nose or eyes to associate with the name, e.g. Jane's wearing jewellery, Tim's tall or Bill's got a beard. If you want to remember numbers try to make associations between numbers in sequence – think of people's ages, special dates, whether they're odd or even.

from *Best* magazine

7 The price of fame

Grammar: error correction

Paper 3, Part 4

Strategy
As you read the text, 'say' the words in your mind.

Read the following text and look carefully at each line. Some of the lines are correct and some have an extra incorrect word that should not be there. If a line is correct, put a tick (✔) next to it. If a line has a word that should not be there, circle the word. There are two examples at the beginning (**0** and **00**).

Stagefright

0 Even the most experienced performers suffer from ✔

00 (the) stagefright. Sometimes this can be so extreme

1 that it almost completely paralyses the person concerned.

2 They stand in the wings, their heart beating at a rate of

3 130 or 135 a minute and often seriously think of about

4 not going on. Some of find they cannot remember

5 the performance at all after it is over. Others genuinely believe

6 they have forgotten all their lines or one of in

7 particular. Most have feel ill. They sweat and shiver and their

8 stomachs are make strange noises. Considering the

9 agonies that even such as well-known actors as Dustin

10 Hoffman or Robert de Niro go through, it is surprising

11 that less experienced performers ever have the courage to walk

12 onto a stage at all. So next time you are feel nervous before a

13 job interview or an oral examination, remember you are in

14 good company. The world's top performers know exactly how do

15 you feel. They should. They often feel a lot worse.

📼 Listening: selecting

Paper 4, Part 4

About the exam
In Paper 4 you may hear different accents such as Australian and Scottish accents as well as speakers whose first language is not English.

Strategy
You will hear the cassette twice. The first time you listen, spend the first half a minute getting used to the accent.

Listen to an interview with Alex Dimitriades, the star of an Australian TV series, and mark the following statements **T** (true) or **F** (false).

1 Alex found it easy to get used to being famous. ....

2 Alex has been in several plays. ....

3 Alex wants to get a part in another film. ....

4 Alex hasn't seen all of Robert de Niro's films. ....

5 The interviewer asks Alex a lot of questions about his private life. ....

6 The interviewer is interested in how he feels about being famous. ....

Learner training
If you have a short wave radio, you can listen to broadcasts in English from all over the world. This will help you get used to the different accents you may hear in Papers 4 and 5.

Vocabulary: entertainment

Look at the following sentences and decide if the people are talking about theatre, music, film, painting or sculpture. Mark the sentences **T** (theatre), **M** (music), **F** (film), **P** (painting) or **S** (sculpture). In some of the sentences more than one category is possible.

1 My audition went really well and I got the part. ....

2 The lead singer also plays guitar. ....

3 His first exhibition opens next week. ....

4 I don't know who composed it, but it's my favourite piece. ....

5 We could only get tickets in the front row so we were much too close to the screen. ....

6 One of the critics said the director should have stuck to acting. ....

7 It had such a sad ending that almost everyone in the audience was crying. ....

8 Are there any well-known heavy metal groups in your country? ....

9 He almost forgot his lines in the performance we saw. ....

10 I thought that young woman conductor was really brilliant. ....

11 He did all the statues in the park. ....

12 The audience went on applauding even after the last curtain call. ....

13 The photography was wonderful, but I didn't think much of the plot. ....

14 Have you heard their latest album? ....

15 They're very modern and the colours are amazing. ....

Vocabulary and grammar: open cloze

> **Paper 3, Part 2**

Strategy
Read the text all the way through and make sure you know what it is about before you begin to answer.

1 Read the following text and answer these questions.

1 Is it about a play or a film? ....

2 How many lines of the text do you have to read before you can be certain? ....

When we got to the booking office, there were very (1).................... tickets left so we couldn't sit (2).................... . George sat in the front (3).................... because he likes to be near the (4).................... and I sat towards the back of the (5).................... .

As soon as it started, I knew I wasn't (6).................... to like it. I really can't (7).................... that kind of thing. Something like ten people were killed in the first ten minutes, and the director (8).................... made sure that he didn't miss a single detail. There was one (9).................... that made me feel quite sick. I don't think they should be allowed to show (10).................... violent films. I'm sure they have a bad effect on people.

I suppose the only good thing about it was the actor who played the (11).................... of the gangster. He was really brilliant. The soundtrack was good, too. There were songs by all the best known (12).................... from the sixties, like the Beatles and the Rolling Stones. I might try and buy the CD when it (13).................... out.

I got the impression the rest of the (14).................... didn't enjoy it much either. It just goes to show you (15).................... never trust what you read in reviews in the press. The critics have such strange taste in films.

2 Now read the text again and fill in the gaps with an appropriate word.

Grammar: Present Perfect

1   Fill in the gaps in the following dialogues with the correct Past Simple, Present Perfect Simple or Present Perfect Continuous form of the verbs in brackets.

A

A: (1)............................. *(see)* the latest Arnold Schwarzenegger film?

B: Yes. I (2)............................. *(see)* it last weekend.

A: What (3)............................. *(think)* of it?

B: I (4)............................. *(like)* it, but I (5)............................. *(think)* it (6)............................. *(be)* a bit violent.

B

A: (7)............................. *(hurt)* your hand? It's all red and swollen.

B: Yes. I (8)............................. *(hit)* it with a hammer this morning. I (9)............................. *(go)* to carpentry classes for the last couple of weeks.

A: (10)............................. *(make)* any furniture yet?

B: Yes, I (11) .... *(make)* a small coffee table for my wife last week. It was her birthday present.

C

A: I (12)............................. *(not/see)* Alex for weeks. (13)............................. *(go)* away somewhere?

B: No. I think he (14)............................. *(study)* for an exam and so he (15)............................. *(not/go)* out very much lately. Hey! (16)............................. *(pass)* your driving test last week?

A: No. I (17)............................. *(fail)* and that's the third time I (18)............................. *(take)* the test!

2   The following sentences were all written by English children. They contain mistakes with the Past Simple and past participle forms of irregular verbs. Find the mistakes and write the sentences out again correctly in your notebook.

1   Our dog has bited me three times.

2   The wind has blowed down all the trees in our street.

3   My daddy builded our house himself.

4   When I throwed the ball yesterday, our dog catched it.

5   My mum and dad buyed me a bicycle.

6   I've falled over at school twice this week.

7   I finded 50p on my way home today.

8   I spended all my pocket money on sweets.

9   I've writed a story about a boy and a cat.

10   My granny sended me a dolly for my birthday.

Writing: report

Paper 2, Part 2

About the exam

In Paper 2, Part 2 you may be asked to write a report on a place you have visited and what it offers a particular group of people.

1 Look at the following task and the answers two candidates wrote which the examiner has already corrected.

> You work in a language school helping to organise excursions and trips for students. The school director has asked you to prepare a report on a museum in your area.
>
> Write your **report** in 120–180 words describing the museum and what it has to offer students of English as a foreign language. Mention both good and bad points in your report.

Candidate A

Last week my classmates and I went on a excursion to the Toy Museum in London. We have left the school at 10 o'clock and reached to the museum at 11, so we have had plenty of time to look around.

The section I liked more was the dolls. There were dolls from all over the world in national dress. There was even one from my country. There were also beautiful dolls from the last century.

On the other hand, Andres and Mehmet really liked the model railway. Jorge and Hiroshi spent most of the time looking at the tin soldiers. We all really loved the collection of teddy bears.

We had lunch in a cafe and travelled back to school by double-decker bus. It was a very nice trip. After I thought that children all over the world are really the same.

Candidate B

Report on the Science Museum
To: School Director
From: Excursions officer
Date of visit: 12 April

I have visited the Science Museum last week to decide if it will be good for students from the school to see. I will make comments on the following: price, interest, language.

1. Price
an
It costs £5 for entrance ticket to the museum. This is much too expensive for most students. There is a special price on Wednesday mornings (£2.50), but most students are in class at this time. However, the museum is very interesting (see next section) so this makes it worth/

2. Interest
There are many exhibits and displays, although the section on astronomy was closed for reforms. Most people will find something that interests them. I liked especially the section on the human body.

3. Language
All of the exhibits have short texts in English expla explicating what is shown. Some exhibits had tapes you could listen/. These were a bit dificult sometimes. In spite of this I think many students could improving improve their English listening to these tapes.

Conclusion: I think levels 4 and 5 should visit this museum. The teachers should prepare some activities to do while we are there.

2 Now read the examiner's comments below. Which comments apply to Candidate A and which to Candidate B?

---

1 Comments: Candidate ....

Grade: Good

The task of writing a report has been done well, with a clear layout and careful attention to the instructions.

There are some errors of tense and vocabulary, but the candidate uses linking words very well.

Although the report contains more than the minimum number of words, the candidate could have used a wider range of vocabulary.

2 Comments: Candidate ....

Grade: Unsatisfactory

There are some good structures and vocabulary, but there is no attempt to write a report or to cover any of the specific points in the instructions.

There is one example of a linking expression used incorrectly and there are also two mistakes with verb tenses.

---

3 Look at the two candidates' answers again. The examiner has marked a number of mistakes in orange. Write the sentences with mistakes out again correctly in your notebook.

4 Join the phrases and sentences in Column A with those in Column B using an appropriate linking word/phrase from the following list. Write the complete sentences in your notebook. You will need to use some of the linking words/phrases more than once. Be careful of punctuation.

- despite/in spite of
- although/even though
- However
- but
- On the other hand

Column A

1 Our visit to the museum was enjoyable
2 We managed to see the exhibits on new technologies
3 Most students thought the museum was interesting.
4 Several students bought copies of the guide
5 We found it a bit difficult to understand all the recorded information with some exhibits
6 Visits to museums can be a bit boring sometimes.

Column B

a) the fact that they cost £15.00.
b) some of that section of the museum was closed.
c) they are an excellent way to learn about the world and to practise our English.
d) the high entrance fee and the crowds.
e) our teachers had taught us a lot of the vocabulary.
f) some of us felt that there wasn't enough information about the exhibits.

5 Now write a report in 120–180 words in answer to the task in Exercise 1.

1 Think of good and bad points about the museum, especially in relation to students of English.
2 Join the good and bad points using the linking expressions listed in Exercise 4.
3 Organise your sentences into numbered paragraphs.
4 Write your report following the layout in Candidate B's answer.
5 Check your answer carefully for mistakes with verb tenses.

> **Strategy**
> Use numbered points in reports. It is much easier to plan and write like this.

Reading: multiple choice

About the exam
In this part of Paper 1 you may be asked questions about the relationship between words in the text.

Strategy
Apart from words like pronouns (e.g. *it, them*) and demonstratives (e.g. *this, that*), nouns and verbs can refer back or forward to other words in the text. For example:

> Making the **wax models** is a highly skilled and lengthy process. From start to finish it takes months of work for the artists and craftsmen to combine who produce the final **figure**. All the **waxworks** are life-size **replicas** of the real person, down to the last detail.

The words 'wax models', 'figure', 'waxworks' and 'replicas' all refer to the same thing. Look for networks of related words like this. This will help you understand the text.

1 Read the following text about guitars and decide which one of the following subjects is **not** referred to.

A companies that make guitars
B materials guitars are made of
C the role of technology
D other musical instruments

2 Answer the following questions about the article.

1 The writer uses the word 'guitar' sixteen times in this text. What two other words does he use instead of 'guitar'?

....

2 In paragraph 1 the writer uses the phrase 'pop stars' to refer to people who play guitars. What word/words does he use before that to refer to pop stars?

....

3 Paragraphs 4 and 5 are about materials used to make guitars. What materials are mentioned?

a) ....

b) ....

c) ....

d) ....

e) ....

f) ....

Guitar Legends

1 Whether it's the melodic sound of an Eric Clapton solo or the growl of a heavy metal band, the electric guitar has influenced popular music and culture more than any other instrument. Rock's greatest musicians have always been closely identified with their guitars. But the instruments being designed for tomorrow's pop
10 stars may look and sound rather different from today's familiar electric and acoustic guitars.

It is only sixty years since the electric guitar was invented. Since then there have been incredible changes to the technical design of the instrument. From what was once a rounded wooden box with a hole in the front, the guitar has evolved into
20 the smooth solid body of the rock guitarist's 'axe'. The most modern guitars are really computer-controlled synthesisers.

Adolph Rickenbacker's Electro String Company produced the world's first electric guitar. It was made of wood and played on the user's lap. The first real breakthrough in design came in 1950 when Leo Fender, a
30 Californian radio repairman, made the first solid-bodied electric guitar, the Fender Telecaster. Soon after the inventor Les Paul made the famous Gibson Les Paul. Fender launched its stylish Stratocaster two years later. These guitars became standard instruments against which newer guitar designs are measured.

All sorts of different materials have
40 been used to make guitars. Acoustic guitars are made from wood, which gives a soft tone. Wood is also a popular material in electric guitar manufacture, but more modern materials such as glass and carbon fibre are also used. There have also been guitars with metal bodies and necks though these were never popular with players, who claim metal
50 feels cold in the hand.

Plastics, on the other hand, have been more used in guitar bodies. A company that makes parts for the aerospace industry has begun to use a kind of fibreglass that was originally used in helicopter blades to make the bodies for its electric-acoustic instruments. Other makers have begun to experiment with graphite, a
60 material that is ten times stiffer than wood but much lighter. It doesn't expand or contract as the temperature or humidity changes either. This makes it particularly suitable for guitar necks and for tennis rackets, for which it is also used.

As long as scientists and musicians work together
70 harmoniously, the electric guitar will continue to benefit from technological innovations. But for all the efforts of the guitar companies' design engineers, production managers and quality controllers, it's the musicians who finally make the instruments sing – and not necessarily in the way the guitar maker intended.

from *Focus* magazine

3 Choose the correct alternative to answer the following questions.

1 'Musicians' *(line 6)* play guitars. Which of the following does not refer back to 'musicians'?

A 'pop stars' *(line 9)*
B 'rock guitarist' *(line 20)*
C 'inventor' *(line 33)*
D 'players' *(line 49)*

2 Who made the first electric guitar?

A Leo Fender
B Adolph Rickenbacker
C Les Paul
D Someone who worked for Adolph Rickenbacker.

3 The guitars that were designed in the fifties

A were not commercially successful.
B are often compared to guitars designed today.
C were made of wood.
D were played sitting down.

4 Wood is used to make

A only acoustic guitars.
B only electric guitars.
C helicopter blades.
D electric and acoustic guitars.

5 Why is graphite a good material for guitar necks?

A It is not affected by temperature or humidity.
B It is stiffer and lighter than wood.
C Both A and B.
D It is used to make tennis rackets.

6 Recent technological innovations

A have not really improved the electric guitar.
B have been ignored by musicians.
C cannot determine the way the guitar will be played.
D are not what musicians hoped for.

Speaking: opinion exchange

Paper 5, Part 4

About the exam
In the last part of Paper 5 the examiner will ask your opinion about something.

Strategy
Make sure you know how to:
● ask someone else what their opinion is.
● express your opinion.
● agree/disagree politely with someone else's opinion.
● ask for/give advice.

1 Listen to two candidates doing Paper 5, Part 4 and fill in the gaps in the following extracts.

1 .... it depends on the instrument.

2 .... if you only want to enjoy playing, ... if you want to have a good time, you can start to learn when you are quite old and it doesn't matter.

3 Well, ... a good teacher ... like me. .... a clarinet at the beginning. .... to see if you like it. .... every day.

4 Well, ... a small drum kit and practise while you listen to albums by your favourite groups. When you are a little bit better, ... a group. Oh, and .... to lots of rock concerts and watch the drummers. That's the best way to learn.

2 In which extract or extracts is the candidate:

a) giving advice. ....

b) giving an opinion. ....

c) disagreeing politely. ....

3 Listen to the following sentences/phrases on the cassette and mark the word on which the main stress falls. Then practise saying the sentences yourself.

EXAMPLE: I don't really agree.

1 As far as I'm concerned ...

2 I completely agree.

3 That's right.

4 From my point of view ...

5 I couldn't agree more.

8 Looking good

Listening: multiple matching

About the exam
You may hear other sounds such as traffic noise, noise from machinery or people talking in the background on the recording. This is to make it more realistic. You will still be able to hear what the speakers say very easily.

Hot tip!
Use the background noises as clues. This may help you to recognise which prompt goes with which speaker(s).

1 You are going to hear five women talking about clothes. Listen and match each extract to a situation below where it is taking place. There is one extra situation which you do not need to use. Write the number of the appropriate extract in the gaps.

A outside	....	**D** in an airport	....
B in a shop	....	**E** at college	....
C at home	....	**F** at a party	....

2 Now listen to the extracts again and match them to the following statements. There is one extra statement which you do not need to use. Write the number of the appropriate extract in the gaps.

A She thinks it looks silly. ....

B She doesn't want to leave the house. ....

C She thought about what he would need. ....

D She didn't know why she had a problem. ....

E She had only worn them once before. ....

F She is very pleased with them. ....

Vocabulary: clothes

1 Write words for the following items of clothing.

2 Read the following descriptions of the models in the pictures below. There are two mistakes of meaning in each sentence. Find the mistakes and write the descriptions out again correctly in your notebooks.

1 Claudia is wearing a high-heeled evening dress and long shoes.

2 Nick is wearing checked trousers and a grey skirt.

3 Paul is wearing a striped blouse, jeans and wellington boots.

4 Kate is wearing a spotted dress and striped tights.

5 Tim is wearing a scarf and dungarees with a plain, leather bow-tie.

3 Mark where the main stress falls in the following words:

EXAMPLE: 'cardigan

1 sandals	6 sweatshirt
2 pullover	7 raincoat
3 bracelet	8 earrings
4 pyjamas	9 waistcoat
5 dungarees	10 T-shirt

Grammar: *used to/would*

1 Match the first parts of the sentences in Column A with the second parts in Column B. Write the appropriate letter in the gaps.

Column A		Column B
1 Did you	....	a) to getting up so early.
2 Are you	....	b) walk along the river holding hands.
3 They used	....	c) use to smoke?
4 We would	....	d) to live near here.
5 I'm not used	....	e) getting used to the food?
6 We didn't	....	f) use to watch so much TV.

2 In which of the following sentences can you use both *would* and *used to*? Mark them with a tick (✔). In which sentences is there only one possibility? Cross out the one you cannot use.

1 When I was younger, we *used to/would* go into town on Saturday night.

2 We *would/used to* spend most of Saturday afternoon getting ready.

3 My friend Diana *would/used to* live only a few minutes walk from my house.

4 She *used to/would* come over to my house after lunch.

5 We *used to/would* wash our hair and decide what to wear.

6 We *used to/would* think we looked really glamorous in our flared trousers, platform shoes and little tops.

7 My older brother *would/used to* give us a lift into town and arrange to pick us up later.

3 Complete the following sentences in your own words.

1 When I was younger, I used to ....
....

2 My friends and I would ....
....

3 One thing I don't think older people will ever get used to is ....
....

Writing: description

Paper 2, Part 2

About the exam
You may be asked to write a description of a
person in Paper 2, Part 2.

1 Read the following task and the answers that
two students wrote. Which one is more interesting,
Description A or Description B?

Write a description of your favourite relative.

Description A

My favourite relative is my grandfather.

The first thing you notice about him is
his huge moustache. He has had it since
he was eighteen and takes very good
care of it. Then you notice his eyes.
They are very dark, almost black, but
sparkling and lively.

He was very tall when he was younger
and he's still quite tall even at eighty-
five. He walks with a stick that he has
had for years now and he always wears
an old black cap when he goes out. My
grandmother bought him a new one last
year, but he won't wear it.

But the most characteristic thing about
my grandfather is his voice. He has the
most wonderful deep voice. You
appreciate this most when he laughs his
big booming laugh. He laughs a lot and
always has a funny story or a joke to
tell to cheer you up.

Description B

My favourite relative is my Aunt Lucy.

She is my mother's older sister. She is
forty years old, but she looks younger
than that. She has dark hair and is slim
with green eyes. She wears glasses.

She likes fashionable clothes. Her
favourite colours are green and blue. She
has a nice green jacket that she wears. It
suits her. She does not wear very much
jewellery apart from a silver ring.

She has a nice voice. She sings in a folk
group in the town where she lives. She is
a teacher at a high school there and her
students like her.

I think she is a very good person.

2 Read the following comments a teacher wrote
on Description B. Then write a description of a relative
following the teacher's advice and using the outline
on page 59.

Your description is very accurate, but you need
to make your writing more interesting.

For example, you say your aunt 'looks younger'.
How much younger? A bit? A lot? Years? You
tell me she has 'dark hair', but you don't say
whether it is curly or straight, thick or shiny. Is it
long or short? And what else can you say about
her eyes? Are they soft and gentle or bright and
sparkling? Are they more or less striking
because of her glasses?

You talk about the jacket she wears and tell me
that it's green. What else can you say about it?
Is it new? What is it made of? Why does it suit
her? And what about the ring? Why does she
always wear it? Because it was a gift?

You comment on her voice, good, but don't use
'nice'. Is it deep or soft and gentle?

And finally why do her students like her? What
do they say about her?

Outline

*I suppose the first thing anyone notices about my ...
is her/his ... . S/he's got ... and ... . S/he's not very ...,
but ... .*

*What I like most about her/him is the way s/he ... .
Once you get to know her/him better you realise
s/he ... .*

S/he always wears ... . S/he's also got ... .

*But the most distinctive thing about her/him is ... .
S/he is ... . I suppose that's why s/he is my favourite
relative.*

3 Now write a description of another person you
like and admire in 120–180 words.

1 Decide which person to write about.

2 Think about this person's
- physical features (hair, beard/moustache, nose,
  eyes, mouth, hands).
- general build.
- unusual habits and/or hobbies.
- favourite items of clothing.
- voice or laugh.

3 Write a plan including the points you thought of.

4 Write your description.

5 As always, check your work carefully.

┌ Hot tip! ◀

DON'T just write a list of details about the person you
are describing! Think of general characteristics and how
they relate to the person's character.

Vocabulary and grammar:
open cloze

Paper 3, Part 2

About the exam
Paper 3, Part 2 tests your knowledge of grammar
and vocabulary. Sometimes there is more than one
possible word for vocabulary gaps.

Strategy
If more than one word seems possible, choose the
one which fits the context best.

For example:

We have to .... for the play we're putting on.

In this sentence *practise* and *rehearse* would both
be possible, but *rehearse* is specific to the context
of theatre and plays.

Two different students have completed the following
sentences from gap fill exercises. Circle the best
answer in each case.

1 When we got to the cinema there were very few
tickets left so we couldn't sit *down/together*.

2 The common cold has been called the single most
expensive *illness/problem* in the world.

3 Runners suffer more injuries than many other
people/athletes.

4 All kinds of *things/materials* have been used to
make guitars: wood, fibre glass, plastic and metal.

5 He is very *strange/secretive*. He never tells anyone
anything about his personal life.

6 She was wearing *shoes/sandals* on her feet even
though it was the middle of winter.

7 He decided to become a *good/professional*
football player and gave up his job at the bank.

8 Do you like to wear a particular *brand/kind* of
trainers such as Nike or Reeboks?

┌ Hot tip! ◀

Even if you can't think of a word that fits the
context exactly, use a general word that is the right
part of speech. You may get some marks for this. If
you leave a gap unfilled, you get no marks.

Reading: gapped text

About the exam

In this part of Paper 1 you decide where to put sentences or paragraphs that have been removed from the text.

Strategy

The sentences that have been removed often express the main idea of the paragraph. As you read, write down what the main idea of each paragraph is.

1 Read the following article about the invention of the safety razor, answering the questions at the end of each paragraph as you read.

A Hairy Problem Solved

(1___) Cave drawings show that the earliest razors were sharks' teeth and clam shells. Sharpened flint was used where it could be found. The Egyptians 6000 years ago made razors from solid gold. By the eighteenth century they had developed into elaborate steel devices. Nevertheless one painful problem remained: men continued to cut themselves.

1 Is this paragraph mainly about
   A the history of the razor?
   B expensive materials used for razors?

In 1762, a Frenchman named Jean-Jacques Perret found a way of protecting the shaver's skin by attaching a safety guard to the steel blade. Perret even wrote a book about shaving called *Pogotonomy or the Art of Learning to Shave*. (2___) As a result, millions of male chins still suffered the consequences daily.

2 Is the main idea that Perret
   A invented a safe way of shaving?
   B wrote a book about shaving?

One such chin belonged to King Camp Gillette, a travelling salesman from Wisconsin, in the United States. One of Gillette's bosses was William Painter, the inventor of the disposable bottle-cap. Painter told Gillette that he would become rich if only he invented 'something which will be used once and thrown away'. (3 ___)

3 Is the main idea that
   A Gillette got some useful advice?
   B Gillette had a boss called Painter?

(4___) He realised that only the straight edge of his old-fashioned razor was doing any work. Why not substitute a thin steel blade that could be held in a clamp and thrown away? 'I stood before the mirror in a trance of joy,' he wrote to his wife. 'Our future is made.'

4 Is the main idea that
   A Gillette suddenly had an idea?
   B he wrote to his wife?

(5___) Finally, Gillette met a mechanic named William Nickerson, and together they formed the American Safety Razor Company. They took out a patent in Boston in 1901. In 1903 they sold just 51 razors and 168 blades. They persevered and by the end of 1904 they had parted with 90,000 razors and 124,000,000 blades.

5 Is the main idea that
   A Gillette formed the company with someone else?
   B the razor was not immediately successful?

2 The following sentences have been removed from the text. Decide in which numbered gap each sentence should go and write in the appropriate letter. Be careful! There is one extra sentence that you do not need to use.

A The answer came to Gillette in front of his shaving mirror in 1895.

B However, his invention remained relatively unknown.

C The customer would have to come back and buy another.

D Men have always searched for the perfect close shave.

E Gillette realized he needed to work with someone else.

F But for six years, he failed to convince people.

Word formation

Paper 3, Part 5

> **Strategy**
> Check your spelling. In the word you form, you may need to:
> - decide if you need to double a consonant.
> - decide if you need to drop an 'e'.
> - decide if the word ends in *-ence* or *-ance*.
> - decide if the word ends in *-sion* or *-tion*.
> - decide if the word ends in *-able* or *-ible*.

1 Fill in the gaps in the following sentences with the correct form of the word in capitals. Use your dictionary if you are uncertain about spelling.

1 We have all got used to .... products such as razors and nappies. (DISPOSE)

2 The telephone is a wonderful .... (INVENT)

3 The .... of the safety razor revolutionised shaving. (PRODUCE)

4 Attacks on young people wearing expensive clothing are a common .... (OCCUR)

5 Nevertheless many young people show a marked .... for particular labels. (PREFER)

6 We visited Stratford-on-Avon and saw a .... of Shakespeare's Romeo and Juliet. (PERFORM)

7 In the .... of her composition she said she did not think co-education was a good idea. (CONCLUDE)

8 When she was offered the part in the film, she accepted without a moment's .... (HESITATE)

> **Learner training**
> Use your dictionary to check spelling and word stress as well as meaning.

2 Mark where the main stress falls in each of the words you formed above.

EXAMPLE: di'sposable

Speaking: problem solving

Paper 5, Part 3

> **About the exam**
> In Paper 5, Part 3 the examiner may ask you to find a solution to a problem. This is so that he or she can hear you speak spontaneously.

> **Hot tip!**
> There is no 'right' or 'wrong' solution, so don't worry if the examiner stops you before you have solved the problem.

bandage antiseptic cotton wool throat lozenges cough mixture plasters muscle pain cream tissues aspirins ear drops eye drops

Listen to an examiner giving two candidates instructions for Part 3 of Paper 5 and look at the pictures. Then decide if the following statements are true or false. Mark them **T** (true) or **F** (false).

1 They have to put the items in order of importance. ....

2 They have to choose a limited number of items. ....

3 They can add other items that are not in the picture. ....

4 They should each decide on their own answer. ....

> **Strategy**
> If you do not understand what you are supposed to do, ask the examiner to explain again. Say: 'I'm sorry. Could you repeat that?' or 'Could you explain again? I'm not sure what we have to do.' You may lose marks if you do not do what the examiner has asked you to do.

Grammar: *can/could/may/might*

1 Rewrite the following sentences using *can*, *could, may* or *might*.

1 It is possible that he is Italian.

  ....

2 Do you know how to play the piano?

  ....

3 You are not allowed to speak during the exam.

  ....

4 It is not possible that they are still on holiday.

  ....

5 You are not allowed to smoke on the plane.

  ....

6 It is possible that it will be a nice day tomorrow.

  ....

7 He didn't know how to spell 'conscious'.

  ....

8 Am I allowed to leave the room?

  ....

2 There are mistakes in all of the following sentences. Find the mistakes and write the sentences out again correctly in your notebooks.

1 That mustn't be the postman. He never comes this early.

2 I might not to come to class on Wednesday. I've got to go to the dentist.

3 Could you riding a bicycle when you were seven?

4 You couldn't borrow my new blouse. I want to wear it myself.

5 I don't think we should buy him a shirt. He could not like the colour.

6 You ought to take a raincoat. It might rained.

Grammar: key word transformations

Paper 3, Part 3

Strategy
In Paper 3, Part 3 there are often questions testing:

a) *-ing/-ed* adjectives.   d) comparatives.
b) structures with *like*.   e) reported speech.
c) gerunds and infinitives.   f) modal verbs.

Try to recognise what the question is testing.

Decide which of the above the following items test. Write the appropriate letter a) – f) in the box. Then complete the second sentence so that it has a similar meaning to the first sentence using the word in **bold** and other words.

1 I will not lend you my jacket.
  refuse
  I .... my jacket. ☐

2 Claudia isn't as thin as Kate.
  than
  Kate is .... Claudia. ☐

3 Psychology interests me.
  am
  I .... psychology. ☐

4 I want a cup of coffee.
  would
  I .... a cup of coffee. ☐

5 'Do you enjoy football?', she asked him.
  if
  She asked.................................. football. ☐

6 He hates travelling by bus.
  stand
  He .... by bus. ☐

7 My advice is to buy a computer.
  ought
  You .... a computer. ☐

8 Tom is a faster worker than Mike.
  works
  Tom .... Mike. ☐

9 You can't smoke here.
  allowed
  You .... here. ☐

9 Too much of a good thing

Vocabulary: multiple choice cloze

About the exam
In this part of Paper 3 you are tested mainly on your knowledge of vocabulary.

Learner training
Instructions for machines are often in English. Practise reading the instructions as you use the machine.

Read the following text and choose the correct alternative to fill each gap.

1 **A** dish   **B** meal   **C** food   **D** plate
2 **A** depending   **B** relying   **C** according   **D** corresponding
3 **A** receipt   **B** menu   **C** prescription   **D** recipe
4 **A** made   **B** served   **C** cooked   **D** prepared
5 **A** peeled   **B** skinned   **C** grated   **D** cracked
6 **A** butter   **B** salt   **C** peas   **D** eggs
7 **A** frying   **B** roasting   **C** cooking   **D** boiling
8 **A** boil   **B** roast   **C** fry   **D** scramble
9 **A** ladle   **B** knife   **C** saucepan   **D** spatula
10 **A** stir   **B** mix   **C** sprinkle   **D** whisk
11 **A** saucepan   **B** plate   **C** bowl   **D** dish
12 **A** drop   **B** pour   **C** put   **D** mix
13 **A** roast   **B** boil   **C** cook   **D** grill
14 **A** edges   **B** bottom   **C** top   **D** middle
15 **A** course   **B** bowl   **C** plate   **D** pan

Spanish Omelette

The traditional Spanish omelette is a full (1).............. in itself. Each Spanish family produces its own individual version of it (2).............. to the season and the availability of vegetables. The following (3).............., however, is the most familiar, often also containing strips of red and green peppers. It can be (4).............. hot or at room temperature.

450 g potatoes, (5).............., washed and finely sliced
Salt
150 ml vegetable oil
1 large onion, peeled and finely chopped
6 eggs
4–5 tablespoons olive oil

Sprinkle the potatoes with (6).............. . In a large (7).............. pan, heat the vegetable oil. Add the potatoes and onions and (8).............. them over a medium heat for 15 minutes, turning them occasionally until they are properly cooked and soft. Remove from the pan with a (9).............. and drain off most of the excess oil.

(10).............. the eggs in a (11).............. with a little salt, add the potato mixture and mix well. In a smaller non-stick frying pan, heat the olive oil and (12).............. in the egg mixture, rotating the pan in order to spread it evenly. (13).............. over a medium heat until it starts to solidify, then turn down the heat. While cooking shape the omelette into a round, pressing the (14).............. away from the sides of the frying pan.

Place a large (15).............. over the pan and quickly invert the omelette on to it. Slide the omelette back into the frying pan and return it to the heat for a further 5–6 minutes, shaping it into a neat circle. Serve with a crisp, green salad.

Grammar: countables / uncountables

Circle the one alternative in the following sentences which is **not** possible.

1 Would you like *some/a little/a few* more chicken?

2 Can I have another *piece/lump/bit* of that delicious chocolate?

3 I had *some/a bit of/a* good news the other day.

4 I tried on *a/some/a pair of* jeans, but they didn't suit me.

5 I don't usually have *much/many/a great deal of* spare time during the week.

6 She gave me *some/a piece of/many* good advice about the exam.

7 *Many/Few/Much* local people came to the meeting.

8 Why not come and stay with us for *a couple of/a pair of/a few* days?

9 Would you like *another/some/more* toast?

10 *The/Some/A* police arrived straight away.

11 We usually have *a lot of/a/some* very nice weather at this time of year.

12 How many *lumps/teaspoons/slices* of sugar do you usually have in your coffee?

13 Could you give me another *piece/sheet/slice* of paper, please?

14 You haven't brought *much/many/a lot of* luggage with you.

15 I would like *some/a bit of/a few* information about your courses.

🖳 Listening: note taking

> **Paper 4, Part 2**

> **About the exam**
> You hear each recording twice. There is a pause before you hear the recording for the second time and another pause before the next recording begins.

Strategy
Make good use of your time during the test.
- The first time you listen, answer as many questions as you can. Write in note form (e.g. *Mon* for *Monday*) and don't worry about spelling.
- Check your answers, especially spelling, in the first pause.
- When you hear the cassette the second time, listen for the information you need to answer the other questions.
- Check your answers to these questions during the second pause.
- You have five minutes after you have listened to the cassette to transfer your answers from the question paper to the answer sheet. Check your answers again.

➤ Hot tip! ◄

DON'T answer on the answer sheet while you are listening to the recordings!

Listen to a doctor talking about foods and how they affect our moods and complete the following notes.

Typical summer foods: (1)..................................
Effect: *good mood*
Contain chemicals such as:

Serotonin
Effect: Makes you feel (2).............................
Found in (3)........................., *ginger* and
(4)..
Best source: spinach

Folic Acid
Deficiency causes (5)............................,
sleeplessness, forgetfulness, irritability

Selenium
Deficiency causes (6)...........................
Found in (7)......................., sunflower seeds,
oysters, cereals, grapes and (8)...........................

DMAE
Effect: Improves (9)........................... and
ability to (10)..
Found in: anchovies and sardines

64

Speaking: planning

Paper 5, Part 3

About the exam
In Paper 5, Part 3 you may be asked to plan something, for example a journey or a meal.

Strategy
You should be able to:
● ask for/make suggestions.
● accept/politely reject other people's suggestions.

1 Listen to two candidates doing Paper 5, Part 3 and complete the following extracts.

1 ....?
They will be very hungry after hiking all morning.

2 It's probably quite cold, ...
.... to start with soup.

3 ....
A fish soup would be good.

4 Mmm ... .
.... serve vegetable soup.

5 OK. We'll serve vegetable soup first. And what shall we have next? ....

6 ....
– with a meat sauce.

7 ....
serve a salad next?

2 In which extract/extracts are the candidates

A asking for suggestions?   ....

B making suggestions?   ....

C accepting suggestions?   ....

D politely rejecting suggestions?   ....

Grammar: error correction

Paper 3, Part 4

Strategy
Look back through the grammar sections in Units 1–9 in the *Exam Maximiser* and the *First Certificate Gold Coursebook*. As you read the following text, look for errors with the language points you have studied.

Read the following text and look carefully at each line. Some of the lines are correct, and some contain an extra incorrect word which should not be there. If a line is correct, put a tick (✔) at the end of the line. If a line has a word which should not be there, circle the word.

Why don't we eat what we should?

1 According to the World Health Organisation almost half our diet
2 should to consist of starchy food such as potatoes, pasta and
3 rice and we should eat five portions of a fresh fruit and
4 vegetables every day. Unfortunately, it will to take a long time
5 for the British diet to approach this ideal. People know what
6 they should eat, but they are not quite so good at when it comes
7 to going to the supermarket to buy food. In fact people usually
8 prefer to eating what they want rather than eating what they are
9 told. Perhaps this is why did the proportion of people
10 considered 'obese' or fat doubled between 1980 and 1991.

'It's fast, but I miss the chewing and swallowing'

Vocabulary: phrasal verbs (*put*)

1 Put the words in the following questions in the correct order.

1 put could the to director you through me?

....

2 they wedding have off put their why?

....

3 put money do rainy day you by for a?

....

4 how put could up you with behaviour rude such?

....

5 prices put they up have again the?

....

6 how firemen fire out did put that the?

....

7 vet why have did to the cat your put down?

....

8 put me could London when come I up you to?

....

9 trying you always why put down me are to?

....

2 Write the following sentences again using a phrasal verb with *put* instead of the underlined words. You may have to change the word order in some sentences.

1 They've <u>increased</u> the price of tinned tomatoes.

....

2 Can you <u>provide accommodation for</u> my nephew when he comes to Madrid?

....

3 I'm just trying to <u>connect</u> you, but the line seems to be busy.

....

4 He's always <u>making her look foolish</u> – I don't know why she goes out with him.

....

5 Please <u>extinguish</u> your cigarettes.

....

6 I think we'll have to <u>postpone</u> the match until after the exam.

....

7 They manage to <u>save</u> some money every week.

....

8 Two horses were so badly injured that they had to be <u>killed</u> after the race.

....

9 I don't know why you <u>tolerate</u> her rudeness.

....

Reading: multiple matching

Paper 1, Part 4

About the exam
In Paper 1 you may be asked where a text comes from (for example, a newspaper or magazine) and what its purpose is (for example, to warn or inform).

Strategy
Pay attention to the **structures** used in various kinds of text.

1 Read the texts opposite and mark with a tick (✔) the geographical regions, countries and continents below which are mentioned.

1	Africa	7	Greece
2	Asia	8	India
3	Australia	9	The Middle East
4	Britain	10	Portugal
5	Europe	11	Spain
6	France	12	The West

Text A

Chillies

Chillies are the seed pods of a South American plant. They contain capsaicin, one of the most powerful substances used by a plant to stop predators eating its seeds. The red colour of the seed pod is nature's customary warning that what is inside is harmful. <u>Chillies were first cultivated in South America 800 years ago.</u> The Incas prized the chilli, valuing it in religious rites, even using the pods as a form of currency. Columbus brought the chilli back to Europe in the 15th century. The Portuguese then carried it to trading colonies in India and Africa, where it quickly became a key flavour in local cooking.

Text B

Eating out

Metrocentre offers more than 50 places to eat and drink, including a 650 seater food court. You can try Mexican chilli beans, the best of Italian pastas and pizzas, paella or seafood from Spain, moussaka and delicious pastries from Greece or a spicy Thai stir fry. <u>If you're more of a traditionalist, you might prefer the good old English pub with excellent pub food and a choice of fine beers and soft drinks.</u> Many of these places to eat are open late to allow you to shop first and relax and enjoy a meal afterwards. Some are open on Sunday as well, so bring the kids for a family day out. They'll love our icecream parlour!

Text C

Indians are mango-mad

Could you eat 3 kilos of fruit in four minutes? Or cross a mango with a rose? **Molly Moore** in New Delhi lives and learns.

Slice them, suck them or slurp them – no matter how you cut them, there's not a fruit on earth that produces more passion among Indians than the mango. Sunny Mohar is the living proof. <u>After eating over 3 kilos of the fruit in four minutes flat, the electronics engineer, aged 24, turned to the cameras and declared, 'I'm crazy about mangoes!'.</u> Javed Faridi, aged 55, while no less enthusiastic, is more reserved in his praise. A mango grower like his father before him, he has created 300 hybrids of India's most popular fruit, including a mango crossed with a rose and another the size of a grape.

Text D

Cooking a Chinese meal

The cooking methods the Chinese use are those that are familiar in the West: boiling, deep-frying, steaming and roasting. In addition there is stir frying, which means stirring and tossing the ingredients in very little oil over high heat. It does mean that all the preparation must be done before the cooking starts, and all the ingredients are cut into pieces of even size and shape. The cooking time is often only five minutes from start to finish. <u>Let your guests wait for the food rather than the other way round.</u> If the food has to wait, it will continue cooking in its own heat and the effect will be spoilt.

2 Look at the underlined sentences in each text and match them to the following labels.

1 Direct speech: Text ....
2 Instructions: Text ....
3 A suggestion: Text ....
4 A statement of fact: Text ....

3 Answer the following questions about the texts.

1 Which text comes from
  a) a newspaper article? Text ....
  b) a cookery book? Text ....
  c) an encyclopedia? Text ....
  d) a brochure? Text ....

2 Which text is mainly intended to
  a) teach people how to do something? Text ....
  b) provide factual information? Text ....
  c) entertain and surprise people? Text ....
  d) attract people and persuade them to do something? Text ....

Learner training

We read different types of text for different purposes. When we read for specific information, we **scan** the text until we have found the information we need. When we read something we know we will probably have to read again, we read quickly or **skim** the first time we read to get a general idea.

Grammar: future forms

1 There is a mistake in each of the following sentences. Find the mistake and write the sentences out again correctly in your notebook.

1 By the time you read this I am sipping champagne in a café near the Eiffel Tower.

2 Tomorrow there is heavy rain in the north.

3 Bye! I see you next week.

4 We've got to be at the airport two hours before our plane will take off.

5 By the time I'm twenty, I will eat 3000 bowls of cornflakes.

6 Look out! That wall will collapse.

7 I don't think I am having dinner. I'm not hungry.

8 I'm afraid I can't come to the cinema with you. I will take my nephew to the circus.

9 I'm sure you are doing very well in the exam.

10 I've made up my mind. I buy a new computer.

2 Fill in the gaps in the following letter with an appropriate form of the verb in brackets.

Dear Sir/Madam,

I (1)........................ (write) in reply to your advertisement for tour guides in last Tuesday's Chronicle.

I (2)........................ (study) tourism at the State Tourism School. I (3)........................ (finish) my course next July and (4)........................ (be) available to start work immediately afterwards.

Apart from the tourism course, I (5)........................ (attend) French classes in the evenings for the next six months and I (6)........................ (go) to France for a month as part of a student exchange programme. I am sure my spoken French (7)........................ (improve) as a result. Furthermore, by the time I complete my tourism diploma I (8)........................ (take) the Cambridge First Certificate in English examination. My teacher is certain I (9)........................ (get) at least a pass grade in the exam. I (10)........................ (start) German classes next week as well.

If you require any further information, I can be contacted by telephone on 0171 734 8972. I (11)........................ (be) at home every afternoon this week and in the mornings until 11 for the next month.

I look forward to hearing from you,

Yours faithfully,

Katerina Geraki

Vocabulary: shopping

Fill in the gaps in the following conversation with an appropriate word.

MOTHER: OK. Let me look at my list. First of all we need to go to the (1)........................ because I want to send some flowers to your Aunt Mary. And then we'll go over to the (2)........................ so that I can send these Christmas cards off.

SARAH: Oh Mum, that'll take ages! There are always long (3)........................ on Fridays. You go and post your letters while I go and get the bread from the (4)........................ .

MOTHER: Could you pop into the (5)........................ and get that cough mixture for your father? It's just next door to the (6)........................ . Actually you could pop in there too and get a couple of onions and a cauliflower. No, let's get all the fruit and vegetables with all the other things we need from the (7)........................ .

SARAH: Didn't you say you wanted to go back to that (8)........................ where you bought those sandals that the heel came off?

MOTHER: Yes, but I doubt that they'll give me a (9)........................ . I bought them in the end of season (10)........................ . And I thought they were such a (11)........................ at only £10. Oh no!

SARAH: What's the matter?

MOTHER: I can't find my (12)........................! I must have left it at home and it's got the original (13)........................ for the sandals and all my credit (14)........................ in it.

SARAH: I've got plenty of money so we can still get the things on the list. We could go over to that big shopping mall in Waverly and I could (15)........................ on another pair of those trousers. They didn't have my (16)........................ in when I was there with Sue last week and the pair I tried on were so (17)........................ around the waist I could hardly breathe.

Writing: letter of application

Paper 2, Part 2

About the exam
In Paper 2, Part 2 you may be asked to write a letter of application.

1 Look at the following job advertisement.

Trading and Commercial Bank
Trainee Managers

We will be recruiting trainee managers to start work in late June or early July in our branches all over Europe. Applicants should have a degree in an appropriate area and a knowledge of English and/or German. Apply in writing to:

The Personnel Officer,
Trading and Commercial Bank,
134 Collins Street,
Manchester

The sentences in this reply are in the wrong order. Put them in the correct order. Write the numbers 1–6 in the gaps.

Dear Sir/Madam,

a) (........) I can be contacted by telephone on 01202 452269 in the mornings or at the above address.

b) (........) I have a working knowledge of German and have recently passed the University of Cambridge First Certificate in English examination.

c) (........) I look forward to receiving your reply.

d) (........) I am writing in reply to your advertisement in last Tuesday's Evening News.

e) (........) I will also complete a degree in Banking and Finance in June and will be available for work immediately afterwards.

f) (........) I would like to apply for one of the trainee manager positions you advertise.

Yours faithfully,

João de Souza

2 Look at the following task.

You see the following advertisement in the newspaper.

Write **a letter** applying for one of these positions and asking for more details about the discounts. Do not write any addresses.

Trainee Travel Agents

We are looking for students who are interested in training to become travel agents. To join our training scheme you must have a knowledge of English and an interest in travelling. These positions are unpaid, but you will receive large discounts on all our organised tours and holidays.

Write to: Maria Sampras,
Director,
TRAVELWISE,
Via Ardipani,
Rome 04100

1 Underline the key words in the instructions.

2 Think about the form of your letter.

- Will your letter begin in the same way as the letter in Exercise 1?

- Will it end in the same way?

3 Plan your letter. Follow the order of the letter in Exercise 1.

4 Write your letter in 120–180 words.

5 Check for errors with future forms.

Learner training
You can practise your letter writing skills by writing to real companies asking for information. Try writing to banks and embassies. They are often willing to send you brochures and even posters.

How to make a fortune

Vocabulary: *do/make*

Fill in the gaps in the following sentences with the correct form of *do* or *make*.

1 Don't .... excuses! You didn't .... your homework and that's that!

2 Could you .... me a favour and lend me your notebook?

3 I want to .... notes while the teacher is explaining.

4 I've lost my wallet. What am I going to ....?

5 My parents expect me to .... things in the house such as .... my bed, helping my brothers .... the washing up and so on.

6 My father .... the ironing and he also .... the best spaghetti sauce in the universe!

7 I didn't realise they were .... fun of me. I suppose I .... a fool of myself.

8 If you want to .... well in the exam, you'll just have to .... more of an effort.

9 I know I always .... a lot of mistakes, but I really am .... my best.

10 .... sure you come to class tomorrow. We're going to .... a test.

11 Take a day off and .... nothing for a change. It won't .... you any harm. In fact it will probably .... you the world of good.

12 I didn't want to .... a fuss, but I really felt I had to .... a formal complaint. They hadn't .... the job properly at all.

13 .... business with you has been a great pleasure. I'm sure both our companies will .... a lot of money out of it.

14 I am afraid that the company has .... a massive loss this financial year.

15 Stop .... so much noise! I've got to .... a very important phone call.

Reading: multiple choice

Paper 1, Part 2

About the exam
In Paper 1 you have **1 hour and 15 minutes** to complete the four parts.

Strategy
Spend an equal amount of time (about 18 minutes) on each of the four parts of Paper 1. Divide each 18 minutes up like this:
- **3 minutes** reading the text and questions once **quickly.**
- **8 minutes** reading the text again and answering the questions.
- **4 minutes** checking your answers and answering any remaining questions.
- **3 minutes** transferring your answers from the question paper to the answer sheet.

1 Read the following text about a woman who has won a lot of competitions and mark with a cross (✗) the things below which are **not** mentioned.

1 a car
2 a TV
3 a fax machine
4 a compact disc system
5 a dog
6 a computer
7 a dishwasher
8 a refrigerator

Enter Mrs Win-a-lot

Introducing the undisputed queen of competitions

Outside Rita Smallburn's home is parked a sparkling blue Renault Clio. Mrs Smallburn won it. It is the fifth car she has won. Inside her sitting room are a video, television, compact disc system, three-piece suite, canteen of cutlery, decanter and glasses, silverware, Trivial Pursuit, Scrabble and an enormous bottle of champagne: all prizes.

In her kitchen are a dishwasher, microwave, French saucepan set, toaster, coffee maker, electric carving knife, kettle, can opener and iron: more prizes.

In fact there is virtually nothing in Mrs Smallburn's entire house, apart from her dog, which she hasn't won. She did not actually win the house she and her family live in, but seven years ago she won another one worth £50,000 which she sold two years later for £100,000. For the last sixteen years she has been the 'Queen of Competitions' or 'compers' as they are known in the trade. Locally she is known as Mrs Win-a-lot.

Since she gave up her job as a geography teacher sixteen years ago, Mrs Smallburn believes she has become much more skilled at winning competitions. 'I expect to win between twenty and forty per cent of the competitions I enter,' she says. 'But my winnings could vary enormously year by year. One year I might win £3,000. The next it could be £100,000.' All her earnings are tax-free.

She enters only about twelve competitions a month now, down from a peak of about fifty when she was younger. Nowadays she is busy running a consultancy in which she shares her competition winning skills with others who would like to achieve success, but the postman's arrival is still a thrill. If her family wants something, she will try to win it. At the moment she is competing for a fax machine. She wouldn't dream of buying anything.

It is an odd life, though Mrs Smallburn denies it is an obsession. 'It's more like an extreme enthusiasm,' she says. To work, the thrill must be in the winning rather than the prizes. The disadvantage is the lack of freedom to buy what you choose. The dog is not allowed to have his favourite brand of pet food. He has to be content with a year's supply of another brand Mrs Smallburn won.

from *The Times* newspaper

---

2 Choose the correct alternative to answer the following questions. **Time yourself!**

1 Which of the following is something that Mrs Smallburn did not win in competitions?

  A A house.
  B The house where the family live.
  C Money and goods to the value of £3,000.
  D Five cars.

2 How does Mrs Smallburn earn a living?

  A She works as a geography teacher.
  B She enters and wins competitions.
  C She runs a service giving advice on how to win competitions.
  D She has her own business and she makes money from competitions.

3 Mrs Smallburn used to

  A win more than she does now.
  B enter more competitions than she does now.
  C be better at winning competitions than she is now.
  D be known as the 'Queen of Competitions'.

4 Mrs Smallburn does not

  A want to buy a fax machine.
  B want to win a fax machine.
  C look forward to the postman coming.
  D try to win things her family want.

5 What is Mrs Smallburn's attitude to entering competitions?

  A She is obsessed with it.
  B She is very keen on it.
  C She is disappointed with the things she wins.
  D She thinks it is a strange way to earn a living.

6 The writer of the text thinks Mrs Smallburn's 'extreme enthusiasm' is the result of

  A the excellent prizes she has won.
  B the feeling she gets from winning.
  C not being free to buy what she wants.
  D an obsession.

7 The article is intended to

  A shock the reader.
  B annoy the reader.
  C entertain the reader.
  D make the reader feel sad.

Grammar: relative clauses/pronouns

1 Make complete sentences by joining one half in Column A with the other half in Column B using an appropriate relative pronoun. If the pronoun can be left out, write it in brackets. Write the complete sentences out in your notebook.

EXAMPLE: **Mrs Win-a-lot is the name (that) Mrs Smallburn's neighbours call her.**

Column A

1 'Mrs Win-a-lot' is the name ✔
2 The £50,000 house is not the one
3 Mrs Smallburn expects to win between twenty and forty per cent of the competitions
4 That is the compact disc system
5 Mrs Smallburn tries to win the things
6 The blue Renault Clio is the fifth car
7 There is hardly anything in Mrs Smallburn's house
8 The dog has to eat a brand of pet food
9 Mrs Smallburn is one of the rare people

Column B

a) she has won in a competition.
b) she hasn't won in a competition.
c) Mrs Smallburn and her family live.
d) earnings are tax-free.
e) Mrs Smallburn's neighbours call her. ✔
f) was a prize.
g) he doesn't like very much.
h) her family needs.
i) she enters.

2 Do the following sentences contain defining or non-defining relative clauses? Mark the sentences **D** (defining) or **N** (non-defining). Add commas where necessary.

1 She lent me a book. I lost the book that she lent me. ....
2 Mrs Smallburn has won five cars. A blue Renault Clio which is one of the cars she won is parked outside her house. ....
3 Pink Floyd who wrote the song 'Money' were performing live in London recently. ....
4 There are several proverbs about money. I agree with the one which says: 'Money is the root of all evil.' ....
5 The Central European University which has its headquarters in Prague has a branch in Budapest. ....
6 My uncle who was very shy when he was a child is now a multimillionaire. ....
7 My uncle who does not show off his wealth by wearing expensive clothes and accessories gives a lot of money to charities. ....
8 Several groups played at the festival. The first group who played were Dire Straits. ....

3 There are mistakes in six of the following sentences. Find the mistakes and write the sentences out again correctly in your notebook.

1 The Spanish omelette she cooked was delicious.
2 The house where we used to live in was bigger than this one.
3 My boyfriend, who used to be a brilliant athlete, has put on five kilos in the last two months.
4 The single object what I treasure most is an old coin my grandfather gave me.
5 The woman I spoke to told me I could have a refund if I brought the original receipt.
6 The waiter, to who I gave a very generous tip, didn't even thank me.
7 The insurance on the house, that was very expensive, didn't cover the cost of the repairs.
8 The loan I took out to pay for my studies has been very useful.
9 Inflation, which has risen to 200 per cent, is crippling the economy.
10 He inherited a lot of money from his grandfather, who he was extremely well-off.
11 The salesman who he sold me this T-shirt didn't tell me I couldn't return it.
12 The town where I was born has changed a lot in the last ten years.

Vocabulary: money

1 Complete this crossword.

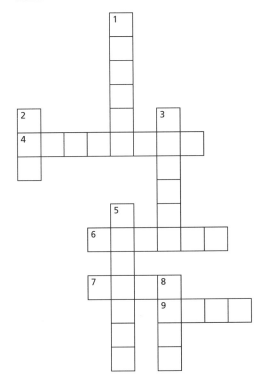

Across
4 to take out money you have put in the bank
6 to use money to make a profit out of something that will increase in value
7 to give someone the use of something, such as money, for a limited period of time
9 to get money by working

Down
1 to have enough money to do or buy something without difficulty
2 to have to pay money to someone because they lent it to you
3 to risk your money or property on horse races, in card games or in business
5 to receive money, goods or property from someone who has died or moved on
8 something that you owe to someone else

2 Now fill in the gaps in the following sentences with an appropriate word. The first two letters of each word have been given to help you.

1 The cashier would not let me take any more money out of my cu.............. account as I was already £50 ov.............. .

2 Excuse me. Would you have ch.............. for a £20 no..............?

3 Would you like to pay ca.............. or by ch.............. or credit card?

4 I wouldn't buy sh.............. in that company if I were you. They made a lo.............. last year.

5 The waiters in that restaurant get low wa.............., but they make a fortune in ti.............. .

6 You can withdraw money and order a bank st.............. from ca.............. machines.

7 If you want to buy a house, go to a building society for your mo.............. .

8 The problems with the ec.............. in my country have affected the ex.............. ra.............. badly.

9 I'm a bit ha.............. up at the moment. Do you think you could le.............. me £10?

10 By donating money to ch.............. you can often get substantial ta.............. deductions.

Writing: discursive

Paper 2, Part 2

> **About the exam**
> In Paper 2, Part 2 you choose **one** of four alternative questions. These may include a report, a story, a description, an article or another letter. You also have the option of writing about one of the set texts.

> **Strategy**
> Make sure your answer is appropriate for the instructions and covers all the points mentioned.

1 Read the following answer a student wrote to a question in Paper 2, Part 2. What kind of answer is this student trying to write?

A a report
B a story
C an article giving an opinion

2 Now look at the answer again. It is very well-structured, but there are five mistakes with verb tenses. Find the mistakes and write the sentences out again correctly in your notebook.

3 There are also two mistakes with vocabulary. Find the mistakes and write the sentences out again correctly in your notebook.

4 What grade would you give this candidate: Excellent, Good, Satisfactory or Unsatisfactory?

In my opinion students should do some paid work while they are studying. There are three main reasons why I am thinking this.

First of all I believe it is important to have work experience. If you had never worked before, it is very difficult to get used to work when you finished your studies. I have a part-time work in my mother's office and I am sure this helps me in the future.

Secondly I think young people must to learn to appreciate the value of money and they can only do this if they earn some themselves. If your parents just gave you money for everything you want, you can never understand about saving for things. My parents give me some money each week, but I also save money from my work.

Finally, by working students can know other people who are not at school. This is good because you can learn new things about the world. At my mother's office I knew a girl who has taught me many things about the environment and pollution.

For these reasons I think it is important for young people to work. Of course they should not work too much. They have to have time to study too!

5 Write your answer to the following question.

A local English language newspaper has asked students to write articles expressing their opinions about this question:

Should students do part-time work?

Write your **article** for the newspaper.

1 Pay attention to the key words in the instructions:
article   English language newspaper   opinion

2 Think of at least three arguments to support your opinion.

3 Write a plan putting your arguments in order.

4 Write your answer in 120–180 words. Use these linkers:
  • First of all/Firstly/In the first place • Finally
  • Secondly/In the second place

5 Check your work very carefully for mistakes with verb tenses, vocabulary and relative clauses.

Listening: multiple choice

Paper 4, Part 1

About the exam
There are always eight extracts in Paper 4, Part 1. Each extract is about **30 seconds** long. You choose between three alternatives to answer each question.

Strategy
Study the questions carefully. Are you asked:
a) what they are talking about?
b) who they are talking to?
c) what they want someone to do?

1 Look at the following questions and write a), b) or c) *(see **Strategy** box above)* in the gaps according to what you are asked.

1 You hear this man talking on a public phone. The man is arranging
  A to hold a meeting.
  B to give a party.
  C to play sport.   ....

2 You are in a community centre. You hear this man talking in a meeting room. The man wants
  A to persuade the audience to buy something.
  B the audience to tell him what they think about something.
  C to get the audience to answer some questions.   ....

3 You walk past a classroom and hear this exchange. The teacher wants Adela to
  A show the others how she found the answer.
  B tell the others the answer.
  C explain why she didn't do the homework.   ....

4 You hear your friend's older sister talking on the telephone. She is talking to
  A a friend who has started a new job.
  B someone who might give her a job.
  C a teacher at the school she attends.   ....

5 You hear this man talking on the radio. The person he is talking about
  A is in the studio now.
  B will be in the studio the next night.
  C was in the studio yesterday.   ....

6 You hear these two people talking in a bank. The woman is unhappy about
  A a cheque.
  B a statement.
  C a credit card.   ....

7 You hear this man talking about a newspaper article he has read. What was the article about?
  A crime
  B health
  C economics   ....

8 You hear this man talking on the telephone. He is talking to
  A a travel agent.
  B a restaurant.
  C a hotel.   ....

2 Now listen and choose the correct alternative in each case.

75

Vocabulary: numbers

1 Listen to the cassette and write the numbers that you hear.

a) ....

b) ....

c) ....

d) ....

e) ....

f) ....

g) ....

h) ....

i) ....

2 What kind of numbers are they? Match the numbers that you wrote above to one of the following categories. Write the appropriate letter in the gaps.

1 a temperature ....
2 a telephone number ....
3 a football score ....
4 the population of a town ....
5 a speed ....
6 a weight ....
7 a decimal ....
8 a fraction ....
9 a price ....

3 Practise saying the following numbers. Then listen to the cassette and check.

a) 0121 730 654   f) 16
b) 13   g) £3.50
c) 50   h) $19.99
d) 1½   i) 647,958
e) 4.75   j) 5,340,414

Speaking: prioritising

Paper 5, Part 3

About the exam
This part of the test lasts for about three minutes.

— **Hot tip!** ◄

DON'T worry if you do not finish putting all the things in order. The examiner will stop you when you have been speaking for three minutes.

Strategy
Don't try to dominate the other candidate. You may also get marks for **interaction**. Encourage the other person to speak by:
● asking her/him questions.
● making suggestions.
● saying a word if s/he hesitates or pauses for too long.
Don't interrupt the other person. Wait until s/he has finished speaking.

Below are some pictures of things which young people like to spend money on. Listen to two pairs of candidates doing Part 3 of Paper 5. They must put the things in order of priority according to how important they think they are. Which candidates do you think got good marks for interaction?

Interview 1: Loukas   Julie   *Interview 2:* Olivier   Dominique

11 The planet Earth

Writing: transactional letter

Paper 2, Part 1

About the exam
Part 1 of Paper 2 is **compulsory**. There is only one question. You always have to write either a formal or informal letter.

1 Look at the instructions below and the letter a candidate wrote in reply. Then decide which of the following examiner's comments were made about the letter. Mark them with a tick (✔).

1 The letter is very accurate.

2 The letter is not well-structured.

3 The letter is in an inappropriate style.

4 The writer has followed the instructions.

5 The letter provides all the necessary information.

You were travelling by train recently and left something that belongs to you on the train. Write a letter to the lost property officer enquiring about the thing you lost. Use these notes in your letter. Do not write any addresses.

– *date of journey*
– *destination and departure time*
– *description of object*

How are you? I'm fine. But I lost something on one of your trains and I'm going to tell you about it. OK?

Well, I got a train to Bristol a couple of weeks ago. Anyway, the train left Paddington station a bit late. It was supposed to leave at eleven, but in the end it left around twelve.

I left my favourite basketball cap on the train. It's bright red with black lettering saying Chicago Bulls. You've got it, haven't you? Let me know if you haven't.

I don't really feel like coming all the way to London to get it. You can send it to me, can't you? Here's my address:

11 St John's Road
Bracknell

Bye for now and thanks.
All the best,

Alex

Strategy
If asked to write to an official or a company, you should not use:
- question tags.
- contractions (e.g. *aren't, it'll, you've*).
- linkers like *well, anyway, by the way.*
- *All the best* or *Love* at the end of your letter.

You should:
- begin your letter with either *Dear Sir/Madam* or *Mr/Ms/Dr* + the person's surname.
- use formal language (e.g. *I look forward to receiving your reply*).
- end your letter with *Yours sincerely/Yours faithfully.*
- sign your letter with your full name.

2 Write a letter in answer to the question in Exercise 1.

1 Write a plan. You should follow this structure.
- Explain why you are writing.
- Say what you lost and when; describe it.
- Ask how you can get it back.
- Thank them in advance

2 Write your letter in the appropriate style in 120–180 words. Check your letter carefully.

Reading: gapped text

About the exam
In Part 3 of Paper 1 you read a text from which various paragraphs (or sentences) have been removed. These paragraphs are in a different order on another page. You decide where to put each paragraph. There is always an extra paragraph that does not belong.

Strategy
- Read the paragraphs that have been removed.
- Then read the text.
- When you think you know which paragraph goes in each gap, check that there is a relationship in meaning between this paragraph and the paragraphs that go before and after it.

Read the following paragraphs and decide in which numbered gap each paragraph goes in the text opposite. There is one paragraph which you do not need to use.

A

Predicting when and where lightning is likely to strike is one of the ways we have made it less of a danger. Forecasting lightning is taken most seriously in America, where scientists keep a constant lookout for weather patterns that could lead to violent storms using weather satellites and ground-based stations. Once the storms appear, teams of observers in the areas at risk report back on where the storm is and where it is going.

B

Things used to be much worse. According to research by Dr Derek Elsom the number of fatalities has dropped by 80 per cent since the mid-1850s. This isn't because lightning is less common, but because fewer people now work in the open.

C

Before scientists started this vital work people could not do very much to protect themselves or their buildings from lightning. In fact up until the eighteenth century people were given dramatic proof that lightning really can strike the same place twice. Between 1388 and 1762, the famous bell tower of San Marco in Venice was severely damaged or completely destroyed nine times.

D

Many people – including scientists – claim to have seen ball lightning and are in no doubt about its existence. The experiences of a certain William Morris during a thunderstorm in 1936 are typical: 'I saw a red-hot ball come down from the sky. It struck our house, cut the telephone wire, burnt the window frame and then buried itself in a tub of hot water. The water boiled for some time afterwards, but when it was cool enough for me to search I could find nothing there.'

LIGHTNING STRIKE

It is not surprising that people in the past were afraid of lightning and thought that it was a sign of anger from their gods. In fact we still find lightning thrilling and fascinating. It is now also an important area of research for scientists, who are trying to uncover its secrets and are looking for ways to predict storms and protect people against lightning strikes.
(1____)
In England and Wales things are not quite as bad as they were in Italy, but about a dozen people are struck by lightning every year and a quarter of those are killed as a result. Men are six times more likely to be struck by lightning than women.
(2____)
The experience of Roy Sullivan just goes to show how dangerous it can be to work outside. Roy, a former park ranger in Virginia, USA, held the world record for being struck by lightning. He was first hit in 1942, losing just the nail from his big toe. He was struck again in 1969, 1970, 1972 and 1973. In 1976 a strike hurt his ankle and in 1977 he suffered chest and stomach burns. After surviving all this, he killed himself in 1983!
(3____)
But even the most advanced forecasting systems can sometimes be caught out when the weather springs one of its surprises. In March 1993, Florida and other states of America were struck by driving blizzards – and severe lightning storms. At the peak the 'Sunshine State' was hit by an astonishing 5,000 strikes an hour. The cause of the storm and the reason it suddenly died out as it travelled north, is yet another mystery of the lightning phenomenon.

Vocabulary: weather

Choose the correct alternative to fill each gap in the following sentences.

1   It's absolutely .... outside, so wear your gloves.

   A cold   **B** chilly   **C** freezing

2   We had to postpone the match because it started to really ....

   A drizzle   **B** pour   **C** shower

3   Tomorrow will be mild with the possibility of a few .... in the evening.

   A rain   **B** showers   **C** sleet

4   It's only a bit of light .... You won't need an umbrella.

   A sleet   **B** drizzle   **C** hail

5   Close to the Equator the weather is hot and .... and there are often electrical storms.

   A damp   **B** mild   **C** humid

6   The old house was very cold and .... in winter.

   A humid   **B** damp   **C** freezing

7   Open the window. There's a lovely cool .... outside .

   A breeze   **B** gale   **C** gust

8   There was such a .... that my umbrella blew inside out.

   A rain   **B** breeze   **C** gale

9   The ground was completely white. I thought it was snow at first, but it was just a heavy ....

   A hail   **B** frost   **C** sleet

Grammar: the article

1   Fill in the gaps in the following dialogue with *a, an, the* or *(-)* if no article is needed.

> **The ghastly guest guide**
>
> A: Working as a hotel manager, you must have some interesting stories to tell about guests.
> B: Yes, indeed. Although we have (1).......... many very charming clients, some of our guests do incredible things.
> A: Such as?
> B: Well, (2).......... people will steal anything. All kinds of things go from (3).......... hotels, including (4).......... dinner plates. One couple stole (5).......... sheets and blankets from their bed, but one of the maids saw them do it. So (6).......... hall porter who carried their luggage down, took (7).......... sheets and blankets out and replaced them with (8).......... set of telephone directories.
>   We also get some very unreasonable requests. I worked at (9).......... hotel in (10).......... London where (11).......... couple wanted to have (12).......... dinner all on their own in (13).......... hotel ballroom, with (14).......... gypsy violinists and (15).......... palm tree. And they also wanted to be able to see (16).......... moon!
>   Some people completely destroy their rooms. One couple managed to spill (17).......... coffee over an area nine metres square. And they didn't even tell us about it. It was everywhere – on (18).......... TV, across (19).......... floor and on (20).......... bedclothes!

2   Read the following text and look carefully at each line. Some of the lines are correct, and some have an extra incorrect word which should not be there. If a line is correct, put a tick (✔) at the end of the line. If a line has a word which should not be there, circle the word. In this case, all of the extra incorrect words are articles.

> **What is jet lag?**
>
> **0**   When you fly from the Europe to the Middle East, America or
> **1**   Asia the flight will be longer than the four hours and
> **2**   will involve crossing several time zones. The time difference
> **3**   between your point of departure and final destination can
> **4**   be as much as the twelve hours. It can also mean flying from
> **5**   winter to summer or spring to autumn. You leave the Athens
> **6**   at seven o'clock on a winter's morning and arrive in Melbourne,
> **7**   which is seven hours ahead, more than a twenty hours later on
> **8**   a hot summer's day. Naturally your body still thinks you are
> **9**   in Athens. Because of this you will almost inevitably
> **10**   suffer from a mild or even quite severe jet lag.

> ***Strategy***
> Sometimes the extra words in this kind of exercise will be articles. Check each line carefully. Are all the articles necessary?

Vocabulary and grammar: open cloze

Paper 3, Part 2

About the exam
There are fifteen gaps in the text. The gaps test your knowledge of **vocabulary and grammar**.

Strategy
These are the most common grammatical words that are removed from the text:
- prepositions (e.g. *on, in, to*).
- quantifiers (e.g. *little, few*).
- auxiliary verbs (e.g. *do, are, have*).
- determiners (e.g. *the, most, another*).
- relative pronouns (e.g. *whom, who, where*).
- possessive adjectives (e.g. *my, his, their*).
Check for these when you fill in the gaps.

Read the following text through once quickly and then fill in the gaps with an appropriate word.

Where are the rainforests?

Rainforests once occupied almost all the land around the Equator, (1)..................... there is hot sun and rainfall almost every day. In these hot, wet areas, trees and (2)..................... kinds of vegetation grow fast, feeding massive (3)..................... of insects and animals.

Until recently, the rainforests filled river valleys in warmer countries (4)..................... Australia. They climbed hillsides of great (5)..................... chains such as the South American Andes, and covered islands (6)..................... Borneo to the West Indies.

In West Africa, (7)..................... rainforests cover a wide strip of the coast from Sierra Leone to Gabon. In the last century these forests (8)..................... mostly uninhabited. The Europeans arrived and soon began chopping (9)..................... the trees for timber and to make way for massive plantations of cocoa, peanuts and cotton.

Today, two thirds of the West African forests (10)..................... gone. But elsewhere in Central Africa it (11)..................... still possible to find huge undisturbed forests. Nineteenth century explorers along (12)..................... river Zaire called Africa the 'dark continent'. Even today (13)..................... are no roads in some places. The inhabitants include pygmies, (14)..................... are trying to lead (15)..................... lives in harmony with the forest.

Grammar: modals of deduction/criticism (past)

1   Match a sentence in Column A with a sentence in Column B. Write the appropriate letter in the gaps.

Column A

1 You must have had a terrible fright.   ....

2 I might be able to come.   ....

3 That can't be Mary.   ....

4 You should take a coat.   ....

5 He can't have forgotten again.   ....

6 That must be Michael.   ....

7 You should have told me.   ....

8 She might not know.   ....

9 You can't have spent it all.   ....

10 They might have seen it.   ....

Column B

a) He always gets home from work at about this time.

b) I only gave it to you yesterday.

c) It's been on for a couple of weeks.

d) I reminded him about fifty times.

e) I would have got you a present.

f) It's going to get cold later.

g) You're still trembling.

h) I certainly haven't told her.

i) She is supposed to be at school.

j) I'll have to ask my parents though.

2 There are mistakes in five of the following sentences. Find the mistakes and write the sentences out again correctly in your notebook.

1 Would you mind buying me a coffee? I must leave my money in my other coat.

2 They can't have left already. We're only five minutes late.

3 You'd better phone him about the match. He might have forgotten.

4 Don't wait for me. I might have been late.

5 It mustn't have been Mary who stole the money. She was with me all evening.

6 She might be offended. She is very sensitive you know.

7 It can't be snowing! It's the middle of July.

8 I might have stayed at home this Saturday night. I've got a test on Monday.

9 That can't be the answer. You must have made a mistake somewhere.

10 You should tell me. I didn't know you were coming.

'You're not thinking of putting me back in there are you?'

Grammar: key word transformations

Paper 3, Part 3

About the exam
There are ten key word transformation questions. They test your knowledge of grammar and vocabulary, such as collocation and idioms, as well as phrasal verbs.

Strategy
Before you complete the sentences try to work out what the question is testing.

1 Look at the following questions. Are they testing grammar, vocabulary or phrasal verbs? Mark them **G** (grammar), **V** (vocabulary) or **PV** (phrasal verbs).

1 Could I stay with you for the weekend?
put
Could you .... for the weekend?   ....

2 It is not possible that Tim was angry.
can't
Tim .... angry.   ....

3 What is the price of this bag?
much
How .... cost?   ....

4 I don't like this wet, windy weather at all.
stand
I .... this wet, windy weather.   ....

5 You should stop smoking.
give
You should .... smoking.   ....

6 You are not allowed to speak during the examination.
may
You .... during the examination.   ....

7 She was imitating a teacher when the headmaster walked in.
taking
She was .... a teacher when the headmaster walked in.   ....

2 Now complete each sentence so that it has a similar meaning to the first sentence. Use the word in **bold** and other words. You must use between two and five words.

Speaking: picture prompts

Paper 5, Part 2

About the exam
Sometimes the photographs in Paper 5, Part 2 will be designed to make you speculate.

Strategy
Make sure that you can use modals of deduction accurately.

Hot tip!
You may get better marks in this part of Paper 5 if you say how you feel about the photograph and give a personal comment.

Listen to a candidate doing Part 2 of Paper 5, look at the photos and write down:

1 three examples of deductions about the past.

a) ....

   ....

b) ....

   ....

c) ....

   ....

2 three examples of deductions about the present.

a) ....

   ....

b) ....

   ....

c) ....

   ....

3 two examples of Eleni making personal comments about the photos.

a) ....

   ....

b) ....

   ....

Vocabulary: problems/disasters

1 Complete this crossword puzzle.

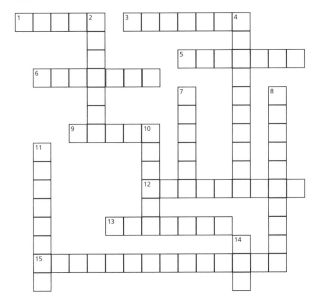

Across

1 a great overflow of water onto a place that is usually dry
3 an illness caused by an infection or disorder in the body or mind, not by accident
5 an organisation that gives money and help to people who are poor, sick or in difficulty
6 a person who has been forced to leave their country for political or religious reasons
9 bad weather conditions with strong wind and often rain, lightning and thunder
12 an unexpected and dangerous situation that must be dealt with quickly
13 a very violent wind that spins at great speed
15 the situation in which there are too many people living in one place

Down

2 a long period of dry weather when there is not enough water
4 a sudden, violent shaking of the Earth's surface
7 a very serious lack of food
8 the killing or death of the last remaining animals of a certain kind
10 a small piece of rock or metal that burns brightly when it falls into the air round the Earth
11 the noun from *solve*
14 money, food and services given to people who need them

Listening: selecting

Paper 4, Part 4

About the exam
In this part of Paper 4 you may have to answer True/False or Yes/No questions about a conversation or an interview.

Strategy
Listen for details that make the statements true or false or provide a 'yes' or 'no' answer to the questions.

— Hot tip! ◄
You have a fifty per cent chance of being right, so **never** leave a question unanswered.

You are going to hear an interview with Dr Goodman, a scientist who works with UNESCO's biosphere programme. Listen and answer 'Yes' or 'No' to the following questions.

1 Did the project start recently? ....
2 Are there biosphere reserves in a lot of different countries? ....
3 Is the new Brazilian reserve far from the capital city? ....
4 Are there animals and plants that are threatened with extinction on this reserve? ....
5 Do UNESCO scientists work on their own on the reserves? ....
6 Does Brazil have more than one reserve? ....
7 Are all the reserves the same size? ....
8 Are all the reserves in warmer parts of the world? ....
9 Do scientists working on the reserves ever get to meet? ....
10 Do some reserves share very similar circumstances and experiences? ....

The great persuaders

Speaking: opinion

About the exam
The examiner asks you to express your opinion about questions related to the task in Part 3.

Strategy
You are asked for your opinion. There is no 'right' answer. For example, if the examiner asks you: 'What is the best age to start learning a foreign language?', pause for a moment to work out what you think. Use expressions like:
- *Well, it depends ...*
- *I'm not sure, but I think ...*
- *I suppose ...*

If the examiner says something like: 'Do you think so?', it is because s/he wants you to say a bit more or give reasons for your opinion, not because you are wrong.

Listen to two candidates doing Part 4 of Paper 5 and make notes of all the words/phrases they use to express their opinions and to agree/disagree.

....

....

....

....

....

Writing: linking expressions

Read the text below and circle the alternative which is **not** possible in each case.

1 **A** On the other hand   **B** Furthermore   **C** However

2 **A** therefore   **B** however   **C** as well as these

3 **A** Furthermore   **B** However   **C** In addition

4 **A** Despite   **B** However   **C** Nevertheless

5 **A** So   **B** Although   **C** Therefore

6 **A** on the other hand   **B** as well as this   **C** however

7 **A** Although   **B** Despite   **C** In spite of

8 **A** In addition to this   **B** Furthermore   **C** Although

9 **A** because   **B** because of   **C** as

10 **A** Because   **B** Therefore   **C** So

A lot of people think that television in my country has improved over the last few years. (1)........., there are people who think it has got worse.

Only ten years ago the only television channels were the two state-owned stations. Nowadays, (2)........., in almost every part of the country you can receive as many as four more channels with your normal TV set. (3)......... you can buy a satellite dish or pay to receive cable television.

(4)........., does this mean the quality of what is shown has improved? There are a lot more movies, game shows, sports programmes and the so-called reality shows in which real people talk about dramatic things that have happened to them. (5)....... if you like a lot of choice and want to be entertained more than anything else, you would probably say that television has improved.

If, (6)........., you thought of television as an educational aid, you are probably very disappointed with what is on offer. (7)......... the large number of channels, there are definitely fewer documentary programmes. (8)........., the documentaries that are shown are of poorer quality than they were a few years ago. There are also fewer programmes about art and music (9)......... advertisers have found that these programmes attract only a small audience.

(10)......... television has improved in terms of the number of channels and the choice of programmes, but, in my opinion, it does not provide as much information as it used to, which is its main purpose.

Writing: discursive

Paper 2, Part 2

About the exam
In Paper 2, Part 2 you may have the option of writing an article in which you talk about the advantages and disadvantages of something, the arguments for and against something or in which you write your opinion about a subject.

1 The article on page 84 was written in answer to the following task.

> You have been asked to write an article for a student newspaper on the following topic:
>
> *Has television improved in your country over the last ten years?*
>
> Write your **article** saying what most people think and giving your own point of view.

Read these two plans and decide which one the writer followed.

Plan A

Introduction: my opinion about the statement (television <u>has</u> improved).

Paragraph 1: describe a situation.

Paragraph 2: first reason for my opinion (more channels = more programmes = more choice).

Examples: movies, game shows, sports programmes, reality shows.

Paragraph 3: second reason for my opinion (no more boring educational programmes).

Examples: documentaries, programmes about art and culture.

Conclusion: state my opinion again: television has improved because it's more entertaining.

Plan B

Introduction: question as a statement; two points of view;

Paragraph 1: describe a situation – more channels than before.

Paragraph 2: more choice; entertainment mainly.

Paragraph 3: not educational; fewer documentaries; fewer cultural programmes.

Conclusion: what most people think; what I think.

Did the writer of the text on page 84 follow the right plan for the task?

2 Write your answer to the question in Exercise 1.

1 Underline key words in the instructions.

2 Think of arguments for and against.

3 Write a plan using Plan B above as a basis.

4 Write your article in 120–180 words using appropriate linking expressions from page 84.

5 Check your work carefully.
   - Does it answer the question?
   - Have you used linking expressions correctly?
   - Is your answer grammatically correct?

► Hot tip! ◄

From now until the exam write at least one extra composition a week. Spend 45 minutes (no more, no less) planning, writing and checking your answer. Give it to your teacher. If your teacher is too busy, exchange answers with a friend.

Grammar: modifiers/intensifiers

Circle the correct alternative in the following sentences.

1 Thanks. The party was *very/really* fantastic.

2 I thought the film was *absolutely/very* terrible, but Mary quite enjoyed it.

3 Their house is *really/very* enormous. Even the bathroom is *absolutely/very* big.

4 My boss is *really/absolutely* good-looking.

5 See you soon! Have a *terrific/terrifying* time.

6 I'd certainly go there again. The staff were *very/absolutely* helpful.

7 The amount of rubbish along the side of the road was *quite/very* incredible.

8 She cooked a(n) *absolutely/quite* terrible meal.

9 I haven't seen such a *delicious/superb* match for a long time.

10 Their new secretary is *very/absolutely* efficient.

Vocabulary: phrasal verbs (*get*)

There are mistakes with word order or the particle in all of the following sentences. Find the mistakes and write the sentences out again correctly in your notebook.

1 I've been trying to get him through to on the telephone all afternoon, but the line is engaged.

2 You really must get up to some work. The exam is in a few weeks' time.

3 I know how to get over our Mum. She always lets me do what I want.

4 I don't get Mary on with very well. She's not my kind of person.

5 I hope you won't get anything up to while we're out. The babysitter will tell me if you do.

6 She doesn't earn a lot – just enough to get down.

7 I'd never do anything dishonest because I'm sure I'd never get away it with.

Grammar: *have to/don't have to/ must/need*

1 Put the words in the following sentences in the correct order.

1 have how we to do many write compositions?

....

2 with you help needn't the shopping.

....

3 needn't you gone much to so have trouble.

....

4 to just I've got pass.

....

5 to you often have do weekend study at the?

....

6 are how words write we to many supposed?

....

7 mustn't ink use you.

....

8 draft to we need do write a?

....

2 Now match each of the sentences above to an appropriate response below. Write the number of the sentence in the gap.

a) Between 120 and 180.   ....

b) I know, but I'd like to.   ....

c) What am I supposed to write with then?   ....

d) Don't worry. I'm sure you will.   ....

e) The letter from Part 1 and another question from Part 2.   ....

f) Yes, I'm afraid I do.   ....

g) It was a pleasure.   ....

h) No, but you should always plan your work before you start to write.   ....

3 Choose the correct alternative to fill in the gaps in the following sentences.

1 I .... go to the supermarket. My Mum asked me to get some things for lunch.

   A have to   **B** needn't

2 I .... go to the dentist. I haven't been for more than two years.

   A don't have to   **B** must

3 She said she .... go to the supermarket.

   A must   **B** had to

4 You .... drive me to the airport. I can get the bus.

   A don't need to   **B** must

5 How wonderful! Tomorrow's Saturday and we .... get up at 6·45.

   A mustn't   **B** don't have to

6 You .... tell anybody. It's a secret.

   A needn't   **B** mustn't

7 She .... retake any of her examinations. She passed them all in June.

   A didn't need   **B** needn't

8 You .... get a good night's sleep before the exam.

   A must   **B** have to

Grammar: error correction

Paper 3, Part 4

About the exam
The texts used for error correction are always at least seventeen lines long. The first two lines are examples and you have to check another fifteen lines. You write your answers on the separate answer sheet.

Strategy
Answer in the question booklet first. When you are sure, transfer your answers to the answer sheet.

Look at each line of the following text. Some of the lines are correct and some have a word which should not be there. If a line is correct, put a tick (✔) by the number **on the separate answer sheet.** If a line has a word which should **not** be there, write the word **on the separate answer sheet.** There are two examples at the beginning (**0** and **00**).

How TV helped me learn a language

0   When I first came to live in Spain, I could not (to)
00 speak any Spanish. I had to learn to speak quickly ✔
1   because of my job. Some friends suggested to buying a
2   television and this turned out to be a really good advice.
3   At the first, I did not really understand anything at
4   all, but little by little I began to pick up the main ideas.
5   I would been read an English newspaper the same day
6   so I knew that what was happening around the world
7   anyway and I could understand the news. But the best of
8   programmes for learning Spanish were the game shows.
9   I must have watched hundreds of them in the first few
10 months after I came to live here. Because of the same
11 patterns are repeated again and again, you learn the rules
12 of the language almost automatically. Despite of the fact
13 that they were not the kinds of programmes I would normally
14 have watched, I began to quite enjoy of them. Although I
15 speak Spanish well now, I still watch them sometimes.

Part 4			
0	*to*	**8**	
00	✔	**9**	
1		**10**	
2		**11**	
3		**12**	
4		**13**	
5		**14**	
6		**15**	
7			

Reading: multiple matching

Paper 1, Part 4

About the exam
You normally have to answer between thirteen and fifteen questions in this part of the exam.

Strategy
- Read the questions or statements that you have to match to the texts once very quickly.
- Underline or circle key words.
- Read the text or texts very quickly.
- Underline key words.
- Match the questions or prompts to the texts.
- Check your answers and transfer them to the answer sheet.

You are going to read some information about television programmes. For questions **1–12** choose from the programmes **A–H**. Some of the programmes may be chosen more than once. There is an example at the beginning (**0**). For questions **13** and **14**, choose the answer (**A**, **B**, **C** or **D**) which you think fits best according to the text.

• Which programme would you watch if you wanted to know about:

technology and the human body ?	0 ...*D*...
how people relate to their environment?	1 ....
animals and their young?	2 ....
how human ingenuity solved a pollution problem?	3 ....

• Which programmes would you recommend to someone who is interested in:

cars?	4	5		
animals?	6	7	8	
sports?	9	10		
medicine?	11	12		

13 What do all the programmes have in common?
- **A** They are all about science.
- **B** They are all about Britain.
- **C** They all provide information.
- **D** They are all part of a series.

14 Why would someone read texts like these?
- **A** To find out what's on TV on a particular night.
- **B** To find out how long the programmes are.
- **C** To find out what channel a programme will be shown on.
- **D** To learn about the environment, sports and science.

A

CHILDREN OF THE STORM
Channel 7
September 12   8.00 pm
About two-thirds of the world's Atlantic Grey seals live around the western shores of the British Isles. This film by Chris Doncaster looks at their breeding colonies on Ramsey Island on the west coast of Wales. Doncaster started watching the seals while on his summer holidays, then became so involved that he is now an acknowledged expert.

B

TOP GEAR
Channel 10
Starts *August 29   2.00 pm*
Join Jeremy Clarkson, Tiff Needell, Quentin Wilson and others as they embark on a brand new series covering all things motoring. Will include road tests and reports, plus sporting coverage such as the British Rally Championships and the Network Q rally.

C

EQUINOX: AUTOMATIC AUTOSTRADA
Channel 2
August 28   9.30 pm
In a change to the programme we published last month, Automatic Autostrada looks at the inevitable issue of 'pay as you drive' roads. The race is on for collecting and monitoring fees from millions of cars.

D

THE BODY ELECTRIC
Channel 10
September 15   8 pm
From the metal fillings in our teeth to high-tech diets and gene therapy, we're all living techno-hybrids. This is a 'visual essay' on how technology has affected the human body this century.

E

ANIMAL HOSPITAL LIVE
Channel 2
August 29– September 4 7.00 pm
Six programmes about a week at the Royal Society for the Prevention of Cruelty to Animals' hospital, one of only three in the country. Backstage drama with staff, pets and owners.

F

HELLFIGHTERS OF KUWAIT
Channel 7
September 17   10 pm
The story of the firefighters flown in to deal with the environmental catastrophe following the Gulf war, when many people believed the oilfields would blaze for years.

G

THE CROSSOVER
Channel 10
September 23   4.00 pm
Another gripping film from
John Varty, this one about life
in the wilds of Africa from the
point of view of the indigenous
people. Explains how Shangaan
hunter-gatherers understand
conservation, and shows life-or-
death battles between man and
lion, leopard and cheetah.

H

NBA RISING STARS
Channel 9
September 20   6.00 pm
Basketball is the world's
fastest-growing sport. With the
arrival of the legendary Magic
Johnson on our shores this
month, British people are likely
to catch the basketball bug. Get
into the spirit of things with
this definitive guide, which
highlights all the hottest talent
of the moment, and showcases
those who are up and coming.

Vocabulary: media

1 Find words in this word search grid to match the following definitions.

J	H	E	A	D	L	I	N	E	T
C	O	Y	E	S	L	G	R	G	R
R	F	U	D	M	K	R	F	O	S
O	C	A	R	T	O	O	N	S	L
S	A	K	N	N	X	V	U	S	T
S	P	O	C	H	A	H	E	I	Q
W	G	B	A	W	K	L	Z	P	S
O	E	D	I	T	O	R	I	A	L
R	Q	P	B	I	L	V	W	S	X
D	C	D	X	J	U	X	P	O	T

1 humorous drawing often dealing with something in the news in an amusing way ....

2 the part of the newspaper giving the opinion of the person in charge of the newspaper on a problem or event ....

3 the title printed in large letters above a story in a newspaper ....

4 informal talk or writing about other people's private lives ....

5 a person whose job consists of collecting information and writing things for newspapers and magazines ....

6 a printed word game which you do by fitting words guessed from questions and information into a pattern of numbered squares going down and across ....

2 Fill in the gaps in the following dialogue with an appropriate word. The first letter of each word has been given to help you.

A: I can't seem to find the BBC World Service on this radio. Perhaps the (1) f.................... has changed.

B: It might just be that the (2) b.................... are getting low. Shall I get some when I go out to the newsagent's?

A: Could you? I want to listen to the news (3) h.................... at eight.

B: I'll go just as soon as this has finished. These (4) s.................... are absolute rubbish, but once you've seen a couple of episodes you're hooked.

A: You don't seem to be getting very good reception. Perhaps you should move the (5) a.................... .

B: Oh, we never get Channel 5 very clearly. Pass me the (6) r.................... c...................., will you? I just want to change over to see if the match has started.

A: I thought you said you were going to the shops as soon as 'Days of Our Lives' had finished.

B: Couldn't you go instead?

🔊 Listening: multiple matching

About the exam
There are always five different speakers who talk about a theme such as travel, the media or health.

Strategy
• Read the instructions and ask any questions before the cassette starts.
• Listen for clues to match each speaker to the prompts.
• Check your answers when you hear the cassette again.
• Don't leave any questions unanswered on the answer sheet – guess if necessary!

You will hear five different men talking about experiences they have had with the media. For questions **1–5** look at the statements **A–F** and match them to the speakers. There is one extra statement which you do not need to use. Use the letters once only.

Speaker 1 .... Speaker 4 ....

Speaker 2 .... Speaker 5 ....

Speaker 3 ....

A He was taken in by an advertisement.
B He was interviewed on the radio.
C He was in a television advertisement.
D Something he wrote was in a newspaper.
E He was rejected because he didn't seem natural.
F He was worried that people would notice something.

Word formation

Paper 3, Part 5

About the exam
There are ten gaps in each word formation text. You write the words you form on a separate answer sheet.

Strategy
• Read the text through once to get a general idea of what it is about.
• Decide what part of speech is missing for each gap.
• Form words to fill each gap and write them above the gaps.
• Read the completed text to check that it makes sense.
• Check that the words are spelt correctly.
• Transfer your answers to the answer sheet.

Read the following text and use the word given in capitals at the end of each line to form a word that fits in the gap in the same line. There is an example at the beginning (**0**). Write your answers on the answer sheet.

EXAMPLE: **0** *variety*

Media career opportunities

Nowadays there is a (0).............. of career opportunities **VARY**
in the media. It is possible to study (1).............. **JOURNALIST**
at most universities, many of which offer (2).............. **OPTION**
courses in reporting on sports and (3).............. . Newer **ENTERTAIN**
degrees in media studies, which were (4).............. **AVAILABLE**
as recently as ten years ago, attract (5).............. **ENTHUSIASM**
students from all over the country.

Some graduates prefer to work in (6).............. **ADVERTISE**
as it allows them to use their (7).............. in the **CREATE**
(8).............. of increasingly sophisticated TV and **PRODUCE**
press advertisements.

(9).............. not all graduates find work easily as **FORTUNATE**
there is still a lot of (10).............. in the media **EMPLOY**
industry, but things are improving.

Part 5			
1		6	
2		7	
3		8	
4		9	
5		10	

13 It's a mad world

Vocabulary: animals

1 Match the sentences in Column A to a response in Column B. Write the appropriate letter in the gaps.

Column A

1 Are you sure it's true that they're getting married? ....

2 I'll never meet a girl as beautiful as Helen. ....

3 It was meant to have been a surprise party, but it was obvious he knew about it all along. ....

4 What did your Dad say when you told him you'd decided not to sit for your exams? ....

5 She'll be furious when she finds out I broke her favourite vase. ....

6 I've got to go into town to the doctor tomorrow morning. ....

7 She told him she thought he was a really terrible manager. ....

Column B

a) Why don't you kill two birds with one stone and go to the bank as well?

b) That must have really put the cat among the pigeons.

c) He nearly had kittens at first, but then he calmed down and was quite nice about it.

d) Wouldn't it be better to take the bull by the horns and tell her?

e) What nonsense! There are plenty more fish in the sea.

f) So who do you think let the cat out of the bag?

g) Well, I heard it straight from the horse's mouth.

2 Label the features on these animals and then write the name of one real animal which has each feature.

1	7 ....
2	8 ....
3	9 ....
4	10 ....
5	11 ....
6	

3 What animal is being talked about in the following sentences?

1 He always barks at the postman. ....

2 I can hear them mooing from over the hill. ....

3 He gave a mighty roar. ....

4 It raised its head and hissed. ....

5 She neighed as I came into the field. ....

6 If you stroke her, she purrs loudly. ....

Speaking: problem solving

About the exam
In Paper 5 you are given marks for use of grammar and vocabulary, pronunciation, fluency, and ability to communicate. The examiner may also assess you on task achievement (how well you do each of the things you are asked to do in Paper 5).

Strategy
When you do a problem solving task:
- make sure you understand what to do.
- cover all the points you are asked to talk about.
- ask for the other candidate's opinion.

1 Listen to the interlocutor giving two candidates instructions for a task and study the map below. Mark the following statements **T** (true) or **F** (false).

1 Each candidate has to talk for three minutes. ....

2 The candidates should decide together which animals they want to see. ....

3 The problem is that the zoo is going to close soon. ....

4 The candidates will need to know the words for various kinds of animals. ....

2 Listen to Dimitra and Giorgos doing the task. Who got good marks for task achievement?

Grammar: conditionals

1 Fill in the gaps in the following sentences with the most likely form of the verbs in brackets.

1 If you .... (be) happy, your immune system .... (work) well.

2 What .... (you/buy) if you .... (win) the lottery?

3 I .... (be) home by six thirty unless my plane .... (be) late.

4 If I .... (have) time tomorrow evening, I .... (sew) those green buttons on your jacket.

5 No matter how hard you .... (try), you .... (not/convince) me you're right.

6 We .... (not/drive) all the way to the airport if we .... (know) their plane had been delayed.

7 If you .... (divide) two thousand five hundred and ninety-six by fifty-four, you .... (get) forty-eight point oh seven.

8 They .... (meet) three years earlier if she .... (come) to my eighteenth birthday party.

9 I .... (lend) you my new shirt to wear to the party, so long as you .... (promise) to give it back.

10 If I .... (be) you, I .... (tell) him.

11 If you .... (mix) an alkali with a fat, you .... (make) soap.

12 I .... (let) you stay up and watch TV tonight provided that you .... (finish) your homework first.

13 If he .... (not/stand) under that tree during the thunderstorm last week, he .... (not/get) struck by lightning.

14 What .... (you/do) if you .... (be) Prime Minister?

2 Complete the following sentences in an appropriate way.

1 If I do well in my exams, my parents ....
....

2 I might not have met my best friend if ....
....

3 If I could change one thing about myself, I ....
....

4 The world would be a better place if ....
....

5 If I stay out in the sun in the summer, I ....
....

6 If I had to choose two records (or CDs or cassettes) to take to a desert island, I ....
....

7 I wouldn't live anywhere else in the world unless
....

Vocabulary and grammar:
open cloze

Paper 3, Part 2

About the exam
You have 1 hour and 15 minutes to do the five tasks in Paper 3 and transfer your answers to the answer sheet.

Strategy
- Read the text once quickly to find out what it is about.
- Read it again, paying attention to the words around the gap.
- Decide what part of speech is missing.
- Fill in the gaps on the question paper.
- Read the text again to make sure it makes sense.
- Make guesses for any gaps you cannot fill.
- Transfer your answers to the answer sheet.
- All of this should take you **no more than** fifteen minutes.

Spend a maximum of fifteen minutes filling in the gaps in the following text and copying them on to the answer sheet.

Life of a tiger

The tiger can live in almost any natural environment from hot, steamy jungles to snowfields with sub-zero temperatures. A female tiger has her first cubs when she is less (1).................. four years old. About half usually die before they (2).................. a year old. They kill their first small animals when they are about one and leave their mother a year (3).................. .

Tigers are good swimmers, can climb trees (4).................. eat 23 kilos of meat in a night. They can jump nearly nine metres, (5).................. is about the length of a double-decker bus. A tiger depends (6).................. its sharp eyes and keen ears. It waits in cover and rushes at the animals it hunts, jumping on (7).................. . If it fails, it often (8).................. up because it gets tired very easily. It can go for more than a week (9).................. catching anything.

Tigers communicate by many sounds, including a roar that can be (10).................. over several miles. Adult tigers usually live alone, (11).................. they are quite friendly with each other. They mostly hunt (12).................. night. They often meet while they (13).................. out hunting, rub heads together and then part.

They have similar bodies (14).................. lions. Nevertheless, (15).................. never mate together in the wild. Occasionally they do in zoos and their offspring are called 'tiglons' or 'tigons'.

Part 2		Do not write here
1		1
2		2
3		3
4		4
5		5
6		6
7		7
8		8
9		9
10		10
11		11
12		12
13		13
14		14
15		15

Vocabulary: places

1 Label these pictures.

1 ....   4 ....   7 ....

2 ....   5 ....   8 ....

3 ....   6 ....

2 Fill in the gaps in the following sentences with an appropriate word. The first letter of each word has been given to help you.

1 My father expects me to help mow the l.................... at the weekends.

2 He keeps all the gardening tools in a s.................... in the corner of the garden.

3 There's no room for those suitcases down here. Put them up in the a.................... .

4 The burglars got in by climbing up a d.................... and through the bathroom window.

5 They got on so well with their neighbours they decided to take down the f.................... between their gardens.

6 There must be someone home. I can see smoke coming out of their c.................... .

7 We keep all the wine in the c.................... because it's so much cooler down there.

8 I couldn't see over the h...................., but I could hear children playing in the front garden.

Writing: describing places

Paper 2, Part 2

About the exam
Another option you may have to choose from in Paper 2 is describing a place or building.

— **Hot tip!** ◀
You will get better marks if your description is interesting to read.

1 Circle the best alternative in the following sentences.

1 If you like water sports, your visit to Lake Eildon will certainly be *spectacular/enjoyable*.

2 The new campsite and sports centre are located just outside the town in *colourful/glorious* countryside.

3 One thing that makes the cathedral different is its *exotic/unusual* spire.

4 Vienna is the place to visit for music-lovers and its cafés are famous for their *charming/delicious* cakes and pastries.

5 The landscape is varied, offering *spectacular/colourful* views of the valleys.

6 The market is very *colourful/delicious* with stall-holders in traditional costume selling *exotic/glorious* fruit and vegetables.

7 If you visit the mountain villages, have lunch in one of the *charming/enjoyable* taverns where the local wine is served.

2 Look at the following task and the answers two candidates wrote. Then match the candidates' answers to the examiner's comments.

Describe your ideal home, saying where it would be and how you would decorate one of the rooms.

Candidate A

My ideal home would be a bungalow in the country not far from where I live.

I would build my bungalow on a hill just outside the village of Saint Andrew. It would have spectacular views of the village, which is very charming, and the sea. There would be a large garden around the house, full of colourful flowering plants and exotic fruit trees.

The living room would have huge windows so that I could sit and watch the small fishing boats coming into the harbour. I would build a large terrace outside the living room so that we could go out there on summer evenings and look at the stars. Inside I would build a big chimney so that we could be warm in winter. There would be huge sofas and comfortable armchairs covered in skin.

My house would also have lots of spare bedrooms so that all my family and friends could come and visit me. Maybe you would like to come and visit too.

---

1 Comments on Candidate........'s answer

Grade: Unsatisfactory

There is little attempt to structure the answer in terms of the instructions.

The vocabulary used is very simple and not entirely appropriate to the task.

There are basic errors with verb forms and word order.

The use of the Present Simple would confuse the reader, making it difficult to tell if the writer was describing an ideal or simply his actual home.

2 Comments on Candidate........'s answer

Grade: Very good

A well-organised piece of writing which meets the requirements of the instructions.

A range of ideas is communicated with a good range of vocabulary and structures, though there are two minor errors with vocabulary.

The use of the conditional (*would*) makes it clear that the writer is talking about an ideal, though the last sentence is inappropriate in a description of this kind.

Candidate B

I live in the city in a appartment. I like very much. It is very nice. It have four bedrooms, a kitchen, a bathroom and a living room.

In the my bedroom there are a bed, a desk, a chair and other furnitures. All is paint in pink. I have on the wall a poster of Johnny Depp. He is my favourite actor. In the desk there is a lamp and a computter. I like play computter game.

I have one brother. My brother like her bedroom too. We are all very contents living in the centre of the city, because of we can to go out to the street which is very excited.

---

3 Find the two vocabulary mistakes the examiner mentions in the good composition. Write the sentences with these mistakes out again correctly in your notebook. Then write the unsatisfactory composition again in better English.

4 Now write your answer to the task in Exercise 2.

1 Underline key words in the instructions.

2 Think of ideas: What kind of house or flat would you choose? Would you build it in the country or in a city, town or village? What would you be able to see/do there? Which room will you describe?

3 Write a plan of your composition following Candidate A's answer.

4 Write your description in 120–180 words making sure that you use some of the vocabulary you studied in this unit and appropriate conditional forms.

5 Check carefully for spelling errors and mistakes with verbs.

Grammar: key word transformations

Paper 3, Part 3

Strategy
- Complete the sentences on the question paper **without** changing the form of the word given.
- Check for spelling and verb form mistakes.
- Write only the missing words in the space on your answer sheet.
- Check that you have copied your answers accurately.

Complete the second sentence so that it has a similar meaning to the first sentence. Use the word in **bold** and other words to complete each sentence.

1 She said she would lend me her notes.
   promised
   She .... me her notes.

2 Although she studied very hard, she didn't do very well in the exam.
   despite
   She didn't do very well in the exam
   .... very hard.

3 My father often played the piano while we sang.
   used
   My father .... while we sang.

4 If I don't feel better tomorrow, I'll go to the doctor.
   unless
   I'll go to the doctor tomorrow
   .... better.

5 You mustn't talk during the test.
   supposed
   You .... during the test.

6 I couldn't tolerate her bad behaviour any longer.
   put
   I couldn't .... her bad behaviour any longer.

7 I have a degree and also extensive sales experience.
   addition
   I have extensive sales experience
   .... a degree.

8 She lost her job because her work was careless.
   carefully
   If she ...., she would not have lost her job.

Listening: gap fill

Paper 4, Part 2

Strategy
- Listen for the general idea and specific information.
- Answer as many questions as you can the first time you hear the recording.
- Fill in the other answers the second time you listen.
- In the pause check spelling and grammar.

You will hear a man being interviewed about ghosts and haunted buildings in Europe. Listen and complete the gaps in these notes which summarise what the speaker says. After you have heard the recording for the second time, transfer your answers to the answer sheet. Spend only **one minute** doing this.

Simon Marsden has photographed more than (1)........................ places in (2)........................ .

He has also visited Tirgoviste the (3)........................ of the part of (4)........................ which was ruled by Dracula in (5)........................ . He is supposed to have had more than (6)........................ people killed during his reign of terror.

The castle that was probably the model for Dracula's castle is in Scotland. One of the ancestors of the family who own the castle was the commander of (7)........................ . He died in mysterious circumstances. His body was (8)........................ .

The dungeon of Dunnottar castle was used to imprison 160 royalist rebels in 1685. Many of these people died of (9)........................ .

Simon was very frightened once in a castle in (10)........................ . He took his photographs, but left as quickly as he could.

Part 2			
1		6	
2		7	
3		8	
4		9	
5		10	

Reading: multiple matching

Strategy

- Read the paragraph headings and the text once quickly to get a general idea.
- Pay attention to the structure of the text.
- Find the main idea in each paragraph.
- Write the paragraph headings in the spaces on the question paper.
- Read the text through with the headings.
- Transfer your answers to the answer sheet.
- Do not spend more than **eighteen minutes** on this part of the test.

Read this magazine article about a pet bear. Choose the most suitable heading from the list **A–I** for each part of the article **1–7**. There is one extra heading which you do not need to use. Transfer your answers to the answer sheet below. Do not spend more than eighteen minutes on this task.

A A big appetite.
B Make yourself at home.
C Specially designed.
D A nasty temper.
E A bit of luxury.
F Too gentle for his own good.
G A dream come true.
H Keep out!

Bear necessities

(1 _H_)
The solidly built house of wood and stone is set amid fifty acres of Scottish forest in the hills above Gleneagles. A sign by the gates warns that this is private property. A custom-built coach parked in front cost £120,000, but as we all know stars are very fussy about these things.

(2___)
There's a forty-five foot swimming pool in the garden – but when this particular star was working in Hollywood he had his own jacuzzi too. Beside the pool is a little log cabin with a pile of rubber tyres inside. Go into the house itself and you notice that everything is big — up to and including the meals.

(3___)
In the kitchen most of the food is firmly locked away, but on the breakfast bar in the morning you'll find a healthy portion of baked beans with bread and eggs, plus coffee with lots of sugar and cream. And at teatime, a dish cooked with tomato soup, potatoes and fifteen pounds of fresh meat. It makes you wonder who on earth lives here.
The solution is provided by a sign outside Andy and Maggie Robins' home. It reads: 'Warning – Hercules the bear walks free beyond this gate.'

(4___)
It all started back in the days when Andy was still a professional wrestler.

He went to the USA and met an Indian who kept a bear. When Andy got married, he confessed to his wife that he wanted a bear as part of the family. Most women would probably have begun divorce proceedings, but not Maggie, a farmer's daughter and keen horse-rider. Hercules was bought almost fifteen years ago from the wildlife park in Scotland where he was born. He was four feet tall, but very wild then. Today it's eight feet from the ground to the tip of his nose.

(5___)
Commercials and films have made him famous, and when he was lost a few years ago it was headline news. But there was nothing for the public to worry about. Hercules is a very friendly bear. His owners say this has stood in his way professionally when he has gone for roles that need a big bad bear. 'He's tried to get serious parts in films – but he's got an awfully soft face,' says Maggie.

(6___)
At home, three children up the road often come round to tea. This is Hercules's house as much as it is the Robins' so he goes where he likes. He'll watch TV when there's something good and loud on, like a Tom and Jerry cartoon. And he appreciates an occasional curry or perhaps something Italian for supper for a change.

(7___)
He sleeps in the log cabin by the pool, but he loves the pretty four-poster bed in the Robins' bedroom. To some degree this house has been made 'Hercules-proof' with bare walls and corridors that have been made wider than usual. 'It's true there aren't that many ornaments about,' says Maggie, 'but that's really more because of Andy than Hercules.'

from TV Quick

1	A	B	C	D	E	F	G	**H**
2	A	B	C	D	E	F	G	H
3	A	B	C	D	E	F	G	H
4	A	B	C	D	E	F	G	H
5	A	B	C	D	E	F	G	H
6	A	B	C	D	E	F	G	H
7	A	B	C	D	E	F	G	H

Guilty or not guilty?

Vocabulary: crime

Choose the best alternative to fill the gaps in the following sentences.

1 She was .... by a man who threatened to tell her employer about her past.

   A hijacked   **B** blackmailed

2 The .... had a knife so she gave him her bag.

   A smuggler   **B** mugger

3 Department stores lose millions from ....

   A pickpocketing   **B** shoplifting

4 The police think a/an .... lit the fire.

   A arsonist   **B** forger

5 He .... his father's signature on £20,000 worth of cheques.

   A forged   **B** smuggled

6 When you travel on public transport, always keep your bag carefully closed in case of ....

   A hijackers   **B** pickpockets

7 The .... said she was sure he was the man she had seen running away from the bank.

   A witness   **B** judge

8 It took the .... twenty-four hours to decide.

   A accused   **B** jury

9 Eventually they managed to reach a ....

   A plea   **B** verdict

10 The judge gave him a suspended ....

   A punishment   **B** sentence

11 .... exists in some parts of the USA.

   A Probation   **B** Capital punishment

12 The police have .... a woman in connection with last Tuesday's robbery.

   A arrested   **B** accused

13 The judge agreed to .... her on bail.

   A acquit   **B** release

Reading: multiple choice

> **Paper 1, Part 2**

About the exam

There are four types of questions you may be asked in this part of the exam.

1 Questions about what the text means.
2 Questions about the meaning of pronouns (e.g. *it, them*) and demonstratives (e.g. *this, that, those*).
3 Questions about the individual words.
4 Questions about where the text comes from or what its purpose is.

Strategy

For questions which ask you about what the text means you should:

- answer without looking at the alternatives.
- find evidence for your answer in the text.
- find the alternative closest to your answer.
- make sure the other answers are wrong. Do they say the opposite of what the text says? Do they say something that may be true but which is not in the text? Do they say something similar but not exactly the same as the text?

Spend **eighteen minutes only** reading the text opposite, answering the questions and transferring your answers to the answer sheet.

1 What did the court decide about Mr Howarth?

   A That he should never be allowed to drive again.
   B That he should pay a fine and be prohibited from driving for a year.
   C That he should take another driving test at once.
   D That he should not be punished.

2 How did the police learn about Mr Howarth?

   A They saw him.
   B Other drivers reported him.
   C A police car had to swerve to avoid him.
   D Another driver telephoned them.

3 Why did Mr Howarth stop in the end?

   A Some policemen managed to stop him.

   B Another driver stopped him.

   C He realised they would catch him eventually.

   D There were road works on the road and he had to stop.

4 Mr Howarth did not realise his mistake at first because

   A there were other cars travelling in the same direction.

   B the incident happened at night.

   C there were not many cars and he couldn't see the other side of the road clearly.

   D he was not wearing his glasses.

5 Why did Mr Howarth plead guilty?

   A Because he thought he had done a terrible thing.

   B Because he was dazed and confused.

   C Because he had driven off when the policeman stopped him.

   D Because he had not stopped as soon as he could have done.

6 Mr Howarth

   A was not aware he was on the wrong side of the road when the police stopped him.

   B did not realise he was on the wrong side of the road until he had driven seventeen miles.

   C realised he was on the wrong side of the road when he saw other cars swerving to avoid him.

   D realised he was on the wrong side of the road after he had driven about a mile.

7 How did Mr Howarth feel about the incident?

   A Terrified and upset.

   B Angry and frustrated.

   C He did not think he had done anything wrong.

   D He was glad it was over.

8 Mr Howarth's lawyer claimed that

   A he had done a very wicked thing.

   B this was not typical of his normal behaviour.

   C he was not to blame for what happened.

   D he was too old to be driving.

An 82-year-old chartered accountant who has had a perfect driving record since passing his test before the Second World War was banned for a year yesterday for travelling seventeen miles in the wrong direction on a dual carriage way.

William Howarth became confused as he tried to avoid roadworks and set off on a road between Oxford and Newbury in the wrong direction, magistrates at Abingdon were told.

Howarth, who uses a hearing aid and wears glasses, was driving in the fast lane of the northbound carriageway as he travelled south causing several drivers to swerve on a dark January afternoon. A police car in the correct lane drove alongside Howarth's car and stopped him, but as the policeman climbed over the central barrier Howarth set off again. He continued for another ten miles until a police road block forced him to stop.

Howarth pleaded guilty to dangerous driving and was also fined £175. He was ordered to re-take his test if he wants to drive again after the year in which he is banned from driving is over.

He leaned forward as he strained to hear yesterday as Mr John Horn, prosecuting, said police received a number of 999 calls saying a car was travelling in the wrong direction.

Mr Robert Hawes, defending said Howarth still worked five days a week as an accountant, sometimes until eight at night, and had a 'perfect' 60-year driving record. He had driven on to the road as he tried to avoid roadworks and had not at first realised he was in the wrong lane because traffic was light and trees blocked his view of the opposite carriageway.

'Within a mile, he realised he was on the wrong carriageway and his intention was to get off as quickly as possible and get back on to the right road.

'There were in fact eight lay-bys along the route where he could have stopped and for that reason he accepts that he is guilty.

'This was not a wicked piece of driving. Mr Howarth was disorientated. It was a nightmare journey for him and he was dazed, confused and in obvious shock.'

1	A	B	C	D
2	A	B	C	D
3	A	B	C	D
4	A	B	C	D
5	A	B	C	D
6	A	B	C	D
7	A	B	C	D
8	A	B	C	D

from *The Daily Telegraph* newspaper

Grammar: *make/let/allow*

1 There are mistakes in seven of the following sentences. Find the mistakes and write the sentences out again correctly.

1 The police made him to stop.

2 The judge decided not to allow him to drive.

3 Are you allow to stay out after ten o'clock?

4 Do your parents make you studying English?

5 Will the teacher let us go home early?

6 They allowed us going to the party.

7 Does she let you stay up late on Fridays?

8 My parents make me wear clothes I didn't like.

9 When I was younger, I didn't allowed to go swimming unless my parents were with me.

10 They wouldn't let me to go.

2 Complete the following paragraphs in your own words.

Children of your own
I wouldn't let my sons or daughters ....
.... I probably wouldn't allow
them .... either.
And I think I would probably make them ....
....

The society we live in
I don't think people should be allowed ....
.... In fact I think they
should be made ....
.... What's more we shouldn't let our
politicians ....

Crime
I don't think the police should be allowed ....
.... I think people who
commit violent crimes should be made ....
.... And I don't think we
should let ....

Vocabulary: phrasal verbs (*make*)

1 Match the following phrasal verbs with *make* to a definition below. One of the verbs goes with two of the definitions. Write the numbers 1–5 in the gaps.

1 make up
2 make out
3 make for
4 make out (that)
5 make up for

a) to see, hear or understand something with difficulty   ....

b) to prepare something by putting different parts together e.g. a bed   ....

c) to reduce the bad effect of something   ....

d) to pretend   ....

e) to move towards something   ....

f) to invent a story or piece of information in order to deceive people   ....

2 There is a mistake with word order in each of the following sentences. Find the mistakes and write the sentences out again correctly in your notebooks.

1 You won't make for lost time up by working all night. You'll be too tired to work tomorrow.

2 What he told me wasn't true. He just made up it.

3 When the police asked him where he had been that night, he made that he had been with me out, but I was in France that week.

4 The escaped prisoners tried to make the mountains for where they thought they would be able to hide.

5 She muttered something under her breath, but I couldn't make exactly out what she said.

6 If your friend wants to spend a couple of days here, we could make a bed for her in the spare room up.

7 They had a terrible row and didn't speak to each other for a couple of days, but they've made up it and are the best of friends again.

Writing: narrative

About the exam
Most of the questions in Paper 2, Part 2 involve writing for a particular situation and audience.

Strategy
● Pay attention to the situation described in the instructions.
● Decide how the situation will affect the style of your answer.

Hot tip! ◀
NEVER memorise a composition to use in the exam! It may not be an appropriate answer to the question.

Choose between the alternatives in Column A to find a word that matches a definition from Column B. Write the words in the gaps.

Column A

a) fidget/writhe/wriggle
b) wonder/consider/reckon
c) exclaim/mutter/insist
d) lob/hurl/toss
e) inform/insist/order
f) stagger/tiptoe/wander
g) chuckle/giggle/snigger
h) munch/nibble/swallow
i) grasp/clutch/hug

Column B

1 to speak (usually angry and complaining words) in a low voice ....

2 to laugh quietly ....

3 to think about, especially in order to make a decision ....

4 to eat with small repeated bites ....

5 to take and keep a firm hold of ....

6 to walk on one's toes with the rest of the feet raised above the ground ....

7 to hit or throw in a slow high curve ....

8 to move one's body around restlessly, so that one annoys other people ....

9 to command ....

2 Use as many of the words in groups a)–i) as you can to make the paragraph below a more interesting piece of writing. Write it out again in your notebook.

He walked along the corridor quietly, thinking about what he would do if the gang were still there. When he was about to climb the stairs, he heard someone laughing in one of the rooms on the second floor. He held the gun and continued to climb the stairs. Suddenly he felt someone hit him very hard from behind and he walked a few steps further and then fell and moved on the ground in pain, telling himself that he had been a fool to try this on his own. The man who had hit him told him to give him the gun and with what little energy he had left he threw it to him. The man laughed and said, 'Now you're really in trouble, Mason.' He took a bottle from his jacket and drank half the contents in one go. Mason thought he would be lucky to get out of there alive.

3 Here are two questions which ask you to write a narrative. Answer both of them. Spend **45 minutes** on each.

You work as a journalist for a local English language newspaper. Write a news story for the following headline:

Local girls home after cycling journey across the USA.

You have entered a detective story competition. Write a story that begins with the following words:

He woke quite suddenly to the sound of someone opening the back door of the house.

1 Study the instructions carefully and underline key words.

2 Think of ideas and write them down in any order. Ask yourself questions about the situation if you have difficulty thinking of original ideas.

3 Write a plan, putting your ideas in order in paragraphs.

4 Write your answer in 120–180 words. Use narrative tenses (Unit 5) carefully and make your writing interesting.

5 Check your work carefully. Exchange answers with a classmate and check their work, too.

Vocabulary: multiple choice cloze

Paper 3, Part 1

Strategy
- Read the text all the way through to find out what it is about.
- Read the text again and choose the best alternative.
- Check that you have not made mistakes with commonly confused words or 'false friends'.
- Mark your answers on the answer sheet.

For questions **1–15** read the text and decide which word **A**, **B**, **C** or **D** best fits each space. There is an example at the beginning (**0**). Mark your answers on **the separate answer sheet**.

EXAMPLE:

0 A hurt   **B** damage   **C** illness   **D** injury

0	A	B	C	D
	⊔	⊔	⊔	▬

1   **A** discovered   **B** invented   **C** done   **D** manufactured
2   **A** extremely   **B** scarcely   **C** slightly   **D** hardly
3   **A** Despite   **B** However   **C** Although   **D** Otherwise
4   **A** does   **B** has   **C** is   **D** makes
5   **A** controlling   **B** preventing   **C** dealing   **D** stopping
6   **A** along   **B** around   **C** at   **D** over
7   **A** under   **B** less   **C** more   **D** below
8   **A** extends   **B** shrinks   **C** reduces   **D** expands
9   **A** suspect   **B** guilty   **C** accused   **D** arrested
10   **A** Few   **B** The   **C** Several   **D** These
11   **A** include   **B** are   **C** create   **D** involve
12   **A** because   **B** because of   **C** as   **D** therefore
13   **A** thought   **B** reckoned   **C** considered   **D** wondered
14   **A** approved   **B** granted   **C** allowed   **D** let
15   **A** expect   **B** hope   **C** anticipate   **D** wait

Foam gun will prevent escapes

DEALING with prison escapes and riots without serious (0).......... to prisoners or guards would still be a major problem without the invention of a new range of non-lethal weapons.

A sticky-foam gun has been (1).......... by scientists at the Sandia National Laboratories in New Mexico. The gun sprays you with (2).......... sticky spaghetti-like material which makes movement absolutely impossible.

(3).......... it sounds like something from a cartoon, the sticky foam has a serious purpose. It (4).......... it impossible for anyone hit to reach for a gun or run away. This means that the guns could be an ideal way of (5).......... with escaping prisoners or criminals. They may also be used with rioting prisoners or violent criminals who have to be moved (6).......... the country.

In (7).......... two seconds, the gun can squirt half a litre of foam. This then (8).......... to fifty times its original size. 'If the foam is sprayed at arms and legs, the (9).......... would stick to himself and anything he touches, including the floor,' says Tom Goolby, one of the researchers working on the gun.

(10).......... other non-lethal weapons have also been developed. These (11).......... instruments that make low-frequency sounds that make you feel as if you are going to be sick and non-toxic chemicals called 'stickums' or 'slickums'. These make roads sticky or slippery and (12).......... impossible to drive on.

All these weapons are being (13).......... by the Department of Justice. It is expected that the foam guns will be (14).......... for use in prisons later this year. The other weapons will have to (15).......... a little longer.

from *Focus* magazine

Part 1				
1	A	B	C	D
2	A	B	C	D
3	A	B	C	D
4	A	B	C	D
5	A	B	C	D

6	A	B	C	D
7	A	B	C	D
8	A	B	C	D
9	A	B	C	D
10	A	B	C	D

11	A	B	C	D
12	A	B	C	D
13	A	B	C	D
14	A	B	C	D
15	A	B	C	D

Listening: multiple choice

Paper 4, Part 1

About the exam
The eight extracts you hear in this part of the exam are completely unrelated.

Strategy
Listen for clues to help you decide:
● what they are talking about.
● where they are.
● what the relationship between the speakers is.

 You will hear people talking in eight different situations. For questions **1–8**, choose the best answer **A**, **B** or **C**.

1 You are on a plane. You hear this woman speaking. She is speaking to
   A her husband.
   B another passenger.
   C a flight attendant.

2 You are visiting a friend. You hear his two younger brothers talking in another room. They are
   A doing their homework.
   B arguing about a computer game.
   C watching television.

3 You are waiting to use a public telephone. You hear this woman talking. She is talking about
   A a problem with an electrical appliance.
   B a problem with a dentist's appointment.
   C a problem with one of her customers.

4 You are in the kitchen. Your friend is watching television in another room. You hear this man speaking. Your friend is watching
   A the news.
   B a film.
   C a quiz programme.

5 You hear these two women talking on a bus. The first woman
   A is criticising the second woman.
   B is giving the second woman some advice.
   C is agreeing with the second woman.

6 You hear this man talking to another man. He is talking about
   A taking a cat to the vet.
   B taking a dog to the vet.
   C taking a baby to the doctor.

7 You hear this man talking on the telephone. He is talking to
   A a business associate.
   B someone he hasn't met before.
   C his wife.

8 You are in the bathroom. You hear this woman talking on the TV. She is
   A in a restaurant.
   B in an office.
   C in a kitchen.

Speaking: opinion

Paper 5, Part 4

About the exam
The examiner will assess you on the following categories:
● use of grammar
● use of vocabulary
● pronunciation
● fluency
● ability to communicate

Strategy
If you do the exam with another candidate, remember you are not competing against this person. Ask their opinion as well as giving your own.

 Listen to two candidates doing Paper 5, Part 4 and assess them on the categories listed below. Was their performance: poor/satisfactory/good/excellent? Write **P** (poor), **S** (satisfactory), **G** (good) or **E** (excellent) in the gaps.

	Nicole	Diego
1 use of grammar/vocabulary	....	....
2 pronunciation	....	....
3 ability to communicate	....	....

Grammar: passives

1   Rewrite the following sentences using the correct passive form of the verbs in *italics*.

1   They're *making* a film about Indian tigers.
A film about Indian tigers ....
....

2   No one has *painted* this house for ten years.
This house ....
....

3   They *provide* over one hundred scholarships for students every year.
Over one hundred scholarships for students ....
....

4   I realised someone had *stolen* my wallet.
I realised my wallet ....
....

5   Someone has to *guard* this prisoner day and night.
This prisoner ....
....

6   Water might *affect* the Joker badly.
The Joker ....
....

7   The police *were interviewing* people in the neighbourhood last night.
People in the neighbourhood ....
....

8   A police roadblock finally *forced* Mr Howarth to stop.
Mr Howarth ....
....

2   Rewrite the following sentences using an appropriate passive form so that they sound more formal.

1   You have made some kind of a mistake.
Some kind of a mistake ....
....

2   We remind you not to put bottles in the overhead lockers.
Passengers ....
....

3   We will refund your money in full if you are not satisfied.
Your money ....
....

4   Our customer relations office is dealing with your complaint.
Your complaint ....
....

5   We will send successful candidates a letter inviting them to attend a second interview.
Successful candidates ....
....

6   We sent the goods on 15th April.
The goods ....
....

7   If no one has delivered the equipment by 15th May, please contact us again.
If the equipment ....
....

8   We will replace furniture that our employees damage in transit.
Furniture damaged in transit ....
....

9   Perhaps you would like another cup of coffee while we are preparing your bill.
Perhaps you would like another cup of coffee while your bill ....
....

10 We apologise for the delay. Technicians were checking the plane.
We apologise for the delay. The plane ....
....

15 The power of words

Grammar: hypothetical meaning

1 Fill in the gaps in the following sentences with a correct form of the verbs in brackets. In some of the sentences there is more than one possibility.

1 I wish I .... (*study*) harder. The exam is tomorrow and I've only revised half the course.

2 We wish you .... (*come*) for Christmas. The rest of the family will all be here.

3 I wish I .... (*can/drive*) a car.

4 I wish I .... (*have*) a computer.

5 I wish you .... (*do*) that. It drives me crazy!

6 I wish you .... (*be*) here. You'd love it!

7 I wish you .... (*tell*) me the answer. I'll never guess.

8 I wish I .... (*know*) more vocabulary. I keep forgetting the words for things.

9 If only I .... (*not/do*) that. I'll regret it for the rest of my life.

10 If only I .... (*can/afford*) that dress. It really suits me.

11 I'd rather we .... (*we/stay*) at home tonight. I'm a bit tired.

12 I'd rather you .... (*not/lend*) him that book. It was a present from my grandfather.

13 It's time you .... (*leave*) for the airport. You have to check in two hours before the time on your ticket.

14 Just suppose someone .... (*recognise*) you. They'll probably have reported you to the police.

15 Suppose we .... (*arrive*) a bit earlier. Then we'll be able to help Mary with the food.

2 Complete the second sentence so that it has a similar meaning to the first sentence. Use the word in **bold** and other words.

1 I'm sorry I didn't phone him.
   wish
   I .... him.

2 How about buying her a CD?
   suppose
   Just .... her a CD.

3 I regret saying that to her.
   only
   If .... that to her.

4 You should go to bed now.
   time
   It's .... to bed.

5 I would prefer to have a light lunch.
   rather
   I .... a light lunch.

6 I'd prefer you not to tell him.
   rather
   I .... him.

7 It really annoys me the way you click your fingers.
   wish
   I .... click your fingers.

8 I am really sorry he isn't here.
   only
   If .... here.

9 Shouldn't you start revising for your exams now?
   time
   It's .... for your exams.

Speaking

Strategy

Relax! Many candidates actually enjoy Paper 5.

Part 1 (short responses)
Before
- Revise vocabulary for education, family and free time activities.

During
- If you do the exam with another candidate, listen to what s/he says and show that you are interested.

Part 2 (picture prompts)
Before
- Revise modal verbs.

During:
- If you don't know a word for something, use another word or describe the thing.
- Relate the photograph to your own experience.

Part 3 (problem solving)
Before
- Revise language for agreeing/disagreeing and asking for/making/accepting/rejecting suggestions.

During
- Make sure you understand what you have to do.
- Make sure you do **all** the things the examiner asks you to do.
- Remember there is no 'right' answer.
- If you do Paper 5 with another candidate, ask for and respond to the other person's suggestions.

Part 4 (opinion)
Before
- Revise the language for expressing/asking for opinions.

During
- Remember! There is no 'correct' opinion.
- If you do Paper 5 with another candidate, ask the other person what s/he thinks and respond to what s/he says.
- Don't say: 'I don't know.'

Remember:
- DON'T prepare a speech!
- DON'T try to dominate!
- DON'T treat it as a competition!

1 Listen to two candidates doing Paper 5 and look at the photos and map they refer to. Assess each candidate on the categories listed below. Was their performance: poor/satisfactory/good/excellent? Write **P** (poor), **S** (satisfactory), **G** (good) or **E** (excellent) in the gaps.

	Anna	Francisco
1 use of grammar/vocabulary	....	....
2 pronunciation	....	....
3 ability to communicate	....	....

1

2

3   4

POSSIBLE SITE *for* SHOPPING MALL

- - - PATHS

6 KILOMETRES

CAR PARK

BUS STATION

BANK

BANK

BUS STOP

SHOPS

POST OFFICE

CAR PARK

S H O P S

S.HOPS

LIBRARY

S H O P S

STATION

🔊 **2**   The candidates pronounced the following words incorrectly.

1) saucepans   2) fruit
3) comfortable   4) convenient

How should they be pronounced? Listen to the cassette and check your answers.

🔊 **3**   How do you pronounce the following words.

1) bear	4) clothes	7) wallet
2) stir	5) money	8) occasion
3) weapons	6) scientist	

Listen to the cassette and check your answers.

Grammar: *to have something done*

Rewrite the following sentences using the correct form of *have* + an object + the past participle of an appropriate verb.

1   The hairdresser cut my hair last week.

I ....

....

2   Some painters are painting the Wilson's house.

The Wilsons ....

....

3   The tailor has turned my trousers up.

I ....

....

4   A pickpocket stole my friend's wallet.

My friend ....

....

5   A photographer took a photo of us.

We ....

....

6   An optician tested my eyes.

I ....

....

7   The dry-cleaner is cleaning my new jacket.

I ....

....

8   A repairman has fixed our refrigerator.

We ....

....

9   The man from the supermarket delivers their groceries.

They ....

....

10   There's something wrong with my car. The mechanic is going to service it next week.

I ....

....

Grammar: error correction

Paper 3, Part 4

Strategy
- Read the text very quickly to get a general idea of what it is about.
- Read it again and 'say' the words in your mind.
- Look for errors with: articles, auxiliaries, comparatives, prepositions and pronouns.
- Write your answers in the question booklet first. Then transfer them to the answer sheet.

For questions **1–15**, read the text below and look carefully at each line. Some of the lines are correct and some have a word that should not be there. If a line is correct, put a (✔) at the end of the line. If a line has a word that should **not** be there, circle the word. There are two examples at the beginning (**0** and **00**)

Speed in handwriting

0	The speed of your handwriting can be estimated by the ✔
00	fluency and continuity of your script; (the) disconnected
1	writing is usually slower than connected is writing,
2	which is made in a continuous motion. A very fast script
3	shows intelligence and an ability to be get down to
4	essentials quickly. Very large handwriting is rarely fast,
5	as the writer tends to waste the time and effort. It is a
6	fact that the more articulate you are the faster than you
7	will write, so fast writing is a clear indication of your
8	ability to speak in fluently as well as your mental
9	capacity. In the same the way, the more simplified your
10	writing, the quicker you will write, and the more elaborate
11	your writing, the more time you do take over it. Intelligent
12	writers often depart from the writing style they were
13	taught at school because of they find it too slow. They
14	adopt an original and economical form of writing. Many
15	executives have small, fast writing, but large signatures.

Reading: gapped text

Paper 1, Part 3

Strategy
- Read the text and the sentences/paragraphs that have been removed once quickly.
- Find the main idea in each paragraph of the text.
- In the sentences or paragraphs that have been removed:
  - work out what pronouns, demonstratives and possessive adjectives refer to.
  - look for a meaning/relationship between the sentences or paragraphs and the text.
  - pay attention to linking words like *however, furthermore, therefore,* etc.

DON'T spend more than **18 minutes** answering the questions and transferring your answers to the answer sheet!

Read the magazine article opposite about writing. Seven paragraphs have been removed from the article. Choose from the paragraphs **A–H** the one which fits each gap (**1–6**). There is one extra paragraph which you do not need to use. There is an example at the beginning (**0**). Mark your answers on the answer sheet.

WHO INVENTED WRITING?

Our ability to communicate through the written word is something we all accept. Yet the invention of writing at around 3500 BC was extremely important for modern civilisation.

(0 _H_)

Over the past 3,500 years different civilisations and cultures across the world have created at least 700 different forms of writing. To our eyes most of these scripts look quite distinct, and people who can read only one script cannot understand another.

(1___)

Writing's most successful ancestors were ancient Egyptian hieroglyphs. All European and Arab scripts originally come from hieroglyphs. Most Asian scripts do too, even if the link is less direct. Modern Korean and Vietnamese, however, come from ancient Chinese.

(2___)

The first forms of writing were pictograms: simple pictures of objects. Gradually, the direct link between a symbol and the object it represented disappeared. In the next phase the pictograms were replaced by symbols which represented objects or 'logograms'.

(3___)

In the alphabetic system, words are made up of combinations of characters or letters representing different sounds. This system developed in the Middle East around 3,700 years ago. It spread quickly and formed the basis of Greek and later of the Cyrillic and Roman scripts now used in Europe.

(4___)

For many years people have believed that writing was invented in Mesopotamia. They thought it spread to Ancient Egypt and then to the region that is now Pakistan. Chinese writing, they thought, developed independently one thousand years later .

(5___)

A second discovery will make experts want to change their theories even more. It seems that the ancient Sumerians, who people thought invented the first fully developed writing, did not arrive in the area until 200 to 300 years after the first Mesopotamian script developed.

(6___)

So if China developed the first writing, did the idea spread from East to West, and not the other way round? It will take time and more evidence to convince all archaeologists that this is true, but, as they say, the writing is probably on the wall.

A But although the complicated way the world's writing systems developed is now well understood, there is still a lot of controversy about which of the four original scripts was the first to be used.

B Of these the only script that has survived without many changes is Chinese. Now with over 50,000 characters, it has remained more or less the same for at least 4,000 years.

C The first task for the script specialists is to discover the number, frequency and position of individual signs; the frequency size and position of groups of signs; and the probable identity of any numerals.

D However, the main archaeological discovery shows that at least some Chinese characters were developed 7,500 years ago – much earlier than the accepted date of 1300 BC.

E However, if the evolution of the world's writing systems is traced back through time it becomes clear that nearly all of them originated from just four scripts: ancient Egyptian, ancient Mesopotamian, ancient Chinese, and ancient Zapotec from central Mexico.

F But a series of extraordinary new archaeological discoveries have revealed Egyptian writings dating from 3250 BC – between fifty and a hundred years earlier than the Mesopotamian script.

G Ancient Egyptian hieroglyphs combined pictograms with logograms. But there is a problem with such a system – it requires a new symbol for every new word and so rapidly becomes very complicated.

H With it came the ability to keep administrative records and pass messages over long distances. This made it possible for central governments to organise large populations and economies. And of course it was also a means of passing on knowledge and literature between generations.

1	A	B	C	D	E	F	G	H
2	A	B	C	D	E	F	G	H
3	A	B	C	D	E	F	G	H
4	A	B	C	D	E	F	G	H
5	A	B	C	D	E	F	G	H
6	A	B	C	D	E	F	G	H

Vocabulary: spoken and written language

Complete this crossword.

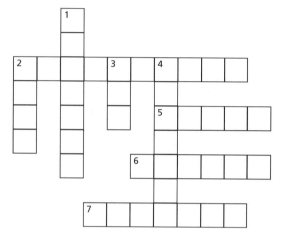

Across
2   correct something which someone has said which you believe is wrong
5   say something very loudly or speak very loudly
6   speak in a low voice, often expressing irritation
7   speak very quietly so only someone nearby hears

Down
1   say or write about something in a few words
2   talk in a friendly and informal way
3   quarrel noisily
4   talk about the details of something with someone

🔲 Listening: selecting

Paper 4, Part 4

Strategy
- Listen carefully to the instructions the supervisor gives.
- Look through the questions before you listen to the cassette.
- The first time you hear the cassette, answer as many questions as you can.
- Answer the other questions the second time you listen.
- Transfer your answers to the answer sheet in the five minutes at the end of the test.

Remember: you only have time to **transfer** your answers, not to think about them and work them out.

You will hear a teacher talking about reading. Choose the best alternatives **A**, **B** or **C** to answer questions **1–7**. Mark your answers on the answer sheet.

1   The speaker says reading and driving are similar because
    A they are both very difficult to learn.
    B you have to practise a lot to be good at them.
    C you have to pass reading and driving tests.

2   The speaker says young people
    A can often only read very slowly.
    B often don't learn to read at all.
    C should read while travelling by car.

3   The problem, according to the speaker, is that
    A they are not given interesting things to read.
    B they don't do what their teachers tell them to do.
    C they are unable to become involved in what they read.

4   One reason some young people read very slowly is
    A they say the words aloud or in their heads.
    B they watch too much TV.
    C they don't recognise all the words.

5   The speaker thinks saying the words aloud
    A is the best way to read.
    B should not be allowed.
    C is a necessary stage children go through.

6   The speaker blames adults because
    A they give children the wrong messages.
    B they complain about children not reading.
    C they make reading seem difficult.

7   The speaker says that
    A we should have learnt to read by the time we leave school.
    B we have to keep practising reading.
    C we should do regular exercise.

Writing: discursive

Strategy

- Remember you **must** answer Part 1. You choose **one** of the alternatives in Part 2.
- If you choose to write a discursive composition, read the instructions **very** carefully and underline key words.
- Think of as many ideas as you can. Ask yourself questions. Think about what people you know would think.
- Plan your answer.
- Write your answer. Use interesting vocabulary and use linking expressions.
- Check your work for your 'typical mistakes'.

Remember in Paper 2:

DON'T write a composition you have memorised!

DON'T spend more than **45 minutes** on each answer!

DON'T answer the set texts question if you have not studied at least one of the books!

DON'T write your answer out again unless it is absolutely necessary!

1 Look at the following task.

> You have been asked to write an article for a local paper on the following theme:
>
> *There should be only one international language.*
>
> Write the **article**, giving arguments for and against this question.

Now look at this answer a candidate wrote. Grade the answer from 0–8 (8 is the top mark) in the following categories.

a) Range of vocabulary and structures.   ....

b) Accuracy of vocabulary and structures.   ....

c) Spelling and punctuation.   ....

d) Appropriacy of style (formal/informal).   ....

e) Organisation and cohesion (structure and making links between ideas).   ....

f) Task achievement.   ....

Should there be one international language? There are points for and against this statment.

To begin with if people used only one language, comunication would be cheaper. There would be no need for translattors because everyone would know a language. On the other hand, perhaps people would stop to use their languages and this is a shame, because all the languages of the world are like a beautiful treasure.

Another point is that there would be less misunderstanding. If everyone spoke the same language, we would all get along well. However, I do not think this is true. Probably many people would not speak the language very well, and they would not always understand everything either. In addition to this the people who are nattive speaker would have a unfair advantage.

As far as I am concerned one international language is not a good thing, because we do not want to loose our languages. It is worth remembering that Esperanto was not so sucessful.

2 The writer has made six spelling mistakes, one mistake with the use of gerunds and infinitives and one mistake with the use of articles. Find the mistakes and write the sentences out again correctly in your notebook.

3 Now write your answer to the question in Exercise 1. Use some of these linking words/phrases:

- *to begin with*
- *on the other hand*
- *another point is that*
- *to sum up*
- *however*
- *in addition to this*
- *it is worth remembering that*
- *as far as I'm concerned*

Practice exam

PAPER 1 – READING

PART 1

You are going to read a magazine article about love. Choose the most suitable heading from the list **A–I** for each part (**1–7**) of the article. There is one extra heading which you do not need to use. There is an example at the beginning (**0**).

A Two magic substances.

B Finding someone who matches us physically.

C Two feelings that are easily confused.

D We don't want to get hurt.

E A silly experiment.

F It's hard to resist.

G We like what we know.

H Spot the difference.

I Most of us feel it.

What is this thing called love?

(0 _I_)

According to a 1991 survey, at any one time about one in ten of us describe ourselves as 'madly in love'. Love is remarkably common; in the survey only one in five of the 1,000 people interviewed said they were 'not really in love', with most of the rest admitting to some kind of romantic involvement. So what is this feeling called love? To many researchers the classic symptoms of butterflies in the tummy, rapid pulse rate and legs turning to jelly are far from mysterious. Many believe it can all be explained by our biochemistry.

(1 ____)

Scientists believe the excitement of that fatal attraction is created by adrenaline – the same hormone that is produced when we are under stress. When stimulated, the adrenal glands also produce a hormone called cortisone, whose side-effects include feelings of great happiness.

(2 ____)

Eyes give away the fact that you are in love, or at least very much attracted to someone because adrenaline enlarges or 'dilates' your pupils. Having large pupils also means that we are more appealing to others. Desmond Morris, a scientist who studies human behaviour, proved this point by showing a picture of a woman to a large number of men. He then told them that she had a twin sister, but presented the same woman with her pupils dilated. When the men were asked which of the twins they'd like to take out for the evening, most chose the one with larger pupils.

(3 ____)

In another study, scientists used two bridges over the Capilano River in British Columbia. One was a very dangerous-looking bridge which was 70 metres above the river, while the other was a solid concrete bridge. An attractive female researcher stopped men coming off each bridge. She managed to give them her phone number while she pretended to get them to fill out a questionnaire. Many more of the men who had crossed the dangerous bridge later phoned the researcher to ask her out than those who had crossed the safe bridge. This made researchers think that love is much like any other

emotional state. Because their adrenaline is flowing and their hearts are beating fast, people believe they are in love even if they are actually only a bit frightened.

(4 ____)

But how do we select our partners from all the thousands of possible people? People are often attracted to others who have a lot in common with them – even if they don't always realise that they have anything in common. We give out unspoken messages about ourselves every day from the way we walk, talk and hold ourselves. It's not just the way we dress, but our posture, facial expressions, movements, tone of voice, accent and so on. If you put a group of people who don't know each other in a room together and ask them to pair up, they will naturally choose partners who are of similar family background, social class and upbringing. We are all looking for something familiar though we may not be aware of exactly what it is.

(5 ____)

Facial attractiveness is a big influence on our choice of partners, too. People have long-lasting relationships with others of a similar level of attractiveness. In a recent study, researchers took a selection of wedding photos and cut them up to separate the bride and groom. They then showed them to people who were asked to rate how attractive each person's face was. When the researchers put the photos back into pairs, they found most of the couples had been rated at similar levels.

(6 ____)

Aside from our ability to rate others, each of us carries a rough estimate in our heads of how facially attractive we might be. We realise subconsciously that if we approach someone who is much better looking than we are, we run the risk of being rejected.

(7 ____)

Whatever the explanation for how and why we fall in love, one thing is clear: Nature has made the whole process as wonderful and as addictive as possible. Perhaps that's why so many of us are at least a little bit 'in love' most of the time.

PART 2

You are going to read an extract from an autobiography. For questions 8–14, choose the answer (**A**, **B**, **C** or **D**) which you think fits best according to the text.

My parents ran a tea-room where they also lived, and I was born in one of the upstairs rooms there. We moved around quite a lot when I was young. I was three or four when we left Upton and went to the Midlands. We seemed to have so many family houses. All the moving also meant changing schools. I attended about four schools and four different technical colleges after that. I did reasonably well at school, finishing up with a couple of O-levels and quite a few CSEs. But it didn't make it any easier switching schools so many times.

The thing I enjoyed most about my first two schools was being captain of the football and cricket teams. I always loved sport and games. At my second school I worked my way into the chess team deliberately to get out of Latin. I had always hated it and it got even worse at this school. In fact I wasn't interested in the academic side at all until I moved to my next school.

Even then, though, it was a rather traumatic experience because I joined in the middle of the year. Previously I'd always been in classes of fifteen; suddenly it was thirty. I'd always been to all-boys schools; now it was mixed. I had no friends there and I got into trouble and fights. It was a difficult time, but I started to learn how to look after myself.

It didn't help when I had to take time off school to race karts. The school was fine about it, but some of the kids weren't. When I was chosen to represent the country in Holland, the headmaster was genuinely pleased for me and announced at assembly that I was getting a special two-week leave. Afterwards in the playground I was beaten up by some older boys. They were presumably a bit jealous and thought it was favouritism. The truth is that getting time off doesn't help anyone, because you have to work harder to catch up on your school work. That's not an easy situation for an eleven-year-old.

Instead of doing my homework in the evening, I used to go home and work on my kart, tuning the engine, fiddling about, polishing it up. If I had polished it one night, I would still go home the next night and polish it again. It was a fascination for me and one I certainly don't regret. It kept me off the streets and I started winning races.

Through those years I never put myself up against anyone and thought: 'I'm better than he is.' I've always preferred to think that given equal opportunity and equipment I do a good job, if not a better one than the next person. The reality of trying to achieve something you want to do is terribly frightening. I went from juniors to seniors to the national and the international races. Each time you move up a level you start at the bottom again. Just because you were champion in the class below does not mean you will be in the next class. All of a sudden you realise how much harder it is.

8 Where was the writer born?

    A In a hospital.
    B In the place where his parents worked.
    C In the house he lived in throughout his childhood.
    D In a restaurant.

9 At the second school the writer attended

    A he began to take an interest in studying.
    B he lost interest in sports.
    C he started to dislike Latin.
    D he took up another activity to avoid a subject he disliked.

10 He found moving to the third school upsetting because

    A it was different to the other schools.
    B the classes were too small.
    C there were no girls there.
    D he had fights with his friends.

11 How did people at the school react to his being chosen to represent his country?

    A Everyone was very proud.
    B The headmaster was angry because he had to take time off.
    C Some of the other pupils resented it.
    D They thought it would make it difficult for him to keep up with the others.

12 What did the author do in the evenings when he was at school?

    A He played in the street with other children.
    B He spent his time at home, but he didn't study.
    C He had a job.
    D He did his homework.

13 The writer believes you can achieve something you want

    A if you believe you are better than other people.
    B if you are lucky.
    C if you are not afraid of trying.
    D if you are very competitive.

14 What would be the most suitable title for this extract?

    A An unhappy childhood.
    B A love of learning.
    C Winning is not always easy.
    D Wasted youth.

PART 3

You are going to read a magazine article about a hotel. Eight sentences have been removed from the article. Choose from the sentences **A–I** the one which fits each gap (**15–21**). There is one extra sentence which you do not need to use. There is an example at the beginning (**0**).

Ice breaks

Holidaymakers who are bored with baking beaches and overheated hotel rooms head for a giant igloo.

Swedish businessman Nils Yngve Bergqvist is delighted with the response to his new accommodation concept, the world's first igloo hotel. Built in Jukkasjärvi, a small town in Lapland, ARTic Hall has been attracting flocks of visitors. (**0** _I_)

In two weeks' time Bergqvist's ice creation will be nothing more than a pool of water. (**15** ____) 'The most interesting thing is designing the igloo,' he says. 'We don't see melting as a big problem. I just look forward to making a bigger one to replace it.'

(**16** ____) It was so successful that he designed the current one, which measures 1,800 square feet. Six workmen spent more than eight weeks piling 1,000 tons of snow on to a wooden base; when the snow froze the base was removed. 'The only wooden thing we have left in the igloo is the front door,' says Bergqvist proudly. (**17** ____)

'I decided to test out some new ideas on the igloo,' he says. (**18** ____) 'Hot red wine with spices is popular, but I always recommend whisky before they go to bed,' explains Bergqvist. 'It warms them up when they get into the cold sleeping bags.'

Bed and breakfast in one of the ice cubicles or the luxury bridal suite is £25–£30 per night. (**19** ____) With no doors, nowhere to hang clothes and temperatures around 0ºC, it may seem more like an endurance test than a relaxing hotel break. 'It's a great novelty for them,' Bergqvist explains, 'as well as being a good start in survival training.' He claims that guests feel warm despite the cold because snow is such a good insulator. (**20** ____)

The popularity of the resort is beyond doubt – it is now attracting tourists from all over the world. (**21** ____) 'You can get a lot of people in,' explains Bergqvist. 'The beds are three metres wide and can fit at least four at one time.' Guests also come to have a drink at the bar and even to get married in the chapel.

Bergqvist is already excited about his next hotel, which will take more than 1,500 tons of snow to construct. 'We're going to concentrate on the architectural features this time,' he says. With summer on its way Bergqvist will soon be holding his annual contest to predict when the igloo will fall. Last year's winner received a large painting from an ARTic Hall exhibition. 'It's great,' says Bergqvist, 'we all sit in a big tent nearby, drinking beer and waiting for it to melt.'

A Strangely enough this seems to be a cause for celebration rather than regret.

B At least eight hundred people have stayed at the igloo this season even though there are only ten rooms.

C Everything else is one hundred per cent snow, including a chapel with pews covered in reindeer fur and a solid ice cross.

D Maximum heat is maintained by ice walls that are about two metres thick.

E Bergqvist built his first igloo in 1991 for a local art exhibition.

F But this is one of the sad things about building an igloo.

G After their stay, all visitors receive a survival certificate recording their accomplishment.

H These include a theatre for slide shows, a jazz club, a radio station and a large ice bar.

I Soon, however, the fun will be over.

PART 4

You are going to read some information about the history of sports. For questions **22–35**, choose from the sports (**A–D**). Some of the sports may be chosen more than once. When more than one answer is required, these may be given in any order. There is an example at the beginning (**0**)

Which sport or sports:

was played all over one European country?	(0 _B_)
could be dangerous?	(22 ____ 23 ____)
was not played in the same way everywhere?	(24 ____)
played a part in religious ceremonies?	(25 ____)
became popular because people read about it?	(26 ____)
includes equipment that developed gradually?	(27 ____)
has uncertain origins?	(28 ____ 29 ____)
caused people to neglect other activities?	(30 ____ 31 ____)
developed in a place that is still very important to people who practise the sport?	(32 ____)
was prohibited by law?	(33 ____)
could take a long time to play?	(34 ____)
is mentioned in historical records?	(35 ____)

Sport A
From the deep blue waters of Waikiki Beach to the cold grey Atlantic of Cornwall, surfers have a strange bond with the sea. They are part of a tradition that stretches back to the people of the Pacific islands, who prayed to the gods for the best waves. From the beginning of the sixteenth century Hawaiian legends and songs describe surfing as an obsession making surfers forget everything, including work and family.

In 1911 America discovered surfing. The journalist and novelist Jack London wrote about surfing in his book *The Snark Hunt*. Soon the craze swept through California and beyond, and surfing has never looked back. Generations of surfers now think of Hawaii as the Mecca for their sport.

Sport B
Four thousand years ago, an Egyptian sculptor carved a picture on a wall of two women hitting a ball back and forth from hand to hand. Is this the ancestor of tennis?

Tennis was brought to northern Europe from Greece in 500 AD. It became so popular between the twelfth and fourteenth century that every town in France had its own court. But this was a very different game from the one we see at Wimbledon today.

At first the game was played bare-handed with a leather ball filled with dog's hair. Later rougher materials like sand and chalk were used, but these caused injuries to the players' hands. This led to the use of protective gloves which got bigger and bigger as time went on until it was necessary to cut out the centres and replace them with tight ropes. Gradually these gloves evolved into rackets.

Sport C
Football is a very old sport, but it was no laughing matter in the early days. Two villages would battle to kick a ball made from a pig's intestine to a goal. The goals were things like trees or buildings and could be as much as five miles apart. The game, which was sometimes extremely violent, could go on from sunrise to sunset.

A more controlled form of the game began to be played in England's public schools in the early nineteenth century. Each school played a different version of the game and the rules varied widely. In 1863 a Football Association was established and the members met to decide on the rules. It took five meetings before they could all agree.

Sport D
No one really knows where the game of golf was first played. The Romans played a game with bent wooden sticks and a leather ball stuffed with feathers, but the details of the game are not known.

In the fifteenth century, golf first appeared in the written history of Scotland. In 1457 the Scottish parliament got very upset about the number of people playing golf instead of training for the army and the game was banned. By 1503 even the King had started playing golf again. Mary, Queen of Scots, is supposed to have been the first woman golfer. People say she played a few rounds of golf just after her husband was murdered.

PAPER 2 – WRITING

PART 1

You **must** answer this question.

1 You and a student of English from another country are going to participate in an exchange programme. She will visit your country for one month and study at the school where you study while you visit her country and attend her school. You have written to her to introduce yourself. You have received the following reply:

> *I'm very excited about the exchange and I can hardly wait to visit your country. Of course, I have all sorts of questions and I'm sure you do too. First, where will I be staying? Will the school arrange accommodation or will I need to arrange it myself?*
>
> *Secondly, I suppose I'll have plenty of time for sightseeing so what would you suggest are the most important things to see? And last but not least, what will the weather be like and what kinds of clothes should I bring?*
>
> *I'm sure there are a lot more things I should ask you, but that's all for now. Is there a time I could phone you so we could talk about the final details? Please let me know.*
>
> *Best wishes,*
> *Maria*

> – *classes every day?*
> – *money: traveller's cheques or cash? How much?*
> – *dates of summer music festival?*

Read carefully Maria's reply and the set of notes which you have made for yourself. Then write a letter arranging a time for her to phone you, answering her questions and covering the points in your notes.

Write a **letter** of between **120 and 180** words in an appropriate style. Do not write any addresses.

PART 2

Write an answer to **one** of the questions **2–5** in this part. Write your answer in **120–180** words in an appropriate style.

2 This is part of a letter you have received from an English pen friend.

> **I am doing a programme on a local radio station on music around the world and I want to include your country. Could you write me a report about music young people like to listen to and play in your country?**

Write a **report** which your pen friend can include on the programme.

3 You have been asked to write an **article** for a local English language newspaper discussing the following question:

Are there more advantages to being famous than there are disadvantages?

Write your **article**.

4 Your school is running a short story competition. You have decided to enter the competition. The rules say you must begin or end your story with the following words:

She put the letter back between the pages of the old book.

Write your **story** for the competition.

5 **Background reading texts**
Answer **one** of the following two questions based on your reading of one of the set books.

(a) Imagine you are one of the characters in the book you have read. Write a letter to a friend who knows nothing about the events described in the book, telling her/him what happened and how you felt about it.

(b) Would you recommend the book you have read to members of your family? What aspects of the book would make it particularly suitable or unsuitable for an older and a younger relative? Write your **composition**.

PAPER 3 – USE OF ENGLISH

PART 1

For questions **1–15**, read the text below and decide which word **A**, **B**, **C** or **D** best fits each space. There is an example at the beginning (**0**).

KEEPING YOUR CAR SAFE

Apart from your home, your car is probably your most (**0**) ....*B*.... possession. It's also your most vulnerable. Car and cassette and radio (**1**) .... make up over a quarter of all recorded crime. Together they (**2**) .... everyone a lot of money. It takes up police time to deal with these offences, taking criminals through the (**3**) .... is expensive and, of course, motorists end up paying higher insurance premiums.

Over 460,000 cars are reported (**4**) .... in Britain each year and many are never found again. Many of those which are found have been (**5**) .... by thieves. A (**6**) .... car is also far more likely to be involved in an accident than the same car driven by its (**7**) ....; car thieves are often young and sometimes drunk.

Yet car crime can be cut drastically if motorists follow a few simple (**8**) .... to keep thieves out of their cars in the first place. Most car thieves are unskilled (**9**) .... and many are under twenty. So make your own car a less inviting target, to (**10**) .... thieves from trying.

Lock your car every time you leave it even for a (**11**) .... minutes. (**12**) ...., one car in every five is left unlocked. Don't leave valuables on (**13**) .... inside or briefcases or even coats which a thief might think (**14**) .... money. If you cannot take valuables with you, lock them in the boot out of sight. (**15**) .... having a car alarm fitted.

0	**A** rich	**B** valuable	**C** worthy	**D** wealthy
1	**A** robberies	**B** steals	**C** thefts	**D** hijacks
2	**A** cost	**B** spend	**C** pay	**D** charge
3	**A** judgements	**B** judges	**C** courts	**D** juries
4	**A** disappeared	**B** lost	**C** gone	**D** missing
5	**A** injured	**B** hurt	**C** damaged	**D** harmed
6	**A** robbed	**B** stolen	**C** taken	**D** lifted
7	**A** owner	**B** holder	**C** master	**D** landlord
8	**A** announcements	**B** rules	**C** laws	**D** warnings
9	**A** kidnappers	**B** criminals	**C** burglars	**D** hijackers
10	**A** put off	**B** put on	**C** put by	**D** put up
11	**A** little	**B** bit	**C** few	**D** five
12	**A** Foolishly	**B** Pleasingly	**C** Excitingly	**D** Astonishingly
13	**A** display	**B** vision	**C** sight	**D** spectacle
14	**A** have	**B** contain	**C** enclose	**D** include
15	**A** Think	**B** Consider	**C** Estimate	**D** Calculate

PART 2

For questions **16–30**, read the text below and think of the word which best fits each space. Use only **one** word in each space. There is an example at the beginning (**0**).

PLASTICS

Plastics are a victim of their (**0**) ...*own*... success. The same properties that make them so popular, such as (**16**) .... ability to resist moisture and last a long time, mean they are very hard to (**17**) .... rid of. The difficulty is making (**18**) .... into a source of food for bacteria.

There are about 80 different types of plastics and about 100 million tonnes (**19**) .... produced worldwide each year. In Britain we throw (**20**) .... about 288,000 tonnes of plastic bottles alone in our domestic waste. An ordinary plastic bottle could (**21**) .... hundreds of years to disappear, if it disappears (**22**) .... all. As plastic has only been around (**23**) .... about a century, we can only guess.

Recently one company has developed what they describe as 'the perfect plastic', (**24**) .... will disappear completely much more quickly. It is made from sugar (**25**) .... once it is buried in the soil it is digested (**26**) .... bacteria. Most environmentalists argue, however, (**27**) .... this is missing the point. They say (**28**) .... only solution is recycling our resources. So (**29**) .... time you are about to put a plastic container in the rubbish bin, think twice. Could you use it again for (**30**) .... purpose?

PART 3

For questions **31–40**, complete the second sentence so that it has a similar meaning to the first sentence, using the word given. **Do not change the word given.** You must use between two and five words, including the word given. There is an example at the beginning (**0**).

Example:

0 Although she had been training for months, she didn't win the match.
spite
She didn't win the match ..*in spite of training*.. for months.

31 'Let's go to the cinema on Tuesday,' said Mary.
suggested
Mary .... to the cinema on Tuesday.

32 The exam started before I arrived.
already
By the time I arrived .... started.

33 I stayed with Martin when I was in London.
put
Martin .... when I was in London.

34 'Where are you from?' she asked.
them
She asked .... from.

35 Smoking is not allowed in here.
supposed
You .... in here.

36 It still feels strange to wear high-heeled shoes.
used
I am still .... high-heeled shoes.

37 He hates people interrupting him.
stand
He .... interrupted.

38 I am sure she knew you were coming.
must
She .... you were coming.

39 A famous artist is painting Michael's portrait.
having
Michael .... by a famous artist.

40 He was angry because she arrived late.
time
If she ...., he would not have been angry.

PART 4

For questions **41–55**, read the text opposite and look carefully at each line. Some of the lines are correct, and some have a word which should not be there.
If a line is correct, put a tick (✔) by it. If a line has a word which should **not** be there, circle the word. There are two examples at the beginning (**0** and **00**).

A JOB INTERVIEW

0 The first job interview I ever had was for a position as ✔
00 a clerk at (the) one of the oldest universities in
41 the city. I bought a new outfit especially for the
42 interview including a pair of lovely suede shoes and a
43 handbag to match. I was not particularly nervous then
44 until I went in and saw that there were four
45 people who were going to do interview me rather than
46 one. They asked me a few questions about my university
47 degree and about why did I wanted the job. One of the
48 people was a very pleasant, smiling woman, who nodded
49 encouragingly every time I have answered a question.
50 Towards the end one of the men asked to me if I had
51 experience with computers. I had to admit I had only
52 used one once. Despite of this I got the job. The pleasant,
53 smiling woman, who turned out to be my boss, told me later
54 that she had argued I should be being given the job because
55 she liked my shoes so much. I was glad I bought them!

PART 5

For questions **56–65**, read the text below. Use the word given in capitals at the end of each line to form a word that fits in the space in the same line. There is an example at the beginning (**0**).

TRAINING SHOES

It is not **(0)** ..*surprising*.. that training shoes have become | **SURPRISE**
such big business. Sporting **(56)** .... of all kinds | **ACTIVE**
have become popular, particularly **(57)** .... | **EXPENSIVE**
sports like running where equipment is **(58)** .... | **NECESSARY**
apart from shoes. Runners suffer more **(59)** .... than | **INJURE**
many other athletes. The runner **(60)** .... strikes | **REPEAT**
the ground with his feet, which can have **(61)** .... | **DISASTER**
effects. Research has led to the **(62)** .... of | **DEVELOP**
running shoes and a considerable **(63)** .... in | **REDUCE**
problems with the feet and ankles. A **(64)** .... of | **COMBINE**
padding and air cushions provide **(65)** .... from | **PROTECT**
hitting the pavement with a force twice your weight.

PAPER 4 – LISTENING

PART 1

You will hear people talking in eight different situations. For Questions **1–8**, choose the best answer **A**, **B** or **C**.

1 You are waiting in a travel agency when you hear this conversation. Why doesn't the woman want the tickets the travel agent offers her?

    A She thinks they are too expensive. _____

    B The return date is not convenient for her. _____

    C She does not want to fly back to Britain. _____

2 Listen to these people talking about what they did on Saturday evening. What are they talking about?

    A a play _____

    B a concert _____

    C a film _____

3 You are in a department store. You hear this woman talking to a shop assistant. What does the woman want?

    A the same item in another size _____

    B her money back _____

    C a different item _____

4 Listen to this newsreader. Why have people been evacuated from Kingsville?

    A Because of an earthquake. _____

    B Because of disease. _____

    C Because of floods. _____

5 Listen to these two men discussing a friend. Why did he lose his job?

    A He was late for a meeting. _____

    B He said what he thought. _____

    C The Managing Director wanted to give the job to his nephew. _____

6 You hear this girl talking on a public telephone. Who is she speaking to?

    A her assistant _____

    B her boss _____

    C her brother _____

7 You are in a restaurant. You hear this man talking to a waiter. What is the man complaining about?

    A the service _____

    B the food _____

    C the bill _____

8 You hear this announcement in a railway station. What does the announcer say about the train on platform 11?

    A It is the next fast train to London. _____

    B It will not be leaving. _____

    C It was late arriving. _____

PART 2

You will hear a doctor talking about common illnesses. For questions **9–18**, complete the notes which summarise what the speaker says. You will need to write a word or a short phrase in each gap.

Number of colds a year

● children: **(9)** ....

● young adults: *two or three*

● old people: **(10)** ....

Caused by virus

● number of viruses: **(11)** ....

● children exposed to more viruses than adults at **(12)** ....

The most expensive illness

● Six million working days lost a year.

● **(13)** .... schooldays lost a year.

Symptoms

● Virus lives for **(14)** ....

● If symptoms last longer than **(15)** .... – probably flu.

Flu epidemics

● World-wide flu epidemics: **(16)** .... and 1957.

● In Britain: every **(17)** ....

● People at risk: **(18)** .... , the weak, tired and unwell.

PART 3

You will hear five people talking about animals. For questions **19–23**, choose from the list of animals **A–F** what each speaker is describing. Use the letters only once. There is one extra letter which you do not need to use.

A camel   **C** cat   **E** horse
B elephant   **D** dog   **F** bird

19 Speaker 1   _____

20 Speaker 2   _____

21 Speaker 3   _____

22 Speaker 4   _____

23 Speaker 5   _____

PART 4

You will hear a woman conducting a market research interview about newspapers. For questions **24–30** decide which of the choices **A**, **B** or **C** is the correct answer.

24 Why doesn't the man read the same number of newspapers every week?

A He sometimes drives to work more often than others.   _____

B He sometimes gives the newspaper to his wife.   _____

C He sometimes has to take his children to the doctor.   _____

25 When the woman asks the man if he buys the newspapers he reads

A he is angry.   _____

B he is pleased.   _____

C he shows that he thinks it is a strange question.   _____

26 When the woman asks him how he reads the newspaper

A he doesn't answer.   _____

B he makes a joke.   _____

C he asks her to repeat the question.   _____

27 Which parts of the newspaper does the man look at first?

A The front page and a section at the back.   _____

B The front pages.   _____

C The middle.   _____

28 Of the newspapers he sees, the man reads

A 50 per cent.   _____

B between 0 and 85 per cent.   _____

C less than 25 per cent.   _____

29 He doesn't look at the crosswords because

A he doesn't have time.   _____

B he doesn't think this is a good way to spend time.   _____

C he doesn't understand them.   _____

30 The man mentions buying

A three different newspapers.   _____

B one newspaper.   _____

C two different newspapers.   _____

PAPER 5 – SPEAKING

PART 1

The interlocutor will ask you to give some personal information about yourself.

 Listen to the cassette and answer the questions the interlocutor will ask you.

PART 2

The interlocutor will ask you and the other candidate to compare and contrast two photos.

 Listen to the cassette, look at the photos below and opposite and follow the interlocutor's instructions.

Candidate A

1

2

Candidate B

3

4

PART 3

The interlocutor will ask you and the other candidate to discuss something together.

Listen to the cassette, look at the photos below and opposite and follow the interlocutor's instructions.

PART 4

The interlocutor will ask you and the other candidate questions related to the theme of Part 3.

📟 Listen to the cassette and answer the interlocutor's questions.

Answer key

UNIT 1

Vocabulary p.7

1 1 sail 2 canoe 3 checking in 4 catching
5 maps 6 visit 7 travelling 8 destination 9 trip

2 1 a platform *cars* 2 a flight *ships* 3 a port *trains*
4 a single *planes* 5 an inspector *cars*
6 a steward *buses* 7 a seatbelt *ships*

Reading pp.8–9

2 3 B 4 B 5 D 6 E 7 B

Word formation pp.9–10

1 2 adverb 3 adjective; noun 4 verb 5 adjective
6 noun 7 adjective 8 adjective

Hot tip! negative (*unfortunately*)

2 2 impatient 3 helpful 4 profitable 5 sunny
6 underestimate 7 overcharge 8 likely
9 homeless 10 disappointment

Listening p.10

1 1 F 2 F 3 T 4 ? 5 T

Tapescript

I flew to Malta and then took a ferry to Gozo where I
stayed in Sannat – a sleepy town away from the
tourist centre. I wanted to explore as much of the
island as I could so I decided that hiring a moped was
probably the best thing to do.

Victoria, the capital, has a good market and Mgarr,
the harbour, is the best place to hire boats to go
water-skiing on the lagoon and to visit the nearby
island of Comino. But *the* place to go on the island is
Marsalforn. It's got the best hotels and the most
fantastic disco called *The Rook* – it's an old castle with
a dance floor in the battlements. Go swimming at
Marsalforn, sandy Ramla bay, the inland sea, or San
Blas bay, which is down a steep incline. Tapinu is
famous for its church where a scene from the film
Clash of the Titans was shot.

I really enjoyed my visit. Gozo in the summer is hot
and arid, but the beaches are great and the nightlife is
fantastic.

2 1 b) 2 e) 3 a) 4 d) 5 c)

Writing p.11

1 1 F 2 I 3 I 4 F 5 F 6 F 7 I 8 F 9 I 10 I
11 F

2 1 informal 2 a) 2 b) 1 c) 4 d) 7 e) 6 f) 5
g) 3

Vocabulary p.12

1 1 e) 2 g) 3 h) 4 d) 5 f) 6 i) 7 c) 8 b)

2 1 ... I'm feeling pretty **pleased**. 2 I was **thrilled** ...
3 My family and I would be **delighted** ...
4 The mountains are really **amazing** ...
5 There are lots of **fascinating** old streets ...
6 The summers can be a bit **exhausting** ...

Grammar pp.12–13

1 1 How do people learn new words? – e)
2 What do we have to do? – f)
3 You don't agree, do you? – i)
4 What do you like doing in your spare
time? – d)
5 Where do you want to go this weekend? – g)
6 Why do you get so nervous? – h)
7 Who were you angry with? – b)
8 What does 'miserable' mean? – a)
9 Are you going to translate each word? – j)
10 Did you write a definition of 'cruise'? – c)

2 1 aren't you – e) 2 haven't I – g) 3 isn't he – h)
4 doesn't she – i) 5 didn't you – c)
6 didn't he – d) 7 hadn't he – a) 8 didn't you – f)
9 won't you – j) 10 would you – b)

3 1 down 2 up 3 down 4 up 5 down 6 down
7 up 8 down 9 up 10 up

When Sam's voice goes up, he is not very sure that
the information is correct; when his voice goes
down, he is fairly sure that the information is
correct.

4 2 I wonder why she said that.
   3 I'd like to know how many tourists visit your country each year.
   4 I wonder if this bus goes to Oxford Street.
   5 Could you tell me where the tourist office is?
   6 Do you know if there are any museums near here?
   7 Would you mind telling me what we are supposed to do?
   8 I don't know if she's English or American.

Speaking p.13

1 KATRINA: How many brothers and sisters **have you got**?/**do you have**?
2 KATRINA: What **does he look like**?
3 SYLVIE: What **do you do**?
4 SYLVIE: What **are you studying**?
5 SYLVIE: And **have you got** any brothers and sisters?

UNIT *2*

Vocabulary p.14

1 1 for   2 from   3 on   4 of   5 to   6 of
2 1 terrified   2 responsible   3 proud   4 satisfied
   5 keen   6 suspicious   7 ashamed   8 good
3 1 B   2 A   3 B   4 A   5 B   6 B   7 A   8 B

Reading p.15

1 1 *These people*   2 *people who do risk sports*
   3 *People*   4 *Risk sports*   5 *executives*
2 1 C   2 A   3 B

Listening p.16

Tapescript

I=interviewer MT=Meregan Turner

I: In today's programme I'll be talking to a woman whose occupation is often thought of as the exclusive province of men. Meregan Turner is one of the very few women who are professional racing drivers. Well, Meregan, I suppose the obvious question is – how does a woman end up in motor racing?

MT: You could say it's in the blood. You see my father was also a racing driver. But I didn't realise how much I wanted to race until some friends took me to Silverstone race track and booked me on to actually drive one day. I just couldn't believe that anything could be so wonderful, that there was anything in the world so super. When I got out of the car, I simply jumped up and down on the spot. And from there on in, I couldn't think about doing anything else at all but motor racing. It's just like falling in love. It's completely taken over my life.

I: How have you found it working in this man's world? Were men protective of you on the track?

MT: No, of course not, and they shouldn't be. But sometimes you get real hostility. One man just wouldn't let me overtake him. When I finally succeeded, he actually turned into my wheels. Then he went straight into the pit and ended up in hospital. But that kind of thing doesn't often happen. Anyway, it's all irrelevant. I didn't go into it thinking, 'I am going to be a female racing driver.' I went into it because I wanted to race. The fact that I was a girl didn't come into it.

I: And ... and what about the men in your life? Do they worry about you?

MT: Well, my father comes to the track and times me. He says he doesn't worry once I start going round. I suppose because he understands what it's actually like he's less likely to think it's dangerous. My boyfriend, Iannis gets terribly worried. He won't watch me because he's terrified I'm going to kill myself.

I: So I don't suppose Iannis ever goes to the track?

MT: No, no. In fact he spends almost a third of the year back in Greece where he comes from. He owns one of the biggest and nicest hotels on Corfu. I applied for a job there once. That's how we met.

I: Don't you miss him when he goes away?

MT: Yes. Terribly. I just don't know what to do with myself. It's like driving backwards down the motorway.

1 racing driver   2 racing driver   3 falling in love
4 Her father   5 Greek   6 hotel owner

Word formation p.16

1 1 adjective   2 adverb   3 adjective   4 noun
   5 adverb; adverb   6 adjective

2 1 complete, final, actual   2 *-ity*   3 *-ive*; *-ive*
   4 danger

3 1 dangerous 2 surprising 3 unpleasant
4 unfair 5 abusive 6 seriously 7 variety

Vocabulary p.17

1 1 f) 2 g) 3 d) 4 a) and j) 5 e) 6 b) 7 i) 8 c)
9 h)

2 1 'debt collector 2 'social worker 3 'traffic warden
4 private in'vestigator 5 'tax inspector
6 'nightclub bouncer 7 plastic 'surgeon
8 'bus conductor 9 senior li'brarian
10 'newspaper editor

3 1 salary 2 resign 3 strike 4 commission 5 retire
6 bonus 7 sack 8 skill 9 employee 10 earn

C	B	X	H	S	K	I	L	L	C
L	O	N	R	S	A	P	Q	S	O
M	N	M	O	T	P	C	C	D	M
E	U	S	M	R	C	R	K	K	M
A	S	F	T	I	Z	E	C	R	I
R	G	U	B	K	S	T	X	E	S
N	W	H	V	E	Y	I	F	S	S
S	A	L	A	R	Y	R	O	I	I
K	I	J	X	E	D	E	G	G	O
E	M	P	L	O	Y	E	E	N	N

Speaking p.18

Tapescript

I=Interlocutor A=Anna P=Petra S=Stefan

Interview 1

I: Here are some pictures of various jobs. I'd like you
to talk about the jobs and put them in order of
priority according to how much people doing
these jobs should be paid. Please give your
reasons for the order you decide on as well.

A: First I put referee because it's very hard job. Then I
put the plumber. And after him nurse because she
work a lot and after her I putting traffic warden
and editor.

I: What about dustmen? Where shall we put them?

A: I don't know. At the bottom.

I: And what about the job in this photograph?

A: I don't know how is called in English.

Interview 2

I: Here are some pictures of various jobs. Could you
work together and put the pictures in order of

priority according to how much you think people
doing each of these different jobs should be paid.
As you decide could you also give reasons for your
decisions?

P: I think you should be paid more if you have to
study for a long time. Umm ... let's see ... nurses
have to study for a long time and nursing is a very
responsible job, so I think they should be paid
more than the other jobs on this list.

S: Umm ... yes ... umm, I agree. It's also a bit
unpleasant ... I mean it can be hard work and
sometimes upsetting or even dirty. I think people
should be paid more for doing dirty and
unpleasant jobs. Shall we put dustmen after
nurses?

P: OK. What shall we put next? I think people who
do jobs that are enjoyable should be paid less. So
perhaps the stockbroker should come last.

S: Ah, no, I don't agree. Being a stockbroker is very
difficult. So I'd put it after dustmen. We ... umm,
should decide which jobs are important.

P: OK. Well, plumbers and traffic wardens are
important. And being a traffic warden is probably
quite difficult.

S: Mmm, mmm ... and ... umm ... what about
editors?

P: Oh, I think they should be paid as much as
stockbrokers. It's a very difficult job and it's also
creative. Let's put editors before stockbrokers.

S: Mmm, yes. That's a very good idea. Let's see.
What's left? Referees and bouncers. Do you want
to put them before editors?

P: Yes, because they're not very popular jobs.

1 Petra and Stefan.

2 1 Shall we 2 put next 3 And what about
4 What's left 5 Do you want

3 1 Yes, I agree. 2 OK. 3 That's a very good idea.
4 No, I don't agree.

Grammar p.19

1 1 don't like 2 have 3 sometimes drives; get
4 never get; is always waiting; turn 5 tells; jump
6 are not going 7 are meeting 8 am making; is
bringing; are bringing 9 rings; do we have
10 doesn't listen; gives 11 is always talking; drives
12 rings; always says; are you doing 13 answer;
am talking

2 1 c) 2 e) 3 a) 4 b) 5 d) 6 f) 7 g) 8 j) 9 h) 10 i)

3 1 are sunbathing 2 are walking
3 are coming back 4 looks 5 like 6 think
7 is skiing

Writing p.20

1 a formal letter

2 1 F 2 T 3 F 4 T 5 F

UNIT 3

Vocabulary p.21

1 1 d) 2 f) 3 a) 4 g) 5 c) 6 b) 7 i)

2 1 arrogant 2 naughty 3 mean 4 silly
5 generous 6 modest 7 flexible
8 narrow-minded

Listening p.21

Tapescript

Speaker 1
I would describe myself as self-confident. I suppose some people would even say that I can be a bit bossy. Years of looking after my younger brothers has made me like this – I came first after all. I think I would also describe myself as rather ambitious. I like to be the leader and I suppose this is the result of having had to struggle to win back my parents' attention after my brothers and sisters were born. I know that this also means that sometimes I can be a bit aggressive, particularly if people don't do what I say and I know that I'm right. On a more positive note, I'm a good communicator and I think this comes from acting like a kind of link between my parents and the younger children in my family. For example, if one of my sisters wanted something and she didn't think our parents would agree to it, I'd try to persuade them.

Speaker 2
I'm the middle one in my family – I've got two older brothers and two younger sisters. I think this has made me quite independent as the two older ones used to play together and so did the two younger ones, so I was left to play on my own a lot. If I wanted to play with them, I had to fit in with what they wanted and I think this has taught me to be cooperative. Because I had to learn to be flexible I think I'm quite a good parent myself. I've had so much experience with older and younger brothers and sisters that I'm adaptable and I get on with all sorts of different people. One negative thing is that I was a bit overshadowed by my brothers and often felt left out. I

think this has left me with a feeling of loneliness and lack of self-confidence.

Speaker 3
I'm the baby in my family and even though I'm in my forties, my older sisters still treat me like a bit of a child. I think I would describe myself as relaxed and open-minded. I wasn't expected to conform like my sisters were, and I was certainly allowed to do all kinds of things they wouldn't have dared even attempt. If I'm honest, I'd have to say that I was a bit spoilt. But I think that having all those people looking after me has made me better at coping with problems in later life than my sisters are. Sometimes I tend to be a bit passive and reluctant to take responsibility for things and I do tend to blame others when things go wrong. I don't want to have any children myself. My husband says this is because I want to be the centre of attention.

Speaker 4
I was an only child and I think this made me responsible, organised and serious. All my parents' hopes and expectations rested on me and I got used to trying to live up to what people think of me. I was always very well organised as a child because I had to fill my own time. My wife says I take life too seriously and I suppose this might come from never having joked with brothers and sisters. I also find it difficult to form friendships or to share my thoughts and feelings with others or let them too close to me. I think I got used to receiving all the attention and that this makes it hard for me to direct my attention to others. Some people would probably say I seem a little selfish.

1 1 Y 2 O 3 M 4 E 5 O 6 E 7 E 8 M 9 Y
10 O

2 a) 4 b) 2 c) 3 d) 1 e) 3 f) 3

Reading p.22–23

1 B

2 1 She was seen performing on TV with her brothers.
2 She lived in a big house with its own zoo and cinema and her family were famous.
3 She wanted to be independent.
4 She feels it has helped her learn.

3 1 A 2 B 3 A 4 A

4 1 Question 4 B 2 Question 3 B 3 Question 2 A

5 1 overshadowed 2 handful 3 understandable

Word formation p.24

1 1 *-able* 2 *-ful* 3 *over-*

2 1 alike 2 appearance(s) 3 tendency 4 overeat
5 childhood 6 adaptable 7 characteristic
8 shyness 9 roomful 10 self-conscious
11 fashionable 12 Unfortunately 13 agreement

Grammar pp.24–25

2 1 T 2 F 3 T 4 T 5 T 6 F 7 T 8 T

Writing pp.26–27

2 Report 1: Candidate B; Report 2: Candidate A

3 1 *writting*: writing 2 *arive*: arrive 3 *bluse*: blouse
4 *foto*: photo 5 *tipical*: typical

4 1 *I writting inform you ...* : I am writing to inform
you ... 2 *She is leave ... and arrive ...* : She is
leaving ... and arriving .../She leaves ... and arrives
... 3 *She is studying very hard every day*: She
studies very hard every day. 4 *Sometimes she uses
glasses, but she will use ...* : Sometimes she wears
..., but she will be wearing ... 5 *Do you want that
she bring you a gift?*: Do you want her to bring you
a gift?

5 1 *with a blonde hair*: with blonde hair 2 *she is
good student*: she is a good student 3 *a blue
trouser*: blue trousers 4 *one photo*: a photo
5 *a typical food*: typical food

6 wear

UNIT *4*

Reading p.28

1 Plan A

2 1 F 2 A 3 B 4 E 5 C

3 1 unimaginable 2 dependent 3 traditional
4 catastrophe 5 familiar 6 unacceptable
7 in isolation 8 back up 9 tragedies
10 impending

Grammar p.30

1 1 you like me to help 2 tell me what he looks
3 sounds like 4 plays racket sports like 5 like
going to the beach 6 smells like 7 look very like
8 would like to

2 1 **What's** your sister like? 2 She's the same height
as me ... 3 ... would you like **to go** to the cinema
...? 4 That sounds **like** a good idea. 5 **Would**
you like to see anything in particular? 6 I **like**
comedies. 7 ..., **if you like**. 8 Are you **like** your
brother ...? 9 I**'m like** my mother ...

Vocabulary p.31

1 1 d) – off 2 g) – on 3 c) – up 4 e) – over
5 h) – off 6 b) – up 7 f) – off 8 a) – in

2 1 take up 2 take on 3 take off 4 take up
5 take over

3 1 She **took me off** ... 3 ... I've **taken it up**.
4 ... they only **took them on** a month ago.
5 ... why don't you **take it off**?

Listening p.31

Tapescript

Speaker 1
We went to one of those Virtual Reality places. It was
really funny. You go along and put this kind of helmet
on your head and there's a plastic thing like a gun
that you hold. Anyway, you put some money in the
slot, just like in any amusement arcade, put the
helmet on and then you really do see all these aliens
running towards you and spaceships dive-bombing
and this incredible terrain like on Mars or something.
It's absolutely fantastic! Much better than an ordinary
video game, because it's all around you. You really feel
as if you're there. I was so involved that when it
finished I went on trying to fire the gun thing. All my
friends were laughing at me. I must have looked
pretty silly.

Speaker 2
My father gave it to me for Christmas. It was
supposed to translate thousands of words and
sentences into French, English and German. You just
type in a sentence in your language and press a
button and a translation appears on a small screen.
Well, there must have been something wrong with it
because when we were on holiday in France, I typed
in a sentence meaning: 'Where is the post office?' and
what I thought was the French translation came up on
the screen. I went up to this old lady and read out the
translation and she burst out laughing. You see, the
machine had given me the French for: 'You are the
most beautiful woman I have ever seen.' It was really
embarrassing.

Speaker 3

It tells you the time all over the world, you can wear it when you're scuba diving, it's solar-powered and it's even got a built-in calculator. But the problem with it is that I can't work out how to stop the alarm. The other day I set the alarm so that I'd remember to look at the time when I was studying. You know, if you're really concentrating, you can forget to look at your watch and miss your favourite show on TV or something. If you don't switch the alarm off, it goes off at the same time every day after that. So the next day in class it started going 'beep beep beep' in the middle of a test and I couldn't work out how to stop it. Eventually it stopped, but the teacher and the other students were a bit annoyed.

Speaker 4

I usually walk up the stairs, but that particular day I'd been up and down all day and I was feeling a bit tired. It was there with the door open so I got in and pressed 3 and nothing happened. Then I pressed 3 again and the 'close doors' button and they did close, but nothing happened. So I pressed 3 again and it sort of jumped up and down a couple of times and then shot up really fast to the third floor. I thought I was going to fly through the roof of the building! Well, the doors opened, fortunately, and I literally fell out shaking like a leaf. I've never taken it again needless to say – it's only two flights of stairs to climb anyway.

Speaker 5

I switched it on and nothing happened. Absolutely nothing. None of the lights that tell you that the battery is low or that the hard disk drive is working went on. It was as if it had died. So I took it to the technician and he flicked the switch on and off a couple of times and got about as much response as I'd done. He checked the battery and the power supply, but there didn't seem to be anything wrong there. Then he flicked the switch again and the screen lit up and everything was running perfectly. 'What did you do?' I said. 'I don't know,' he said. 'No. Come on. Tell me,' I said. 'What did you do?' 'I just frightened it a bit,' he said. Well, quite frankly I could have done that myself.

1 F   2 D   3 C   4 A   5 E

Writing pp.32–33

1 1 b) 2 d) 3 a) 4 c) 5 f) 6 e) 7 i) 8 h) 9 k) 10 j) 11 g)

2 1 The captain **did not believe** ...   2 ... **they had been missing** for only a few hours ...   3 when they **were found** ...   4 ... they all **had** long beards   5 ... as if they **had not shaved** for six months or more.   6 ... when they **disappeared**.

Vocabulary and grammar p.33

1 scientific   2 technological   3 laboratories   4 research   5 problems   6 development   7 revolutionised   8 chemical   9 produce   10 inventor

Speaking p.34

Tapescript

I=interlocutor L=Laura A=Ahmet

I: Now, I'm going to give to each of you two different photographs. I'd like you to show each other your pictures and then talk about them. You each have one minute to do this so don't worry if I interrupt you. Laura, here are your two photos. Please let Ahmet see them. They show technological devices. Ahmet, I'll give you your photos in a minute. Laura, I'd like you to compare and contrast your photos and say how you feel about devices like these.

L: My photographs show a row of houses with ... umm ... I think they are called 'parabolic antenna' or aerials. It's a kind of dish. They are used for receiving satellite TV and you put them on the roof of your house or outside near the roof. We haven't got an antenna like those but I think they would be very useful because you can watch TV programmes in other languages. The other photograph is very different because it is taken inside not outside a house. It shows a girl in her bedroom working ... or maybe she's playing some game on her computer. She looks very concentrated. I think computers are very useful. My mother has one and she use it a lot to write reports and work out how much money she has got to spend. She says she couldn't live without it.

I: Ahmet, could you tell us how you feel about the devices in Laura's photos?

A: Yes ... erm ... I like watch TV so I would like one of those ... how did you call it? ... aerials? I have got a computer at home and I use it a lot to play game. Erm ... that's all.

I: Thank you. Now, Ahmet, here are your two photos. They show two different types of accommodation or housing. Could you please compare and contrast the photos and say how you feel about them.

A: Yes. In the ... err ... first photograph I can see a big building with about twenty or thirty ... I don't know what you call them in English. It's a big city, but I don't know where it is. In the other photo there is a house in the country, the house has a ... err ... I don't know how you say in English ... around it. That's all.

I: Thank you. Now, Laura, could you tell me a little bit about how you feel about the two types of accommodation shown in Ahmet's photographs.

L: Yes, of course. Well, I definitely wouldn't want to live in this block of flats. It looks like it is in the middle of a big city and there is probably a lot of noise and traffic. I like the other picture much better. I would like to visit this house. It looks peaceful and quiet. I would like to sit out on the ... mmm ... balcony ... veranda at night.

1 Laura

2 1 I think they are called ...   2 It's a kind of ...
3 They are used for ...

UNIT 5

Grammar p.35

1 1 felt fine   2 were worried about her   3 thought she was acting strangely   4 slept well   5 woke up very early   6 she hadn't eaten   7 felt hungry
8 was a new student

2 1 I have to go out to lunch with my parents on Sunday   2 I don't have any special plans
3 I haven't   4 told me he really enjoyed it
5 sounds great   6 I think   7 is usually less crowded

Grammar p.36

1 his name was   2 I had got to know him   3 what year he was in at school   4 how much older he was
5 we had been   6 the movie had finished   7 we had done   8 long we had been in the restaurant   9 we had got home

Grammar p.37

1 promised not to tell   2 advised Laura to try being
3 warned her not to   4 accused her of meeting
5 threatened to tell   6 denied seeing/having seen
7 admitted trying/having tried to phone

8 suggested meeting   9 refused to speak to
10 encouraged Mrs Carter to be   11 decided to ask
12 invited Steve to have   13 agreed (that) Laura was
14 offered to take   15 recommended going out

Grammar p.38

line 1: delete *to*   line 2: delete *more*   line 3: delete *to*
line 6: delete *that*   line 8: delete *for*   line 9: delete *to*
line 10: delete *of*   line 13: delete *at*
line 15: delete *me*

Vocabulary p.38

1 going out   2 infatuated   3 had fallen in love
4 got married   5 got engaged   6 best man   7 aisle
8 vicar   9 choir   10 bouquet   11 have rows
12 was having/had had an affair   13 to get a divorce

Listening p.39

Tapescript

Extract 1
... this is really beautifully written. Towards the end when Maria and Charles meet again after ten years, I was so involved that I literally couldn't put it down. Anybody who enjoys historical novels will love this. I thoroughly recommend *A Second Chance*.

Extract 2
... and that was Gloria Estefan's latest. For those of you who don't speak Spanish she's singing about devoting the rest of her life to her husband. She's certainly got a great voice in any language. And now it's over to the newsroom for a bulletin of world news.

Extract 3
Mmm ... that sounds great. Perhaps some other time. You see, I'm going to my cousin's wedding on Saturday and I ... next Friday? Umm, let me see. Oh, that's right. I have to take my younger brother to see the latest Walt Disney film. ... Thursday? No. I've got volleyball practice until nine thirty and ...

Extract 4
My friend used to say that he was the best-looking boy at university. I never expected him to notice me, though we actually attended the same history lectures for a term. The first time I spoke to him was when I was queueing for tickets to see a film called *Picnic at Hanging Rock*. He just came up to me and said, 'I know this sounds ridiculous, but haven't I seen you somewhere before?'

Extract 5

A: ... so I'm going round to her house to meet her parents.

B: You must be crazy. They'll kill you!

A: No, I don't think so. Her mother sounded really nice on the phone. I think they were just worried when she got home so late. After all, she left the house at about five and we didn't get back till midnight or something. We waited ...

1 C 2 B 3 A 4 A 5 A

Reading p.40

1 1 this feeling inside 2 have much money
3 your song 4 the sun 5 forget

2 A

3 1 B 2 D 3 A 4 C 5 B

4 1 B 2 A 3 B 4 A

5 1 groom 2 bride 3 bridesmaids 4 engagement
5 anniversary

U N I T 6

Grammar p.42

1 1 ... **denied stealing** the necklace.
4 ... **admitted taking** it. 5 ... **refused to say** where she had hidden it, ... 6 ... **were arranging to take** her to the station, she **agreed to return** it. 9 ... **hoped to find** a job there. 10 ... **try to help** her find work. 11 Mary **stopped crying** ...

2 1 wearing 2 to know 3 waking up 4 to make
5 to talk 6 to go 7 smoking 8 to go

Listening p.43

Tapescript

Most of the time we go through life relatively unaware of the fact that deep within the brain is a body clock that works ... well, like clockwork! It's only really when our normal routine is interrupted that we become conscious of our physical and psychological rhythms. But we *do* disrupt them from time to time: by flying from one side of the world to the other and crossing several time zones, falling asleep at the wrong time of day or staying up all night studying for an exam. These rhythms are almost identical from one person to another because they're determined by the Earth's cycle of day into night, night into day. If you are out of step with this cycle, you feel the effects: jet lag, fatigue or poor concentration and memory. If on the other hand you learn to understand your biological rhythms, if you know at what time of day you remember things more easily, when your reactions are fastest, when you are most creative, you can plan your day and always be at your best.

Short term memory works best around midnight because your temperature is lowest and a cool mind genuinely does memorise more effectively. But luckily your memory is still working well at nine o'clock in the morning. Try learning vocabulary or reading texts and answering comprehension questions first thing in the morning or just before you go to sleep at night. But make sure the texts are not too long and don't try to learn more than ten to twelve words at a time. Short term memory only lasts ten minutes or so. After that it won't absorb information efficiently.

Problem solving is easiest mid to late morning, say around eleven o'clock. Unfortunately we are less and less able to solve problems efficiently as the day goes on because we get more and more tired. So mid-morning is the right time to work on your mathematics and to make any important decisions. If you're preparing for FCE, work on your writing at this time of day. Plan and write reports, articles and stories as well.

Long term memory, the sort we use when recalling what happened yesterday or last month, is working most efficiently at around three in the afternoon. If you have to memorise something important, this is the time to do it, whether it's a piece of music or grammar rules. This is the best time of day to study and probably the best time to do the kind of test that requires you to remember things you learnt a while ago. Your reflexes are quickest between about four and six o'clock, so if you play volleyball or basketball, you'll perform best in the late afternoon or early evening.

But what if you have trouble getting out of bed in the first place? To get your body clock running, try combining a splash of cold water on the face with a blast of bright light. The body clock inside your brain is really two tiny structures about the size of two grains of sand. These structures are connected to the eyes so daylight can penetrate the brain and set the clock running to the right time – in much the same way as you set your watch. If you have to travel to the United States or Australia, spend some time in direct sunlight each morning for the first two or three days. You'll recover from jet lag much more quickly.

2 2 understand our biological rhythms   3 around midnight   5 solving problems   6 three o'clock in the afternoon   7 bright light

Grammar p.43

1 didn't feel like taking   2 can't afford to buy   3 can't stand studying   4 agreed to accept   5 suggest buying/I buy/I bought   6 refused to lend me
7 pretended to be/that they were   8 expect to pass
9 encouraged me/him/us, etc. to do   10 gave up smoking

Vocabulary p.44

1 A   2 B   3 B   4 C   5 B   6 A   7 C   8 A   9 B   10 C

Vocabulary p.45

1

C	A	P	R	C	H	E	A	T	L
L	M	T	G	M	B	A	F	Z	R
A	Y	E	S	E	C	K	P	K	P
S	B	R	M	Q	W	M	A	R	K
S	O	M	T	O	T	X	S	E	L
B	H	V	D	I	R	Z	S	V	E
G	F	V	H	Q	U	I	P	I	S
C	N	A	E	D	A	Y	S	S	S
W	J	F	I	X	N	J	N	E	O
R	Y	K	O	L	T	M	Z	X	N

Possible definitions

term: a period of time into which the school year is divided; *cheat*: act dishonestly in order to gain something; *revise*: prepare for a test by studying; *fail*: be unsuccessful in an exam; *class*: a group of students or pupils who are taught together; *mark*: figures given by a teacher to represent how good someone's work is; *lesson*: a period of time in which students are taught; *pass*: be successful in an examination; *memorise*: learn and remember something exactly

2 a) calendar   b) lamp   c) stapler
d) sharpener   e) notebook   f) pencil
g) highlighter   h) paper clips   i) calculator
j) waste-paper bin   k) bookcase

Speaking p.45

1 1 Nilgün   2 Daniel   3 Nilgün

Writing p.46

1 1 *I am not agree ...* : I do not agree ...   2 *On my opinion ...* : In my opinion ...   3 *I am agree up to a point ...* : I agree up to a point...   4 *This is truth up to a point, ...* : This is true up to a point, ...
5 *As far as I am concerning ...* : As far as I am concerned ...   6 *In my point of view ...* : From my point of view ...

2 1 Dear Mr Lewis,   2 My daughter Helen will not be able to attend school tomorrow morning.
3 She has an appointment with the dentist at nine o'clock.   4 Dr Melrose's surgery is about twenty minutes from the centre of Cambridge.   5 It is unlikely that I can get Helen to school before midday.   6 I would be very grateful if you would excuse her from her English and Mathematics classes.   7 Yours sincerely, Jane Warburton

Reading p.48

2 A   3 D   4 B   5 E   6 F

UNIT 7

Grammar p.49

line 3; delete *of*   line 4: delete *of*   line 6: delete *of*
line 7: delete *have*   line 8: delete *are*   line 9: delete *as*
line 12: delete *are*   line 14: delete *do*

Listening p.49

Tapescript

I=interviewer AD=Alex Dimitriades

I: Well, Alex, it's really great to have you here in the studio. Your very successful film *The Heartbreak Kid*'s just been made into a TV series – *Heartbreak High*. You're almost a household name and I'm sure thousands of girls all over Australia have your photo on their bedroom wall. What's it really like being famous?

AD: I guess when you get invited to all these parties that you never used to get invited to, it is pretty great. But apart from that, it's just like another job really.

I: Do you enjoy it?

AD: Ah, yeah, it's enjoyable, but it has its ups and downs like everything else.

I: Was it hard to adjust to being famous?

AD: Yeah, it was a bit. It was a bit of a shock for me when the movie came out and I got so much attention, but I don't think there'll be such a big fuss when the TV show comes on.

I: How long did it take you to decide to star in the TV version?

AD: The producer had the show in mind for a while and he asked me if I'd be interested. I said I'd think about it and during that time I was doing publicity and promotion for the movie. Once it started quietening down a bit, they came forward and said they were going to make the series. At that stage, I wasn't doing much, so I agreed.

I: Apart from the show, what other plans do you have for the future?

AD: Nothing definite. I'm doing a play at the moment. It's called *The Man Who Became A Dog* and it's showing in Sydney. It's part of an amateur theatre festival and I know a girl who's involved in it. She asked me if I wanted to be in it and I said 'yes' because I've never done live theatre before. I really wanted to experiment.

I: What part do you play?

AD: The dog! It's OK. It's different. It's giving me a bit of variety which is what I like.

I: In the past year you've done film, TV and live theatre. Which do you prefer?

AD: The thing that I'd like to do most is another film, a really good film, a top production.

I: Do you have any idols?

AD: Idols? It's hard to pick someone 'cos I'm not really fanatical about anyone, but I really like Robert De Niro's acting. I like what I've seen him in, but I haven't seen all his films.

I: Do you feel comfortable about being a household name?

AD: I am? Yeah, I guess it's alright. What's wrong with that? I mean, of course, there are going to be people who are going to say bad things about you but as long as I don't feel bad, it's OK.

1 F   2 F   3 T   4 T   5 F   6 T

Vocabulary p.50

1 T/F   2 M   3 P/S   4 M   5 F   6 T/F   7 T/F   8 M   9 T
10 M   11 S   12 T/M   13 F   14 M   15 P/S

Vocabulary and grammar p.50

1 1 a film   2 fifteen

2 1 few   2 together   3 row   4 screen   5 cinema
6 going   7 stand/bear   8 had   9 scene/bit
10 such   11 part/role   12 groups/bands
13 comes   14 audience   15 can/should

Grammar p.51

1 1 Have you seen   2 saw   3 did you think   4 liked
5 thought   6 was   7 Have you hurt   8 hit   9 have been going   10 Have you made   11 made
12 haven't seen   13 Has he gone   14 has been studying   15 hasn't been going   16 Did you pass
17 failed   18 have taken

2 1 bitten   2 blown   3 built   4 threw; caught
5 bought   6 fallen   7 found   8 spent   9 written
10 sent

Writing pp.52–53

2 1 Candidate B   2 Candidate A

3 1 ... an excursion ...   2 We **left** the school ... and **reached the** museum. 3 so we **had** ...   4 The section I liked **most** was the dolls.   5 **But** Andres and Mehmet really liked the model railway.   6 I **visited** the Science Museum last week to decide if **it would** be good ...   7 However, the museum is very interesting so this makes it **worth the money**. 8 ... although the section on astronomy was closed for **repairs/renovation**.   9 All of the exhibits have short texts in English **explaining** what is shown.
10 Some exhibits had tapes you could **listen to**.
11 ... a bit **difficult** ...

4 1 d) despite/in spite of   2 b) although/even though
3 f) However,   4 a) despite/in spite of
5 e) although/even though   6 c) On the other hand,

Reading pp.54–55

1 D

2 1 'axe'; instruments   2 Rock's greatest musicians
3 a) wood b) glass fibre c) carbon fibre d) metal
e) plastics f) graphite

3 1 C   2 D   3 B   4 D   5 C   6 C

Speaking p.55

Tapescript

I=interlocutor S=Sofia P=Pedro

I: What do you think is the best age to start learning to play a musical instrument?

S: In my opinion it depends on the instrument. But I think if you don't start learning when you are young it is difficult to become really ... umm ... really .... to learn to play really well.

P: Yes, that's true, but if you only want to enjoy playing ... if you want to have a good time, you can start to learn when you are quite old and it doesn't matter.

I: Sofia, you told us before that you play the clarinet. What do you think I should do if I want to learn to play the clarinet well?

S: Well, you should find a good teacher ... like me. If I were you, I wouldn't buy a clarinet at the beginning. You should wait to see if you like it. You should practise every day and ... umm ...

I: And ... umm ... Pedro, you play the drums, don't you? What advice would you give me?

P: Well, you ought to buy a small drum kit and practise while you listen to albums by your favourite groups. When you are a little bit better, it would be a good idea to join a group. Oh, and you really must go to lots of rock concerts and watch the drummers. That's the best way to learn.

I: Thank you very much, I'll certainly think about what you both said. Well, ...

1 1 In my opinion 2 Yes, that's true, but 3 you should find; If I were you, I wouldn't buy; You should wait; You should practise 4 you ought to buy; it would be a good idea to join; you really must go

2 a) 3 and 4 b) 1 c) 2

3 1 As far as I'm concerned ... 2 I completely agree. 3 That's right. 4 From my point of view ... 5 I couldn't agree more.

UNIT *8*

Listening p.56

Tapescript

Extract 1

A: This is 509 5505. I'm sorry but we can't answer your call at the moment, but we'll get back to you as soon as we can if you leave your name and number after the tone.

B: Hello. It's me – Jenny. I won't be able to make the rehearsal tomorrow. I seem to have come out in a dreadful rash all over my arms. I've got bright red spots on my chest as well. I think it could be something to do with that new top I bought. I only wore it once, but it felt very strange and uncomfortable. So you'll just have to make do without me. Perhaps Jackie could read my part. I really can't go out looking like this.

Extract 2

A: So I bought these new trainers and they've made a tremendous difference.

B: Oh, yeah?

A: Yes, they're really good. They've got this air bag in the sole to cushion the impact each time your foot hits the ground. Did you know that a marathon runner hits the ground more than 25,000 times a race?

B: No ... I didn't.

A: Yeah, and the force of each impact is two and a half times the runner's body weight. No wonder my ankles and knees were giving me trouble.

Extract 3

A: I think it looked much smarter round the right way. It looks ridiculous like that and it won't even keep the sun out of your eyes.

B: All the kids are wearing them like this now, Mum. I won't be part of the group if I don't get one.

A: Why can't you just be yourself? You don't have to be the same as everyone else. You're an individual. You ought to be proud of that rather than just doing what all the other boys do. And it's ... what? £20! That's absolutely ridiculous.

B: But, Mum, you promised.

C: So, have we made up our mind yet, young man? Is it to be the Chicago Bulls or ...?

Extract 4

A: The first time I wore them she was away visiting my grandparents and Dad wouldn't notice if I was wearing fluorescent pink Wellington boots and a bikini, he's usually so absorbed in the football on Saturday afternoons. But this time when I put them on to go out on Friday evening, she nearly had a fit! 'You can't go out looking like that! What will the neighbours say?' I even tried showing her some pictures in magazines of some of the top models wearing them, but she flatly refused to let me go out unless I got changed.

B: So what did you wear in the end?

A: Oh, my 501s and a body I got in London. Oh no! I've left my shorts and trainers at home and we've got volleyball this afternoon.

Extract 5

A: What on earth have you got in this suitcase? It weighs a ton!

B: Just clothes.

A: We're only going for two weeks and it's supposed to be boiling hot there so I can't imagine that you'll need all this lot.

B: Well, you never know. When the Widdowsons were there, it was really quite cold. They did a lot of hiking in the mountains though, so I popped my walking boots in and a few novels just in case it turns out to be too wet. Oh, and I noticed that you'd only packed two T-shirts and a pair of shorts for yourself so I've put in a couple of your pullovers and your anorak, too. Oh yes, and your good trousers and jacket just in case we go out. Oh, and I saw that you'd forgotten to put in anything to read so I've packed a couple of your favourite detective stories, too. OK?

1 A 2 B 3 C 1 D 5 E 4

2 A 3 B 1 C 5 E 4 F 2

Vocabulary pp.56–57

1 1 a checked shirt 2 a tie 3 a waistcoat
4 a cardigan 5 a raincoat 6 a pair of Wellington boots 7 a cap 8 a suit 9 a blouse 10 a belt
11 a brooch 12 a bracelet 13 a dress 14 a pair of sandals 15 a pair of shorts 16 a T-shirt
17 a pair of trainers

2 1 Claudia is wearing **a long evening dress** and **high-heeled shoes**. 2 Nick is wearing **grey trousers** and a **checked shirt**. 3 Paul is wearing a

striped **T-shirt**, jeans and **trainers**. 4 Kate is wearing a **plain** dress and **spotted** tights. 5 Tim is wearing a **cap**, dungarees and a leather **belt**.

3 1 'sandals 2 'pullover 3 'bracelet 4 py'jamas
5 dunga'rees 6 'sweatshirt 7 'raincoat
8 'earrings 9 'waistcoat 10 'T-shirt

Grammar p.57

1 1 c) 2 e) 3 d) 4 b) 5 a) 6 c)

2 Both *would* and *used to* can be used in sentences 1, 2, 4, 5 and 7. In sentences 3 and 6 *used to* is the only possibility.

Writing pp.58–59

1 Description A

Vocabulary and grammar p.59

1 together 2 illness 3 athletes 4 materials
5 secretive 6 sandals 7 professional 8 brand

Reading p.60

1 1 A 2 A 3 A 4 A 5 B

2 1 D 2 B 3 C 4 A 5 F

Word formation p.61

1 1 disposable 2 invention 3 production
4 occurrence 5 preference 6 performance
7 conclusion 8 hesitation

2 1 di'sposable 2 in'vention 3 pro'duction
4 oc'currence 5 'preference 6 per'formance
7 con'clusion 8 hesi'tation

Speaking p.61

Tapescript

Now Efi and Akiko, here is a picture of a first aid kit and some things that you might put into the kit. Unfortunately, there is only enough space in the kit for five of these items. I'd like you to talk together about this and decide which items you will put into your first aid kit.

1 F 2 T 3 F 4 F

Grammar p.62

1 1 He could/may/might be Italian.   2 Can you play the piano?   3 You may not/ can't speak during the exam.   4 They can't still be on holiday.   5 You may not/can't smoke on the plane.   6 It could/may/might be a nice day tomorrow.   7 He couldn't spell 'conscious'.   8 May/Can I leave the room?

2 1 That **can't be** the postman.   2 I **might not come** to class on Wednesday.   3 **Could you ride** a bicycle when you were seven?   4 You **can't borrow** my new blouse.   5 He **may/might not like** the colour.   6 It **might rain**.

Grammar p.62

1 c) refuse to lend you   2 d) thinner than
3 a) am interested in   4 b) would like
5 e) him if he enjoyed   6 c) can't stand travelling
7 f) ought to buy   8 d) works faster than
9 f) are not allowed to smoke

UNIT 9

Vocabulary p.63

1 B   2 C   3 D   4 B   5 A   6 B   7 A   8 C   9 D   10 D
11 C   12 B   13 C   14 A   15 C

Grammar p.64

1 a few   2 lump   3 a   4 a   5 many   6 many
7 Much   8 a pair of   9 another   10 A   11 a
12 slices   13 slice   14 many   15 a few

Listening p.64

Tapescript

We all feel happy to be alive in the summer, but it may not only be the warmer weather that makes us feel like this. Although we think we choose what to eat because it tastes or looks good, in fact we make unconscious choices based on the way food makes us feel. Summer foods like seafood and salads are full of chemicals that put us in a good mood.

One chemical that is found in high protein foods is serotonin. It makes you feel calm and relaxed. It can also be found in coffee and tea, ginger and honey, but the best source is spinach which also contains folic

acid in large quantities. A deficiency in folic acid can cause depression, sleeplessness, forgetfulness and irritability.

Fish has traditionally been considered an ideal brain food because it contains high levels of the mineral selenium, which can also affect how you feel. A lack of selenium in your diet can produce tiredness and depression. Apart from fish, sunflower seeds, oysters, cereals, grapes and chicken are good sources.

If you want a food that will cheer you up instantly, then chillies are the answer. They can have a dramatic effect on your mood. When you eat a dish containing chillies, your body reacts because it is encountering something that is almost like a poison. This leads to the release of the body's natural pain killers, giving a sense of well-being. But the experience can become addictive, sometimes causing people to search out stronger and stronger chillies. A slower acting but longer lasting antidepressant called DMAE can be found in anchovies and sardines. DMAE also heightens intelligence and makes it easier to learn. So if you've got an important exam coming up, make sure you eat all these foods that keep you feeling good and thinking clearly.

1 1 seafood and salads   2 calm and relaxed
3 coffee, tea   4 honey   5 depression   6 tiredness and depression   7 fish   8 chicken   9 intelligence
10 learn

Speaking p.65

Tapescript

I=interlocutor M=Marcus B=Birgit

I: Now, Marcus and Birgit, here are some pictures of various foods. I'd like you to talk together to plan a healthy lunch for a group of young people on a hiking trip in the mountains.

M: Well, what do you think? They will be very hungry after hiking all morning.

B: Yes, and they'll need lots of energy for the rest of the day.

M: It's probably quite cold, so I think it would be a good idea ... mmm ... to start with soup.

B: Yes, that sounds fine. Mmm ... a fish soup would be good.

M: Mmm ... I don't know. Maybe it would be better to serve vegetable soup. Some people don't like fish.

B: OK. We'll serve vegetable soup first. And what shall we have next? What about spaghetti?

M: Yes, spaghetti would be good – with a meat

sauce.

B: And lots of cheese. Oh, and I think they should have some vegetables.

M: Why don't we serve a salad next?

B: Yes. And what shall we give them for dessert? Perhaps some fruit ... bananas and apples.

M: Mmm ... I'm not sure about that. Perhaps some kind of cake or pie would be better.

B: Yes, but cakes are not very healthy. We could have the fruit and give them a chocolate bar each to eat in the afternoon.

M: Yes, that sounds fine.

1 1 Well, what do you think? 2 so I think it would be a good idea 3 Yes, that sounds fine.
4 I don't know. Maybe it would be better to
5 What about spaghetti? 6 Yes, spaghetti would be good 7 Why don't we

2 A 1 and 5 B 2, 5 and 7 C 3, 5 and 6 D 4

Grammar p.65

line 2: delete *to*   line 3: delete *a*   line 4: delete *to*
line 6: delete *at*   line 8: delete *to*
line 9: delete *did*

Vocabulary p.66

1 1 Could you put me through to the director?
2 Why have they put off their wedding/put their wedding off? 3 Do you put money by for a rainy day? 4 How could you put up with such rude behaviour? 5 Have they put up the prices/put the prices up again? 6 How did the firemen put out that fire/put that fire out? 7 Why did the vet have to put down your cat/put your cat down? 8 Could you put me up when I come to London? 9 Why are you always trying to put me down?

2 1 They've **put up** the price of tinned tomatoes/ **put** the price of tinned tomatoes **up**. 2 Can you **put up** my nephew/**put** my nephew **up** when he comes to Madrid? 3 I'm just trying to **put** you **through**, but the line seems to be busy. 4 He's always **putting** her **down**. I don't know why she goes out with him. 5 Please **put out** your cigarettes/**put** your cigarettes **out**. 6 I think we'll have to **put** the match **off/put off** the match until after the·exam. 7 They managed to **put** some money **by/put by** some money every week. 8 Two horses were so badly injured that they had to be **put down** after the race. 9 I don't know why you **put up with** her rudeness.

Reading pp.66–67

1 Numbers 1, 5, 7, 8, 10, 11 and 12 are mentioned.

2 1 C 2 D 3 B 4 A

3 1 a) C b) D c) A d) B   2 a) D b) A c) C d) B

Grammar p.68

1 1 By the time you read this **I will be sipping** champagne in a café near the Eiffel Tower.
2 Tomorrow there **will be** heavy rain in the north.
3 Bye! **I'll see** you next week.   4 We've got to be at the airport two hours before our plane **takes off**.   5 By the time I'm twenty, **I will have eaten** 3000 bowls of cornflakes.   6 Look out! That wall **is going to collapse**.   7 I don't think **I'll have** dinner. I'm not hungry.   8 I'm afraid I can't come to the cinema with you. **I'm taking** my nephew to the circus.   9 I'm sure **you'll do** very well in the exam.   10 **I'm going to buy** a new computer.

2 1 am writing   2 am studying/study   3 will finish/ will be finishing   4 will be   5 will be attending/am attending   6 am going/will be going
7 will improve   8 will have taken   9 will get
10 am starting/will be starting   11 will be

Vocabulary p.68

1 florist's   2 post office   3 queues   4 baker's
5 chemist's   6 greengrocer's   7 supermarket   8 shoe shop   9 refund   10 sale   11 bargain   12 wallet/purse
13 receipt   14 cards   15 try   16 size   17 tight

Writing p.69

1 d)   2 f)   3 b)   4 e)   5 a)   6 c)

UNIT *10*

Vocabulary p.70

1 make; do 2 do 3 make 4 do 5 do; making; do
6 does; makes 7 making; made 8 do; make
9 make; doing 10 Make; do 11 do; do; do
12 make; make; done 13 Doing; make 14 made
15 making; make

Reading pp.70–71

1 Numbers 6 and 8 are not mentioned.

2 1 B 2 D 3 B 4 A 5 B 6 B 7 C

Grammar p.72

1 2 c) where 3 i) (that) 4 f) that 5 h) (that)
6 a) (that) 7 b) (that) 8 g) (that) 9 d) whose

2 1 D 2 N A blue Renault Clio, which is one of the
cars she won, is parked outside her house. 3 N
Pink Floyd, who wrote the song 'Money', were
performing live in London recently.
4 D 5 N The Central European University, which
has its headquarters in Prague, has a branch in
Budapest. 6 N My uncle, who was very shy when
he was a child, is now a multimillionaire. 7 N My
uncle, who does not show off his wealth by
wearing expensive clothes and accessories, gives a
lot of money to charities. 8 D

3 2 The house **where we used to live** was bigger
than this one. 4 The single object **(that)** I treasure
most is an old coin my grandfather gave me.
6 The waiter, **to whom** I gave a very generous tip,
didn't even thank me. 7 The insurance on the
house, **which** was very expensive, didn't cover the
cost of the repairs. 10 He inherited a lot of money
from his grandfather, **who was** extremely well-off.
11 The salesman **who sold** me this T-shirt didn't
tell me I couldn't return it.

Vocabulary p.73

1 Across 4 withdraw 6 invest 7 lend 9 earn
  Down 1 afford 2 owe 3 gamble 5 inherit
8 debt

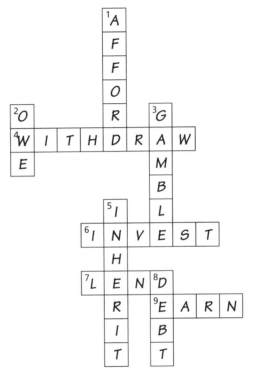

2 1 current; overdrawn 2 change; note 3 cash;
cheque 4 shares; loss 5 wages; tips
6 statement; cash 7 mortgage 8 economy;
exchange rate 9 hard up; lend 10 charity; tax

Writing pp.74–75

1 C

2 1 There are three main reasons why **I think** this.
2 If you **have** never worked before, ... 3 ... when
you **finish** your studies. 4 ... I am sure this **will
help** me in the future. 5 If your parents just **give**
you money ...

3 1 I have a part-time **job** in my mother's office ...
2 At my mother's office I **met** a girl ...

4 Good

Listening p.75

Tapescript

Extract 1

No, I'm not superstitious. I know we'll beat them on any day of the year. Anyway, it's Tuesday the thirteenth that's the unlucky day here – not Friday. And there are three Friday the thirteenths this year so we'll have to cancel two more matches as well as this one. And then we'll never finish the championship.

Extract 2

Right then, ladies and gentlemen, if I could just have your attention. Thank you for coming along this evening. I'll get straight to the point. As you know Tristar Pictures is planning to film a few scenes of our upcoming feature film *It could happen to you* in your neighbourhood. We'll be building the set of the coffee shop on the parking lot at the corner of North Moore and West Broadway. The reason we've invited you along tonight is that we want to give you an opportunity to raise any questions, and to make any comments, complaints or suggestions you might have.

Extract 3

A: OK, let's see Jackie. Could you give us the answer to number five?

B: I'm sorry, Mr Rignall. I haven't done that one.

A: Why not? You were asked to do all the exercises on page 20 for homework. Someone else then. Tom.

C: Four hundred and sixty-eight thousand two hundred and twelve.

A: Does everyone agree? What about you, Adela? How about coming out to the board and showing us how you worked it out.

D: Do I have to?

A: Come on, Adela.

D: OK.

Extract 4

For how many hours did you say that was? ... I see. So that's Saturday morning from 8 till 2 and Thursday evenings from 6 till 9. Umm ... I don't think I understand. That's nine hours work at £3 an hour, which comes to £27 – not £20 – by my calculations. So I would have to pay tax and national insurance even as a part-timer? That doesn't really seem fair ...

Extract 5

And on tomorrow night's show I've invited someone whose latest album is really selling like the proverbial hot cakes. Yes, you guessed it – Mark Williams will be joining us here in the studio to play some of the tracks from the album and to tell us a little more about the dates of his forthcoming world tour. So make sure you tune in around this time tomorrow evening – 740 on your dial, Radio Metro.

Extract 6

A: I don't understand. I paid it in on Monday.

B: I'm sorry. It hasn't been cleared yet.

A: But I expected to be able to make a withdrawal today. I'm going on holiday tomorrow.

B: I'm afraid there's not a lot I can do ... you see I'm not allowed to authorise payment earlier than four working days after it was paid in.

A: But it is four working days today.

B: No. Today's Wednesday. That's only three working days.

A: Look, I'd like to speak to the manager if you don't mind.

Extract 7

It was an amazing thing to say really. I mean imagine saying that to a judge: 'I just like cash.' Who doesn't, after all? Anyway the judge wasn't having any of it. They'd smuggled £600,000 of used bank notes out of the Bank of England. They kept it under the floorboards in their house. Anyway, it said that the judge decided they had to pay it all back plus interest. Oh, and the bank's suing them as well. I can't understand why the police are not involved.

Extract 8

... Yes, a table for thirteen. ... No, not thirty, *thirteen.* ... A private room?... No, I don't think we want that. ... No extra cost? Well, perhaps it wouldn't be such a bad idea. ... Oh, about 8.30 or 9.00. Oh, there may be an extra person, but I'll phone and confirm that tomorrow. ... The set menu?... What exactly does that involve? ... That sounds a bit expensive – look, can I get back to you on that as well?

1 1 a) 2 c) 3 c) 4 b) 5 a) 6 a) 7 a) 8 b)

2 1 C 2 B 3 A 4 B 5 B 6 A 7 A 8 B

Vocabulary p.76

1 *Tapescript*

a) oh one, two four nine, seven four oh, three two five

b) three quarters

c) a hundred thousand

d) six point three seven

e) one and a half kilos

f) fourteen degrees centigrade

g) twenty five pounds fifty

h) thirty five miles per hour

i) two nil

a) 01249 740325   b) ¾   c) 100,000   d) 6.37
e) 1½ kilos   f) 14° C   g) £25.50   h) 35 mph
i) 2–0

2 1 f)   2 a)   3 i)   4 c)   5 h)   6 e)   7 d)   8 b)   9 g)

3 *Tapescript*

a) oh one two one, seven three oh, six five four
b) thirteen
c) fifty
d) one and a half
e) four point seven five
f) sixteen
g) three pounds fifty
h) nineteen dollars ninety-nine cents
i) six hundred and forty-seven thousand nine hundred and fifty-eight
j) five million three hundred and forty thousand four hundred and fourteen

Speaking p.76

Tapescript

L=Loukas   J=Julie   O=Olivier   D=Dominique

Interview 1

L: Shall we start? What do you think is the most important?

J: Erm … I don't know.

L: How about books? I think buying books is never a waste of money. Are you … do you agree?

J: Yes, I agree.

L: What shall we put next?

J: Err … private classes.

L: Do you think private classes are important?

J: Yes, I do.

L: Yes, I think they are too, especially if a subject is difficult for you. … But it's important to get a lot of exercise as well as studying, so perhaps we can put sports next. Do you spend very much money on sports?

J: No. I don't like.

L: I don't like all sports, but I play volleyball so I have to buy good trainers. I don't know what to put after that. What … what do you think?

J: Erm … computer games.

L: OK. We could put that next. I suppose computer games help you … umm … to … ummm … to learn to use a computer.

J: Mmm.

L: Do you think we should put music next?

J: OK.

L: Do you think cassettes and compact discs are too expensive?

J: Err … yes.

Interview 2

O: Well, I think we should put computer games first because this is the age of technology and everybody needs to know use a computer if he wants to get a good work.

D: Yes, I agree that computers ….

O: And after that I think clothes and then cosmetics because it is important to have a good presence … I mean good-lookings.

J: Yes, I think they're important, but for me books and music are more important than make-up and clothes. And spending money on sport is OK, too.

O: I am not agree with you. People spend too much money on buying famous marks. You can get good shoes in the supermarket. My brother, he only wants to wear Nike shoes and I think he is very foolish. The mark doesn't mind. It is the quality. I always buy in the sales because everything is very cheap and good.

D: Yes. That's true, but I mean that it's good to play sport and sometimes you must spend a little money on it. Why don't we put … err … private classes next?

O: Yes. Private classes can help you practise your English very much. You can be with your teacher only you practising speaking and this is very good for you, your English. My teacher is very good and she says I speak English very well. Next year I will have private classes in German and err …

Loukas and Dominique

145

U N I T *11*

Writing p.77

1 Comments 1, 3 and 4

Reading p.78

1 C   2 B   3 A

Vocabulary p.79

1 C   2 B   3 B   4 B   5 C   6 B   7 A   8 C   9 B

Grammar p.79

1 1 (-)   2 (-)   3 (-)   4 the/(-)   5 the   6 the   7 the
8 a   9 a   10 (-)   11 a   12 (-)   13 the   14 (-)   15 a
16 the   17 (-)   18 the   19 the   20 the

2 line 0: delete first *the*   line 1: delete second *the*
line 4: delete *the*   line 5: delete *the*
line 7: delete *a*   line 10: delete *a*

Vocabulary and grammar p.80

1 where   2 all/other   3 numbers/populations   4 like
5 mountain   6 from   7 the   8 were   9 down
10 have   11 is   12 the   13 there   14 who   15 their

Grammar pp.80–81

1 1 g)   2 j)   3 i)   4 f)   5 d)   6 a)   7 e)   8 h)   9 b)
10 c)

2 1 Would you mind buying me a coffee? I **must
       have left** my money in my other coat.
     4 Don't wait for me. I **might be** late.
     5 It **can't have been** Mary who stole the money.
       She was with me all evening.
     8 I **might stay** at home this Saturday night. I've
       got a test on Monday.
    10 You **should have told** me. I didn't know you
       were coming.

Grammar p.81

1 1 PV   2 G   3 G   4 V   5 PV   6 G   7 PV

2 1 put me up   2 can't have been   3 much does
this bag   4 can't stand   5 give up   6 may not
speak   7 taking off

Speaking p.82

Tapescript

I=interlocutor E=Eleni

I: Now I'm going to give you two photographs of
landscapes. I'd like you to talk about your pictures
and say which looks more attractive to you.

E: Erm ... well in the first picture I can see a desert. It
could be Africa or perhaps in the USA. There can't
have been any rain for a long time because the
ground is very dry. There might be a drought. I
wouldn't mind visiting this place, but I wouldn't
like to live there. The second photograph is very
different. It might have been taken in Canada or
Alaska. This is a kind of ... hut or a cabin ... it's
built of wood and I think it looks very attractive. It
must be, must be really ... err ... cosy inside. There
is a lot of snow on the ground, on the trees and on
the roof of the house, but the sky is blue and there
are no clouds. It must have snowed during the
night. I think this would be a good place to go for
a holiday.

1 1 a) There can't have been any rain for a long time
because the ground is very dry.   b) It might have
been taken in Canada or Alaska.   c) It must have
snowed during the night.
2 a) It could be Africa or perhaps in the USA.
b) There might be a drought   c) It must be really
cosy inside.
3 a) I wouldn't mind visiting this place, but I
wouldn't like to live there.   b) I think this would be
a good place to go for a holiday.

Vocabulary p.83

Across: 1 FLOOD 3 DISEASE 5 CHARITY 6 REFUGEE 9 STORM 12 EMERGENCY 13 TORNADO 15 OVERPOPULATION

Down: 2 DROUGHT 4 EARTHQUAKE 7 FAMINE 8 EXTINCTION 10 METEOR 11 SOLUTION 14 AID

Listening p.83

Tapescript

P=presenter DG=Dr Goodman

P: And so. Welcome to the studio, Dr Goodman.

DG: It's a pleasure to be here.

P: Now, I know that many of our listeners are already familiar with the biosphere project, but many others are not. Perhaps you could start off by telling us exactly what a biosphere reserve is?

DG: Biosphere reserves are areas that are specially protected by conservationists so that scientists and others can study them. We hope this will make it easier to preserve such areas in other parts of the world.

P: And has this project just started?

DG: No, no. In fact the first biosphere reserves were established over twenty years ago. There are 324 biosphere reserves in 82 countries now,

P: 82 countries! Can you tell us a bit about some of the more recent projects?

DG: Well, we've established a 226,000 hectare biosphere reserve in Brazil, quite near the Brazilian capital Brasilia, and a 2.57 million hectare reserve in the Wadi Allaqui valley near the Nile valley in Egypt. The Brazilian reserve has 44 endangered or threatened animal species and 41 endangered or threatened plant species.

P: And are there only UNESCO scientists working on these reserves?

DG: No. In fact the local community always makes an important contribution to the research and the management of the reserve. In the case of the Brazilian reserve, Brazil has made a big contribution because they already had a lot of experience. You see they already had another reserve – the Atlantic Forest Biosphere. Now that reserve has recently been extended to cover 3,000 kilometres. This is a particularly large reserve.

P: In fact all the reserves you've mentioned so far sound very large. I suppose there are also smaller reserves.

DG: Yes. We have a couple of reserves which are islands. Err, Lanzarote in the Canary Islands is one example, it measures 70,000 hectares, and Menorca in the Balearic islands is another. Menorca is a little smaller.

P: And what about the colder parts of the world? Are there any biosphere reserves in Scandinavia, for example?

DG: Yes, in fact there's the Sea Area Biosphere reserve in Finland. This reserve includes pine forest and small sandy islands so it has quite a lot of variety.

P: And the idea is that scientists working on these projects should share their experiences with others working on reserves in other parts of the world. Now, how do they communicate with each other?

DG: In all sorts of ways. We're about to hold an international conference which will be attended by between 300 and 400 people. This should give everybody an excellent opportunity to compare notes and improve the biosphere project in a number of ways. Apart from the conference, computer technology has made rapid communication very much easier and we also have a news bulletin which provides up to date information for the local community.

P: I imagine that many of the reserves share similar problems.

DG: Yes, indeed they do. We've actually begun to 'twin' reserves with very similar problems so that the people working on them can establish stronger links. For example, a reserve in France and one in Spain have recently been twinned.

P: Well, thank you very much for telling us about the biosphere reserve project, Dr Goodman. I'm sure we all hope that the project is a great success. Now also with me in the studio tonight I have ...

1 No 2 Yes 3 No 4 Yes 5 No 6 Yes 7 No 8 No
9 Yes 10 Yes

U N I T *12*

Speaking p.84

Tapescript

I=Interlocutor H=Helmut G=Gloria

I: Tell us, what do you think of television nowadays?

H: Well, in my opinion television is not as good as it used to be. There are a lot more channels, but ... umm ... there is a lot of rubbish on them.

I: Do you agree, Gloria?

G: I agree up to a point, but because there are more channels, there's more choice. There might be a movie on one channel, a quiz programme on another and a documentary on another. So even if you don't like one thing, you can always find something ...

H: Always?

G: OK, often find something you like.

I: So do you think parents should limit the amount of television their children watch?

G: Yes, definitely. I think that unless they limit their children, they will be watching all the time.

H: Yeah, I agree completely. My younger brothers switch the television on as soon as they come home from school and unless my parents made them turn it off, they'd still be watching it at midnight.

I: Is there too much advertising on television?

H/G: Yes!

G: But sometimes ... well ... I enjoy watching the advertisements. I think they can be very original.

H: Yes, I agree with you. Sometimes the advertisements are better than the programmes!

I: Well, thank you both very much for coming.

in my opinion ... ; I agree up to a point, but ... ; Yes, definitely. I think that ... ; I agree completely.; Yes. I agree with you.

Writing p.84

1 B 2 A 3 B 4 A 5 B 6 B 7 A 8 C 9 B 10 A

Writing p.85

1 The writer followed Plan B. Yes.

Grammar p.86

1 really   2 absolutely   3 really; very   4 really
5 terrific   6 very   7 quite   8 absolutely   9 superb
10 very

Vocabulary p.86

1 I've been trying to **get through to him** ...   2 You really must **get down to** some work.   3 I know how to **get round** our Mum.   4 I don't **get on with Mary** very well.   5 I hope you won't **get up to** anything while we're out.   6 She doesn't earn a lot – just enough to **get by**.   7 I'd never do anything dishonest because I'm sure I'd never **get away with it**.

Grammar p.86

1 1 How many compositions do we have to write?
2 You needn't help with the shopping.   3 You needn't have gone to so much trouble.   4 I've just got to pass.   5 Do you often have to study at the weekend?   6 How many words are we supposed to write?   7 You mustn't use ink.   8 Do we need to write a draft?

2 1 e) 2 b) 3 g) 4 d) 5 f) 6 a) 7 c) 8 h)

3 1 A 2 B 3 B 4 A 5 B 6 B 7 B 8 A

Grammar p.87

line 1: delete *to*   line 2: delete *a*   line 3: delete *the*
line 5: delete *been*   line 6: delete *that*
line 7: delete *of*   line 10: delete *of*
line 12: delete *of*   line 14: delete *of*

Reading pp.88–89

1 G 2 A 3 F 4 B 5 C 6 A 7 E 8 G 9 B 10 H
11 D 12 E 13 C 14 C

Vocabulary p.89

1 1 cartoon 2 editorial 3 headline 4 gossip
5 journalist 6 crossword

```
J H E A D L I N E T
C O Y E S L G R G R
R F U D M K R F O S
O C A R T O O N S L
S A K N N X V U S T
S P O C H A H E I Q
W G B A W K L Z P S
O E D I T O R I A L
R Q P B I L V W S X
D C D X J U X P O T
```

2 1 frequency 2 batteries 3 headlines 4 soaps
5 aerial 6 remote control

Listening p.90

Tapescript

Speaker 1
We were waiting outside the manager's office when this guy came up to us and asked if we'd mind being filmed for an ad they were making about the bank. I wasn't too sure, but Sharon was quite keen. So when we actually went in to discuss our mortgage repayments, there were hidden cameras filming us having this discussion with the manager. They filmed lots of other people, too. Erm ... it was a bit disappointing really because they didn't use us in the end. They said we seemed as if we were acting.

Speaker 2
Of course I'd sent in lots of others and I'd basically given up hope of ever getting one published. But there it was. I couldn't believe my eyes. I was on the train on my way to work and I opened my copy of *The Times*, turned to the 'Letters to the editor' page and ... well, I just burst out laughing. It really is difficult to get one published in *The Times*, or at least that's what they say. There were a whole lot of replies about two days later. Some of them really made my blood boil, but I suppose that's democracy for you – people expressing their views.

Speaker 3
It was an absolute pack of lies. Not just exaggerated claims, completely false. Not only did the stuff have absolutely no effect whatsoever on the amount of hair on my head, it smelt really disgusting, a bit like turpentine. 'A fine head of thick glossy hair will be yours within weeks.' Haa! So I reported them to one of those consumer protection authorities. I haven't seen it for weeks now, so they must have had other complaints and decided to take it off. Needless to say, I threw the stuff away.

Speaker 4
I was incredibly nervous. I had to get there a couple of hours before though they hadn't actually told me why. I'd never done anything like that before so I didn't know you had to wear make-up. Apparently your face would be too shiny otherwise what with all the very bright lights and you'd look terrible on the screen. So this girl put all this powder and stuff all over my face. She even insisted on that black stuff women use on their eyelashes and lipstick. I was going to nip off to the toilets and wash it all off, but the next thing I knew, I was sitting on a kind of sofa being interviewed. I didn't even see the programme until a couple of days later, because it went out live. You couldn't actually tell I was wearing lipstick – thankfully!

Speaker 5
We'd hardly got out of the plane when this mass of reporters descended on us all shoving microphones and personal stereo recorders in our faces and literally firing questions at us. How did we feel now that we were back home? Could we describe how we felt when Diego kicked the third goal? When were we going to start training again? Lots of people I know heard it on the local station. It was during the nightly sports broadcast. No one managed to record it for us, though. So my one moment of glory is lost for ever. Who knows? Perhaps we'll win again next year.

1 E 2 D 3 A 4 F 5 B

Word formation p.90

1 journalism 2 optional 3 entertainment
4 unavailable 5 enthusiastic 6 advertising
7 creativity 8 production 9 Unfortunately
10 unemployment

UNIT 13

Vocabulary p.91

1 1 g) 2 e) 3 f) 4 c) 5 d) 6 a) 7 b)

2 1 tail: dog 2 feathers: bird 3 beak: bird
4 claws: cat 5 wings: bird 6 horn: rhinoceros
7 mane: lion 8 hump: camel
9 hooves: horse 10 trunk: elephant
11 fur: tiger

3 1 dog 2 cows 3 lion 4 snake 5 horse 6 cat

Speaking p.92

Tapescript

Here is a map of a zoo. You are at the entrance to the zoo. Unfortunately, you only have half an hour before the zoo closes and you want to see as many animals as possible. I'd like you to talk together to plan which route you will take from the entrance to the exit. You have about three minutes to do this. Would you like to start?

1 1 F 2 T 3 T 4 T

Tapescript

D=Dimitra G=Giorgos

G: What do you want to see first?

D: Well, if we take this path, we could see the koalas and the seals. They're quite close together so we could see both of them and then have a drink at the café which is next to the seals.

G: Yes, that's O.K. What other animals do you want to see?

D: Err, well I really like the giraffes, so perhaps we could go and see them after we've had a drink. See – they're just along this path here. Oh, and then we could have a look at the zebras. They're almost next door to the lions so we could have a look at them as well. What would you like to see?

G: I like to see the lions, too.

D: OK. So after the lions we could go along this path. Are you interested in any of these animals?

G: Yes, I like them.

D: OK, well, err, perhaps we could go and look at the monkeys and the polar bears and after that the butterflies – then we're quite near the exit. I think that's probably all we could do in half an hour.

2 Dimitra

Grammar pp.92–93

1 1 are; works 2 would you buy; won
3 will be; is 4 have; will sew 5 try; won't convince 6 wouldn't have driven; had known
7 divide; get 8 would have met; had come 9 will lend; promise 10 were; would tell 11 mix; make
12 will let; finish 13 hadn't stood; wouldn't have got 14 would you do; were

Vocabulary and grammar p.93

1 than 2 are/reach 3 later 4 and 5 which 6 on 7 them 8 gives 9 without 10 heard 11 but 12 at 13 are 14 to 15 they

Vocabulary p.94

1 1 terraced houses 2 semi-detached houses
3 detached house 4 bungalow 5 block of flats
6 cottage 7 hut 8 caravan

2 1 lawn 2 shed 3 attic 4 drainpipe 5 fence
6 chimney 7 cellar 8 hedge

Writing pp.94–95

1 1 enjoyable 2 glorious 3 unusual 4 delicious
5 spectacular 6 colourful; exotic 7 charming

2 Report 1: Candidate B Report 2: Candidate A

3 Inside I would build a big **fireplace** so that we could be warm in winter. There would be huge sofas and comfortable armchairs covered in **leather**.

Grammar p.96

1 promised to lend 2 despite studying/having studied 3 used to play the piano 4 unless I feel 5 are not supposed to talk 6 put up with 7 in addition to (having) 8 had worked more carefully

Listening p.96

Tapescript

I=interviewer SM=Simon Marsden

I: Here in the studio tonight we have Simon Marsden, a self-confessed ghost hunter. Simon has devoted his life to photographing ghostly sites all over Europe. He has now visited over 6,000 sites in Britain alone. Simon, do you really believe these places are haunted?

SM: Yes, I do. I think violent events or emotions in the past leave a kind of mark on their surrounding which can then be released in the right circumstances – either atmospheric conditions or by people sensitive enough to pick up on them.

I: And of course one of these places is Dracula's castle. How true is Bram Stoker's story of Dracula?

SM: Well, Dracula was a real person who ruled part of Romania in the fifteenth century. Tirgoviste was his capital city and the palace was an ideal place for the tyrant to watch his victims being tortured and executed in the courtyard below. During his lifetime he is said to have killed over 100,000 men, women and children. There's not much left of the actual buildings now, though.

I: But I understand it was in fact another castle that inspired Bram Stoker.

SM: Yes, that's right. Ecclescrieg House in Aberdeenshire in Scotland is thought to be the model Bram Stoker used for Dracula's castle. And it certainly is a very haunting place. There's a legend attached to the family who lived there until very recently. Earlier this century, Osbert Clare Forsyth-Grant was the commander of a ship with a mixed crew of Scots and Eskimos. He offended the Eskimos in some way and it is claimed they put a curse on him and his family. Soon afterwards his ship went missing and was wrecked in a storm. Forsyth-Grant and the Scots died but all the Eskimos survived. His body was never found.

I: There are quite a lot of haunted castles in Scotland, aren't there?

SM: Yes, indeed. One with a particularly dark history is Dunnottar Castle in Kincardineshire. There was a Royalist rebellion and in 1685 over 160 men, women and children were kept in the dark dungeon and fed on a diet of rotten meat, raw fish and salt water. Many died of starvation and some say their screams and cries can still be heard at night. The cold dark cellar where they were held can still be seen today.

I: Haven't you ever felt scared when you've been photographing one of these places?

SM: Well, yes. I visited one castle in Ireland where the atmosphere was pure evil, the most disturbing I've ever come across. I usually photograph alone, but I got out of there as fast as I could. People say I must be crazy, but I actually prefer this 'other world' to the one everyone else lives in. Now walking down a busy street in a big city like London, to me that's scary.

1 6,000 2 Britain 3 capital 4 Romania 5 the fifteenth century 6 100,000 7 a ship 8 never found 9 starvation 10 Ireland

Reading p.97

2 E 3 A 4 G 5 F 6 B 7 C

UNIT *14*

Vocabulary p.98

1 B 2 B 3 B 4 A 5 A 6 B 7 A 8 B 9 B 10 B
11 B 12 A 13 B

Reading pp.98-99

1 B 2 A 3 A 4 C 5 D 6 D 7 A 8 B

Grammar p.100

1 The police **made him stop**. 3 Are you **allowed** to stay out after ten o'clock? 4 Do your parents **make you study** English? 6 They allowed us **to go** to the party. 8 My parents **made** me wear clothes I didn't like. 9 When I was younger, I **wasn't allowed** to go swimming unless my parents were with me. 10 They wouldn't **let me go**.

Vocabulary p.100

1 1 b) and f) 2 a) 3 e) 4 d) 5 c)

2 1 You won't **make up for** lost time by working all night. 2 He just **made it up**. 3 When the police asked him where he had been that night, he **made out** that he had been with me, ... 4 The escaped prisoners tried to **make for** the mountains ... 5 She muttered something under her breath, but I couldn't **make out** exactly what she said.
6 If your friend wants to spend a couple of days here, we could **make up** a bed for her ...
7 ..., but they've **made it up** and are the best of friends again.

Writing p.101

1 1c) mutter   2g) chuckle   3b) consider   4h) nibble
5i) grasp   6f) tiptoe   7d) lob   8a) fidget
9e) order

2 *Possible answer*

He **tiptoed** along the corridor **wondering** what he
would do if the gang were still there. When he was
about to climb the stairs, he heard someone
chuckling in one of the rooms on the second floor.
He **clutched** the gun and continued to climb the
stairs. Suddenly he felt someone hit him very hard
from behind and he **staggered** a few steps further
and then fell and **writhed** on the ground in pain,
telling himself that he had been a fool to try this on
his own. The man who had hit him **ordered** him to
give him the gun and with what little energy he
had left he **tossed** it to him. The man **sniggered**
and said, 'Now you're really in trouble, Mason.' He
took a bottle from his jacket and drank half the
contents in one go. Mason thought he would be
lucky to get out of there alive.

Vocabulary p.102

1 B 2 A 3 C 4 D 5 C 6 B 7 A 8 D 9 A
10 C 11 A 12 D 13 C 14 A 15 D

Listening p.103

Tapescript

Extract 1

Excuse me, miss. I'm sorry to bother you, but there
doesn't seem to be any space in the overhead locker. I
know we're only supposed to have one piece of hand
luggage, but my grandson gave me this as a present
just before I left. Could you possibly find a space for it
further down the plane? You see I've already got my
bag under the seat in front of me and if I put
anything else there, I won't have any room to put my
feet.

Extract 2

A: But you said I could have a go when you'd
finished.

B: Well, I haven't finished, have I?

A: But you started to play another one after you
finished the first one. It's not fair. I'm going to tell
Dad.

B: OK. You can have a go now. But don't break it!

Extract 3

Yes. About two weeks ago. But it's making a very
funny noise and it doesn't keep things cold enough.
... My customer service number? Let me see. Would it
be this one? 0765872? ... Can't they come any earlier
than Wednesday? ... Could you possibly give me some
idea of when they'll be here? ... That's fine. I'll be in
all morning.

Extract 4

Police were involved in a car chase earlier today after
two bank robbers fled from the scene of a hold-up in
Malvern Road. The robbers entered the bank at about
midday and told the three customers who were
waiting to withdraw money, to lie down on the floor.
They then forced one of the bank tellers to open the
safe and empty the contents into a bag. She was able
to give the alarm by pressing a button inside the safe
door.

Extract 5

A: Why don't you make it up with her? You're
obviously just as unhappy as she is.

B: I just can't. You wouldn't believe the things she
said to me. And to think I'd always thought she
was such a sweet gentle person.

A: I know she's been under a lot of pressure at work
lately. She's really not herself at all.

B: Well, as far as I'm concerned that's no excuse ...

Extract 6

It was fine really. He was so gentle with her that she
was even purring for a while. Of course she didn't like
it much when he gave her the injection, but then he
stroked her and calmed her down so well, she almost
rolled over and let him rub her tummy.

Extract 7

Hello ... Hello ... I can hardly ... I can hardly hear you.
This is a really bad line. Look, I'm at the station and I
just wondered if you wanted anything from the
supermarket? ... What was that? You'll have to speak
up a bit. ... OK. I'll see you in a minute then, love.

Extract 8

Now we whisk them until they are snowy white and
standing up in peaks. And then we pour that in with
the melted chocolate and stir ever so gently. And then
into the little soufflé dishes and now we'll just pop
them in the oven. I'll be back with you to try our
soufflés after a short break.

1 C 2 B 3 A 4 A 5 B 6 A 7 C 8 C

Speaking p.103

Tapescript

I=interlocutor N=Nicole D=Diego

I: Do you think young offenders should be sent to prison?

N: No. I am definitely not agree with this. If they go in prison, they will become much worser. Because if a young man he is in prison, he meet other delinquents and he learns new ways to make crime. I think they must to do works in the society like help the old people who is often very alone and need someone take care of them.

I: Do you agree with Nicole, Diego?

D: Yes, I think she's quite right.

I: Why do you think young people commit crimes?

D: Well, there are many reasons for this. Unemployment is an important one.

I: Why do you think unemployment is important?

D: If young people cannot get jobs, they become frustrated.

N: Yes. This is truth. If they cannot to find a work, they cannot get any money and they must to stay in their house all day watching TV. This is very bad. I think another problem is that the young people are not educate. They do not know that crime is a so bad thing.

I: Do you think education is important Diego?

D: Of course, I think it's important ...

1 Nicole P Diego G
2 Nicole S Diego G
3 Nicole G Diego S

Grammar p.104

1 1 is being made. 2 has not been painted for ten years. 3 are provided every year. 4 had been stolen. 5 has to be guarded day and night. 6 might be badly affected by water. 7 were being interviewed (by the police) last night. 8 was finally forced to stop by a police roadblock.

2 1 has been made. 2 are reminded not to put bottles in the overhead lockers. 3 will be refunded in full if you are not satisfied. 4 is being dealt with (by our customer relations office). 5 will be sent a letter inviting them to attend a second interview. 6 were sent on 15th April. 7 has not been delivered by 15th May, please contact us again. 8 will be replaced. 9 is being prepared. 10 was being checked (by technicians).

UNIT 15

Grammar p.105

1 1 had studied 2 were coming/could come/would come 3 could drive 4 had 5 wouldn't do 6 were 7 would tell 8 knew 9 hadn't done 10 could afford 11 we stayed 12 didn't lend/hadn't lent 13 left 14 recognised 15 arrive

2 1 wish I had phoned 2 suppose we buy/bought 3 only I hadn't said 4 time you went 5 would/'d rather have 6 would/'d rather you didn't tell 7 wish you wouldn't 8 only he were 9 time you started revising

Speaking p.106

Tapescript

I=interlocutor A=Anna F=Francisco

Part 1

I: Good morning.

A/F: Good morning.

I: My name is Sally and this is my colleague Pam.

A/F: Hello.

I: Pam, this is Anna and Francisco. Well, do you two know each other?

A: Yes, we go to the same school.

I: I see. Well, Francisco, let's start with you. Where are you from?

F: I am from here in Madrid. I live very close by.

I: And Anna are you from Madrid, too?

A: No, I come from Alicante, but I live here now.

I: How long have you lived here?

A: Almost three years.

I: Tell us what it's like living here, Francisco.

F: It is great. The weather is good in spring and summer, but it gets quite cold in winter. You can go out to a pub in the evening and listen to jazz or go to a café to meet your friends.

I: Anna, how do you like to spend your free time?

A: I like playing basketball and going to the cinema. But I don't have so much free time because I study a lot.

I: What are you studying?

A: I am studying Economics at the university.

I: And, Francisco, are you studying too?

F: No, I finish my studies last year. I am working in a bank now.

Part 2

I: Now, I'm going to give each of you two pictures and ask you to talk about them. You have one minute to do this so don't worry if I interrupt you. Anna, here are your two pictures. They show people playing games. I'd like you to say how you feel about games like these. Francisco, I'll give you your two pictures in a minute.

A: Well, there are both pictures of people playing games, as you said. In the first picture there are some old men playing cards at a table outside a café I think. They look very concentrated on what they are doing. Some of the men are not playing but just watching what the others are doing. The second picture shows some boys, some teenagers playing games in a ... I think that you call it an amusement arcade. They look as if they are enjoying themselves. I quite like playing this kind of games too, but I don't like playing cards so much. I sometimes play with my grandmother, though.

I: Thank you, Anna. Now, Francisco, here are your two pictures.

F: Well, my two pictures are of chickens ... I mean kitchens. The first kitchen is very modern. It is all in white and it looks a bit like a hospital ... it is very clean. But it doesn't look ... it looks like nobody ever cooked in it. I like the other kitchen more. It looks like my grandmother's house. It have ... I means *has* ... some saucepans hanging up as well as herbs and dry flowers and there is fresh fruit on a plate on the table. I think the second kitchen looks a lot more warm and comfortable than the first one.

I: Thank you, Francisco. So, Anna, which kitchen do you prefer?

A: I like the modern kitchen best.

Part 3

I: Now, Anna and Francisco, I'm going to give you a map of a town in Britain. The local council are trying to decide where to build the new shopping mall. I'd like you to talk together about this and decide which position on the map would be most suitable for the shopping mall. Then I'd like you to say what sorts of shops and facilities the shopping mall should have.

F: I'm sorry. Do we have to decide where each shop should be?

I: No. You need to decide where the shopping mall should be and then decide what kinds of shops should be *in* the shopping mall.

F: OK. Umm ... let's see. We could put it here in the centre near to the post office. What do you think?

A: Yes. But I think it would be a problem for people to park their cars there. There is more space over here near bus station.

F: Mmm ... I don't think there is a very big space there and we don't want it to be only a very small shopping mall.

A: No, that's true. What about outside the, of the town? Here near the motorway.

F: Yes, that's a good idea. I think that would be a perfect place. Then everybody could drive there and there would be no problem for traffic.

A: But what about the people who do not have cars. Can you see any bus stop near there?

F: No, I can't. Perhaps we should build it here, near the bus station.

A: Yes, I think that's better. And what shops and ... shall we have?

F: A sports shop and a shop for animals.

A: A pet shop .... yes, that's a good idea. And boutiques with the last fashions, do you agree?

F: Yes, of course. And a newsagent's. Oh, I think we forgot something.

A: What?

F: Banks. We need banks so that people can get money to spend in the shops.

A: Yes. And a supermarket. We definitely need a supermarket, don't we?

F: Oh, yes. And what else ... a ...?

Part 4

I: Do you enjoy shopping in big shopping malls or do you prefer to go to markets and smaller shops?

A: I like shopping malls because they are very ... umm ... convenient and you don't have to walk too much.

F: Yes, it is much easier to make all your shopping in one place. And you can sometimes meet your friends there, too.

I: In Britain people sometimes think that shopping malls are destroying the small shops in town centres. What do you think about that?

F: My uncle has a shop in the centre of our town and he has lost a lot of customers because of the shopping mall.

A: Yes, not many people want to shop in the centre now and it must be very bad for the shop ... err ... people.

I: Do you think people spend too much time on shopping?

A: Yes, I do. It has become like a hobby. People go shopping instead of playing sport or going for a walk in the country.

F: I am sorry, but I don't agree. I think it is good for the economy of the country if everybody buy a lot of things. And anyway is good fun. Don't you like shopping?

A: Yes, I do. Sometimes, but not with my mother she always wants me to buy really horrible clothes.

F: Yes, my mother is the same way.

I: So who do you prefer to go shopping with?

A: With my best friend. But we don't have much money so we only look at the things in the umm ... in the ...

F: ... the window displays? Yes, I go with my cousin sometimes, but we don't usually buy too much.

I: I don't like shopping at all myself and if I do go shopping I generally go on my own. Well, thank you both for coming. Goodbye.

A/F: Goodbye.

1 1 Anna G   Francisco G
       2 Anna S   Francisco G
       3 Anna E   Francisco E

2 1 saucepans: /ˈsɔːspænz/
       2 fruit: /fruːt/
       3 comfortable: /ˈkʌmftəbəl/
       4 convenient: /kənˈviːniənt/

3 1) bear: /beə/   2) stir: /stɜː/
       3) weapons: /ˈwepənz/   4) clothes: /kləʊðz/
       5) money: /ˈmʌni/   6) scientist: /ˈsaɪəntɪst/
       7) wallet: /ˈwɒlɪt/   8) occasion: /əˈkeɪʒən/

Grammar p.107

1 had my hair cut last week.   2 are having their house painted.   3 have had my trousers turned up.   4 had her/his wallet stolen.   5 had our photograph taken.   6 had my eyes tested.   7 am having my new jacket cleaned.   8 have had our refrigerator fixed.   9 have their groceries delivered.   10 am going to have my car serviced next week.

Grammar p.108

line 1: delete second *is*   line 3: delete *be*   line 5: delete *the*   line 6: delete *than*   line 8: delete *in*   line 9: delete second *the*   line 11; delete *do*   line 13; delete *of*

Reading pp.108–109

1 E   2 B   3 G   4 A   5 F   6 D

Vocabulary p.110

```
        ¹M
         E
²C O N T ³R A ⁴D I C T
 H       T     I
 A       I     ⁵S H O U T
 T       O     C
 N           ⁶M U T T E R
               S
         ⁷W H I S P E R
```

Listening p.110

Tapescript

Learning to read is an infinite, continuous, life-long process, not something that takes place at primary school to be quickly and thankfully ticked off the list before you go on to the next thing.

It's like learning to drive. When you pass your test, you've been taught the basics, but you're still a very inexpert beginner who needs to get out on to the road and learn to drive properly. New readers face a similar challenge. They can do it, but it's not yet second nature. And it will only become so through routine daily practice.

Many young people never learn to read other than very slowly. Fourteen and fifteen-year-olds who should have become fluent readers a long time ago, carry the same book around with them in school for weeks.

They read very slowly through a page or two when the teacher tells them to, but their attention is on the mechanics of reading and they never really have the chance to become interested in the content.

Someone who's stuck in this limited position will inevitably turn to television or video because it's faster and easier.

If children are to become 'natural' readers, their reading must be developed and speeded up. No fluent reader, for example, slowly pronounces the words very quietly or reads aloud in his head, mentally articulating every word, apart from when we do this deliberately if we're reading something very complicated like a scientific article.

But many young and adult readers never get beyond the stage of pronouncing every word, which is why they're so slow. When seven or eight-year-olds read 'to themselves' you can sometimes see their lips moving. This should be a brief stage in the process of learning to read, not the end result.

The answer for children lies in giving them lots of accessible books quickly, and plenty of time both at school and at home to read them. It probably means deliberate restriction of television exposure time, too.

It's also crucial that children see reading as an ordinary part of adult behaviour. Children copy adults. I frequently hear teachers and parents complaining that children won't read. In the next breath these same adults are either explaining that they themselves are too busy to read or discussing the previous evening's television programmes at length. Two unmistakable messages are being transmitted to children: Don't read, watch TV.

Learning to read doesn't stop when children leave primary school to go on to secondary school. It doesn't even end when you leave school, but should go on throughout life. Sadly you can lose your ability to read if you don't use it regularly – just like the ability to type, run, swim or play the violin.

Teaching children to read is just the beginning. It's what happens after that that makes the difference.

1 B 2 A 3 C 4 A 5 C 6 A 7 B

Writing p.111

1 a) 8 b) 7 c) 6 d) 8 e) 8 f) 8

2 *statment*: statement; *comunication*: communication; *translattors*: translators; *nattive*: native; *loose*: lose; *sucessful*: successful
people would stop to use: people would **stop using**; *everyone would know a language*: everyone would know **one** language

PRACTICE EXAM

Paper 1 Reading

PART 1   1 A 2 H 3 C 4 G 5 B 6 D 7 F
Distractor E

PART 2   8 B 9 D 10 A 11 C 12 B 13 C 14 C

PART 3   15 A 16 E 17 C 18 H 19 G 20 D
21 B Distractor F

PART 4   22 B 23 C 24 C 25 A 26 A 27 B
28 B 29 D 30 A 31 D 32 A 33 D
34 C 35 D

Paper 3 Use of English

PART 1   1 C 2 A 3 C 4 D 5 C 6 B 7 A 8 B
9 B 10 A 11 C 12 D 13 A 14 B 15 B

PART 2   16 the/their/an 17 get 18 them 19 are
20 away 21 take 22 at 23 for 24 which
25 and/so 26 by 27 that 28 the 29 next
30 another

PART 3   31 suggested going 32 the exam had
already 33 put me up 34 them where
they were 35 are not supposed to smoke
36 not used to wearing 37 can't stand
being 38 must have known 39 is having
his portrait painted 40 had arrived on time

PART 4   line 43: delete *then* line 45; delete *do*
line 47: delete *did* line 49: delete *have*
line 50: delete *to* line 52: delete *of*
line 54: delete *being*

PART 5   56 activities 57 inexpensive
58 unnecessary 59 injuries 60 repeatedly
61 disastrous 62 development
63 reduction 64 combination
65 protection

Paper 4 Listening

Tapescript

Hello. I'm going to give you the instructions for this test. I'll introduce each part of the test and give you time to look at the questions. At the start of each piece you'll hear this sound (tone). You'll hear each piece twice. Now look at Part 1. You'll hear people talking in eight different situations. For questions 1–8 choose the best answer A, B or C.

PART 1

Extract 1

A: I'm looking for two one-way tickets to Crete next Thursday.

B: OK, I'll just have a look for you. I'm afraid there's not very much available at the moment. You see it's mid-term next week. I can do two-week returns from Gatwick for £189. That means you'll get back on the fourteenth.

A: But I wanted one-way tickets.

B: Oh, I'm sorry. So you did. Let me try this company.

Extract 2

A: We'd been wanting to see it for absolutely ages and when Tom's mother gave us tickets for our wedding anniversary, we were really thrilled.

B: Yes, I mean it's booked solid until October, you know.

C: I'm not surprised. It had such fantastic reviews.

B: Maybe we just got a bad night, but I don't think I've ever seen such a poor performance. The leading man actually forgot his lines.

A: We were so disappointed and when Tom's mother asked us if we'd enjoyed it, we just didn't know what to say.

Extract 3

But I was not told that there was no return of sale goods. In fact I didn't even notice that it had been reduced. Obviously if I'd realised I couldn't exchange it, I never would have bought it in the first place. You must have realised it wasn't for me. I mean, how many women of my age wear things like this? My daughter loves it, but it's far too tight so if you would just be good enough to see if you have it in a 14, I'd be most grateful.

Extract 4

For the third successive day Kingsville in the northwest has been lashed by torrential rain. The River Leech burst its banks late last night and many townspeople were stranded on the upper floors of buildings and had to be rescued by helicopter. The town has been evacuated. Meteorologists blame the freak storms on global warming, but local people say the government should have been better prepared for the disaster. Damage to property is estimated to be in the millions.

Extract 5

A: Well, he's always been like that, you know.

B: But contradicting the Managing Director in a meeting, that's going too far.

A: That wasn't the only time either. Apparently he was always expressing his view that they were misjudging the market badly with that new software they launched last month and it was designed by the managing director's nephew.

Extract 6

Hello, it's me. Look – I'm at the station, but there are no taxis. ... A bus? But the bus stop's miles away and it's pouring. ... No, I haven't got an umbrella. I lent it to Dad this morning. Look – can't you just jump in the car and come and get me? It'll only take you ten minutes. And it is Mum's car after all. ... Oh, you're impossible!

Extract 7

I'm sorry, but there seems to be some mistake. My wife had the chicken not the duck and there's a £2 difference in price. And another thing. You've charged us for a bottle of mineral water. My wife had a glass of water, but it certainly didn't look like that expensive fizzy stuff to me. Even if it was, that seems far too much.

Extract 8

We apologise to passengers waiting to board the next fast train to London. The train is now ready for boarding on platform seven. Repeat platform seven. The train on platform eleven is out of service. Passengers awaiting the 10.52 service to Bournemouth are advised that there is a ten-minute delay due to signal failure.

That's the end of Part 1. Now look at Part 2.

PART 2

You'll hear a doctor talking about common illnesses. For questions 9–18 complete the notes which summarise what the speaker says. You'll need to write a word or a short phrase in each box. Before you start spend 45 seconds looking through Part 2.

There is one positive thing about getting older: you get fewer colds. Children catch about ten colds a year, young adults two or three and old people can expect to pick up just one. This is partly due to the way our immune system works – once you've been infected by a particular virus, you tend not to get it again. There are about 200 different cold viruses and the more of them you've already had, the fewer you have left to get in the future. That's why children are more vulnerable than adults. Children also catch more colds because, at school, they're exposed to many more viruses than adults.

The common cold has been called the single most expensive illness in the world. In the UK alone it accounts for the loss of about six million working days each year and the same number of schooldays.

Each cold means about two days of sheer misery. The virus usually dies within 48 hours and the stuffed-up feeling should clear up within a week. If the illness goes on for longer than this, it's likely to be either flu or an infection. Flu is caused by a virus too, but unlike colds, it can kill. The worldwide flu epidemics of 1918 and 1957 killed millions of people. Major epidemics tend to occur in Britain about once every three years, but the modern types of flu are very rarely life-threatening. Flu typically lasts about a week and causes fever and a sore nose and throat. You also ache all over. Unlike colds, which tend to be more common in winter, flu is a year-round disease.

The only people who are at risk of colds and flu becoming serious are those who are very old,

157

weak or already tired and unwell. If after a week or so the symptoms of a cold or flu seem to be getting worse, it's worth visiting your doctor.

Now you'll hear Part 2 again. (Part 2 tapescript repeated.) That's the end of Part 2. Now look at Part 3.

PART 3

You'll hear five people talking about animals. For questions 19–23 choose from the list of animals A–F what each speaker is describing. Use the letters only once. There is one extra letter which you do not need to use.

Speaker 1
Of course we had no way of knowing, but he was barking constantly while we were at work and it was driving the neighbours crazy. It wasn't really fair to have him when we were both away all day. Luckily my brother and sister-in-law have got a big garden and they'd been thinking of getting one anyway so they took him. I think we'll just have to wait a while before we get another pet.

Speaker 2
Oh, mum, please can I have one? They're so cute. There's one that's black with two white paws and the tip of his tail is white, too. He's just gorgeous. When he tries to meow, he just makes this squeaking noise. Jenny's mum says they'll be big enough to take away from their mother next week. Perhaps we could even get two and then they could play together. They won't scratch the furniture, I promise. Jenny's mum says you can get their claws clipped.

Speaker 3
I hadn't been anywhere near one for years, so I'd forgotten how big they look and how difficult it is to actually get on. I was absolutely terrified and I'm sure it could tell, because it kept stopping and no amount of kicking would get it going again. The instructor told me to hold the reins differently and that did seem to make a bit of a difference. We just walked at first and then we tried some trotting and cantering. I thought I was going to fall off at one point, but I somehow managed to hang on to its mane.

Speaker 4
It was wonderful to see it happening in our own back garden. It was up in that old oak tree. She spent about two weeks building it with all sorts of things including plastic straws and then she laid her eggs. When they hatched, they looked like such fragile little creatures. Whenever she brought them something to eat, they had their beaks wide open and their little

wings flapping just desperately. One of them fell out of the nest, which was a shame though.

Speaker 5
People say they feel real affection for each other – a bit like humans really. Apparently when one of them gets sick or is going to die, the others all gather around it and sort of stroke it with their trunks. They really do have fantastic memories. They say they can recognise people they haven't seen for years and years. They're such wonderful animals. It's terrible to think they're endangered.

Now you'll hear Part 3 again. (Part 3 tapescript repeated.) That's the end of Part 3. Now look at Part 4.

PART 4

You'll hear a woman conducting a market research interview about newspapers. For questions 24–30 decide which of the choices A, B or C is the correct answer. Before you start, spend thirty seconds looking through Part 4.

WOMAN: Excuse me. I wonder if you'd be willing to answer a few questions about newspapers for a market research survey.

MAN: Yes, I suppose so. If it won't take too long that is. I've got to be back in the office by two.

WOMAN: It should only take about five minutes.

MAN: OK, fire away then.

WOMAN: Right. How many times a week do you read a newspaper?

MAN: Well, it varies a bit. I suppose three or four.

WOMAN: You say it varies. What do you mean exactly?

MAN: Well, some weeks I get the train to work more than others and when I get the train I buy a paper. You see my wife and I share the one car and if she needs to take the kids to the doctor or whatever, I leave it with her.

WOMAN: And do you actually buy all the newspapers you read?

MAN: Well, I don't go through rubbish bins picking out old newspapers other people have thrown away, if that's what you mean, no.

WOMAN: No, what I meant was does your wife buy newspapers too or do they perhaps get the papers where you work?

MAN: No, we don't get them at work, but my wife does buy the papers on Saturdays and Sundays and occasionally during the week as well.

WOMAN: I see. How do you read the newspaper?

MAN: Well, I sort of hold it like this and look at the words.

WOMAN: No, I mean do you read the front page first or do you go straight to a particular section.

MAN: Umm ... I think I usually look at the front page and then I probably have a look at the sports pages towards the back and then I kind of work my way back through to the beginning again.

WOMAN: What proportion of the newspaper would you say you actually read: 85 per cent, 50 per cent, 25 per cent or less than 25 per cent?

MAN: Well, again that depends. If I've got loads of time, say on a Sunday, well, I might read most of the articles, providing they're interesting, that is. But during the week if I've got work to do on the train, I probably only glance at the headlines and then I might read one or two articles when I get home in the evening. Just occasionally I buy a paper and forget to look at it at all.

WOMAN: Are there any sections you particularly dislike?

MAN: Yes. I never look at the cartoons or crosswords. I can't understand how people can waste their time on things like that.

WOMAN: And is there a section that you think is particularly important?

MAN: Well, from a professional point of view I would have to say the business section, but I suppose that on a more general level the international news is the most important.

WOMAN: Do you always buy the same newspaper?

MAN: Well, I generally buy *The Argus* on weekdays and Saturdays and *The Sunday Chronicle* on Sundays. Just lately I've bought *The Herald* a couple of times. I thought it was rather good, though I don't think it can expect to compete with *The Echo*.

WOMAN: OK. Thanks very much and here's a free copy of *The Herald*. I hope you'll get time to read it.

Now you'll hear Part 4 again. (Part 4 repeated.) That's the end of Part 4.

PART 1   1 C   2 A   3 A   4 C   5 B   6 C   7 C   8 B

PART 2   9 ten   10 one   11 two hundred   12 school
          13 six million   14 48 hours   15 a week
          16 1918   17 three years   18 the very old

PART 3   19 D   20 C   21 E   22 F   23 B

PART 4   24 A   25 C   26 B   27 A   28 B   29 B
          30 A

Paper 5 Speaking

Tapescript

PART 1

Where are you from?
How long have you been living there?
What's it like living there?
How do you usually spend your free time?
What are your plans for the future?

PART 2

I'm going to give each of you two different photographs. I'd like you both to show each other your photos and then talk about them. You each have only one minute for this, so don't worry if I interrupt you. Candidate A, here are your two pictures. Please let Candidate B see them. They show different people doing different types of jobs. I'd like you to compare and contrast these pictures saying which you prefer and why.

Now, Candidate B, here are your pictures. Please let Candidate A see them. They show two different types of social occasion. I'd like you to compare and contrast these pictures saying which type of occasion you prefer and why.

PART 3

Now, Candidates A and B, here are some photographs showing things which represent a threat to our natural environment. I'd like you to talk together about these things and decide which two threats are the most serious. You only have about three minutes for this, so don't worry if I stop you.

PART 4

Which of the things shown in the photographs is a problem in your country?
What do you think can and should be done to solve problems like these?
Do you think individual people can do anything to stop the spread of pollution? If so, what can they do?

Addison Wesley Longman Limited,
Edinburgh Gate,
Harlow,
Essex
CM20 2JE
England
and Associated Companies throughout the world.

First published 1996

Fifth impression 1996

Set in 10/12.5pt Frutiger 45 Light

Printed in Spain by Mateu Cromo

ISBN 0 582 27856 2

We are grateful to the following for permission to reproduce copyright material:

Attic Futura Ltd for an extract from the article 'Alex Dimitriades' by Elisha Wadick in *Girlfriend* Magazine, March 1994; Ewan MacNaughton Associates for an extract from an article by David Fleet in *Daily Telegraph* 14.04.94; Gruner & Jahr Ltd for extracts from the articles 'Our Sports are Ancient' by Matt Bacon in *Focus* Magazine, August 1993; 'What is ball lightning?' in *Focus* Magazine, February 1993. 'Foam gun will bring prison escapes to a sticky end' in *Focus* Magazine, September 1994; Guardian Media Group PLC for an extract from the article 'Mango mad Indians drown their capital in orange pulp' by Molly Moore in *The Guardian* 18.8.94. adapted extracts from the articles 'Damn it Janet' by David Toop in *The Observer Magazine* 16.5.93; 'Icebreaks, preamble' by Emma Cook in *The Observer Magazine* 16.5.93; Harper Collins Ltd for an extract (recipe) from *Mediterranean Vegetable Cookery* by Rene Salaman; IPC Magazines Ltd for extracts from *Travel Games Checkpoint Book* by Lynn Guest; the articles 'I couldn't think about doing anything else' by Penny Vincenzi in *Options* Magazine, November 1988; 'The Making of You' by Angela Philipps in *Options* Magazine, August 1994; extracts based on articles 'Body Clock' by Paul Clayton in *Women's Journal*, September 1992; 'Diary of a Ghosthunter' by Simon Marsden in *Options* Magazine, November 1994; NMC Enterprises Division for extracts from 'Screen Test' feature in *She* Magazine, February 1994. © National Magazine Company & 'Destination GOZO' by Dee Pilgrim in *Company* Magazine, February 1989. © National Magazine Company; Newspaper Publishing PLC for an extract from the article 'Faster speeds for learner readers' by Susan Elkin in *Independent* 11.8.95; Random House UK Ltd for extracts from *Driven to Win* by Nigel Mansell & Derekk Allsop, published by Stanley Paul 1988; Times Newspapers Ltd for an extract from the article 'Enter Mrs Win-a-lot' by Rachel Kelly in *The Times* 19.9.94. © Times Newspapers Ltd, 1994; World Publications Ltd for an extract from the article 'Growth of a green network' by Alison Semple in *The Royal Geographical Society Magazine*, February 1995.

We have unfortunately, been unable to trace the copyright holders of extracts from *Earthlings* Magazine, Launch Issue Aug/Sept. 1994; 'Bear Necessities' by Louise West in *TV Quick*, 1991; 'So luv, this is your song' by Alan Attwood in *The Age* (Melbourne, 26.2.95) and would appreciate any information which would enable us to do so.

We are grateful to the following for permission to reproduce the following photographs and copyright material:

Barnabys Picture Library/Parker Hale for page 124(top); Camera Press/Avotakka for page 107(bottom left); J. Allan Cash Photolibrary for pages 34(right), 82(top), 107(top), 127(middle); The Complete Picture/D. Thistlethwaite for page 124(bottom); 1994 © Peter Ginter for page 25(right), 25(left); Robert Harding Picture Library for page 107(bottom right); The Image Bank/Andre Gallant for page 82(bottom), /James H.Carmichael for page 127(bottom); Life File/Jeff Griffin for page 19(bottom), /Andrew Ward for page 126(bottom); 1994 © Peter Menzel for page 25(middle); Network/Mike Goldwater for page 107(middle), /Christian Sappa/Rapho for page 34(middle), /Homer Sykes for page 125(top); Popperfoto/Jon Levy for page 22; Rex Features for page 49; The Spectator for pages 8, 23, 33, 36(bottom), 65, 81; Tony Stone Worldwide for pages 19(top), 34(bottom), 126(top), 127(top); Telegraph Colour Library/Axandre for page 93, /S.Benbow for page 34(left), /Bavaria-Bildagentur for page 125(bottom).

Illustrated by Gary Andrews, Kathy Baxendale, Peter Byatt, Neil Gower Kim Harley, Ed McLachlan, Martin Shovel, Neil Sutton